IMPLEMENTING SYSTEMATIC INTERVENTIONS

Accessibly written and specifically designed for secondary schools, *Implementing Systematic Interventions* provides you with the tools you need to successfully organize for and smoothly implement schoolwide intervention strategies. Discover how to:

- Organize administrative support and leadership teams;
- Create effective communication techniques and protocols;
- Use effective models to select school-specific priorities;
- Support staff and students during the transition;
- Identify desired outcomes and assess whether or not they've been achieved.

Featuring supplemental online resources, this essential guide helps your team avoid common mistakes, identify clear goals, and implement successful interventions to help every student succeed.

Hank Bohanon is Professor of Special Education at Loyola University Chicago, USA.

Lisa Caputo Love is a Learning Behavior Specialist and Bilingual Coordinator in the Chicago Public School District, USA.

Kelly Morrissey is Director of Personal Learning and Student Support at Maine Township High School District 207, USA.

IMPLEMENTING SYSTEMATIC INTERVENTIONS

A Guide for Secondary School Teams

*Hank Bohanon, Lisa Caputo Love,
and Kelly Morrissey*

Routledge
Taylor & Francis Group

NEW YORK AND LONDON

First published 2021
by Routledge
52 Vanderbilt Avenue, New York, NY 10017

and by Routledge
2 Park Square, Milton Park, Abingdon, Oxon, OX14 4RN

Routledge is an imprint of the Taylor & Francis Group, an informa business

Library of Congress Cataloging-in-Publication Data
Names: Bohanon, Hank, author. | Caputo Love, Lisa, author. | Morrissey, Kelly, author.
Title: Implementing systematic interventions : a guide for secondary school teams / Hank Bohanon, Lisa Caputo Love, and Kelly Morrissey.
Description: New York, NY : Routledge, 2021. | Includes bibliographical references. |
Identifiers: LCCN 2020018780 (print) | LCCN 2020018781 (ebook) | ISBN 9780367279103 (hardback) | ISBN 9780367279097 (paperback) | ISBN 9780429298646 (ebook)
Subjects: LCSH: Learning disabled children–Education (Secondary) | Response to intervention (Learning disabled children) | Teaching teams. | Student assistance programs. | Behavior modification.
Classification: LCC LC4704.74 .B65 2021 (print) | LCC LC4704.74 (ebook) | DDC 371.9–dc23
LC record available at https://lccn.loc.gov/2020018780
LC ebook record available at https://lccn.loc.gov/2020018781

ISBN: 978-0-367-27910-3 (hbk)
ISBN: 978-0-367-27909-7 (pbk)
ISBN: 978-0-429-29864-6 (ebk)

Typeset in Minion Pro
by Swales & Willis, Exeter, Devon, UK

Visit the eResources: www.routledge.com/9780367279097

CONTENTS

PREFACE
Using This Book

In a Nutshell

- Keep in mind the following themes: A*sk before you tell, do not train or implement what you cannot support, remember the humanity of your stakeholders*, and *be patient – it won't be perfect right away.*
- Integrate the models of tiered support for effective schoolwide improvement.
- Suggestions for use: Educators, schoolwide leaders and stakeholders, and pre-service teachers can use this book to enhance discussion and drive successful implementation of high-leverage practices in classrooms, schools, and districts.
- Checklist for implementation

Important Themes to Keep in Mind

While reading this book keep several key themes in mind. First, you must **"ask before you tell."** A leader or small team may believe they know what is best, but even if they are correct, it is crucial to base recommendations or directives for change on the needs stakeholders have expressed, as well as the data driving the work. Jumping in before establishing some level of consensus around the need for change can set teams up for an eternal struggle. Second, *do not train or implement what you cannot support*. Sometimes ideas and plans sound wonderful on paper, but unless the systems elements are in place to support the effort, it is likely to be wasted. Next, ***remember the humanity*** of your stakeholders. Students, teachers, and other staff members are contending with many stressors every day, and this can impact how receptive they are to changes. Before recommending a change in practice, think through how it would impact the day-to-day experience for each stakeholder group. Don't forget to think of it in the context of the other four million factors they are juggling each day! And finally, ***don't throw out "better" because it's not perfect.*** Systems change is a marathon, not a sprint. In a large school, it will typically take years to get even a few strategies universally implemented with fidelity.

It would be overwhelming to start from square one and fully build out all the systems, data, and practices described in this book, and we authors would be the first ones to tell you that we have yet to achieve perfection in our own work! It is difficult to find examples of secondary schools that are implementing tiered systems well. But the good news is, even incremental steps forward in schoolwide systems of support can yield a positive impact. So start with one element, one cohort, or one practice and build from there. Keep the big picture and ultimate goal in mind, but use data to choose a step forward that you think will give you the best return on investment with the lowest amount of effort. Rinse and repeat!

Models and Terminology

This book is intended to help educators design and/or refine their efforts to create and sustain systems that support schoolwide improvement. There are a wide variety of models, programs, and practices that can fit within this framework, specifically tiered systems of support for students, known as multi-tiered systems of support (MTSS). Examples of models that fit within MTSS are positive behavior interventions and support (PBIS), social emotional learning (SEL), and response to intervention (RtI). There is considerable overlap between these various MTSS-related approaches, and also with the process of school improvement. Throughout the book, when you see phrases such as "schoolwide efforts" or "school-wide model," we are referring to these practices and models that fall within an MTSS framework.

Originally, tiered systems approaches like RtI, SEL, and PBIS evolved separately, primarily because they were developed by people with different professional orientations (e.g., special education or school psychology), and in some cases because they focus on different (but related) student outcomes (e.g., academic functioning, social skills). To help you visualize this, Figure 0.1 provides an illustration of a general idea of the origins of RtI, PBIS, SEL, and SBMH. However, the way you would approach a school improvement plan and these models are very similar: Look for trends in student outcomes and data, then develop a tiered, targeted system of support to help make improvements. In addition, many times the functions and/or needs of the students transverse multiple categories.

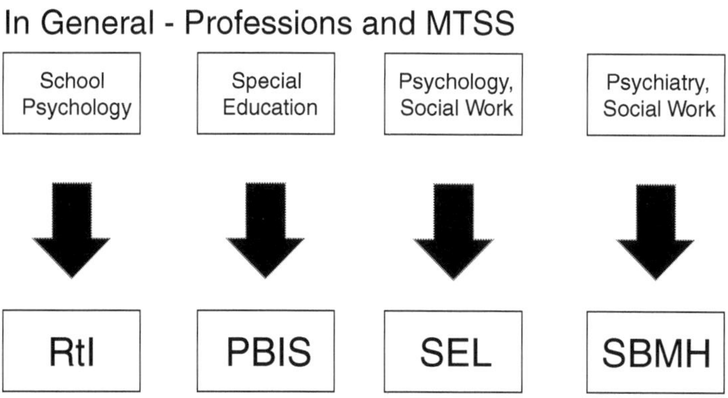

In General - Professions and MTSS

School Psychology	Special Education	Psychology, Social Work	Psychiatry, Social Work
⬇	⬇	⬇	⬇
RtI	**PBIS**	**SEL**	**SBMH**

Figure 0.1 The Origins of MTSS Approaches by Profession

Teams will be able to utilize this book regardless of whether they have adopted (or are considering) a specific model (such as PBIS), or they are selecting one schoolwide practice (such as teaching common steps to organize the writing process) that they would like to put into place with fidelity. However, for long-term planning, we strongly encourage schools to integrate all these into a unified comprehensive school improvement process that is driven by the school's vision and mission. A comprehensive school improvement process that follows the MTSS model (including both academics and the social emotional and behavioral realm, as well as tiered levels of intervention), ensures all efforts are integrated and effective.

Suggestions for Use in Staff Development

This book was designed to be used by staff members in secondary schools, as well as professors and students in higher education programs. The "Application" and "Pondering on Purpose" activities throughout were designed to allow the reader to actively engage in the content, and also to guide the discussion or activities of a book study group. Teams or small groups of stakeholders may wish to read a chapter at a time, and select some of these activities to complete together. Supplemental materials are available on the companion website, and readers are strongly encouraged to utilize that resource.

Checklist for Implementation

As you read through this book, you will encounter many different steps, as developing schoolwide systems of support is a complex and lengthy process. The following checklist is a summary of the steps you will be reading about throughout the book. You may want to refer to this as an anticipation guide, as a review, or as a tool to increase the fidelity of your implementation of what you have learned.

Exploration and Adoption Stage

- Determine areas of need by gathering existing information and data.
- Create an environment of transparency by advertising an outline of the steps including timelines and various formats for input that are accessible to all stakeholders.
- Assess the readiness, perceptions, and existing methods of the stakeholders using surveys and interviews.
- "Dive" into data together using protocols that involve a variety of stakeholders.
- Establish consensus on the area of need and the desired outcomes of any intervention/change implemented.
- Engage in additional (diagnostic) data gathering processes to narrow down on current trends related to the desired outcomes.
- Determine specific training, resources, and environmental needs that may be roadblocks to successful implementation.
- Share findings with stakeholders.
- Establish and train a team that will lead the work to create the change.
- Address the biases and working styles of the team to make the team effective.
- Select the resources and/or interventions to be implemented to create the change.
- Secure and execute the training, resources, and environmental needs that were identified as roadblocks to clear the path for implementation.
- Identify the measures that will be used to monitor the progress of implementation.
- Identify the measures that will be used to monitor the desired outcomes of implementation (outcome assessment).
- Share findings with stakeholders.

Initial Implementation

- Identify a small cohort to pilot the change.
- Use the outcomes assessment to establish a current baseline measure of the desired outcome. (It may be useful to give this assessment to both pilot and non-pilot stakeholders to compare outcomes.)

- Provide training, support, and resources identified in the installation stage.
- Begin implementation.
- Monitor throughout using the measure identified in the installation stage.
- Engage in protocols to analyze outcomes and progress of implementation with all stakeholders.
- Make adjustments as needed and determined by the data.
- Repeat the execution of implementation and outcome assessments and analysis as needed.
- Share findings with stakeholders.

Full Implementation

- Once it is determined using initial implementation findings that the change is beneficial, replicate implementation with additional stakeholders.
- Repeat measuring implementation and outcomes. According to the National Implementation Research Network, full "implementation" has been established when 50% or more of the intended stakeholders are implementing the change as intended while demonstrating the desired outcomes (see https://nirn.fpg.unc.edu/module-4/topic-6-full-implementation).

Checklist for Creating Teams

- Evaluate the level of trust within your team and work to establish and maintain a "safe space."
- Establish a mission and vision for your team.
- Create the roles needed to achieve the mission and vision.
- Set ground rules and norms for team meetings and the team's work.
- Establish structures for agendas, notetaking, and action planning for the team.
- Plot out data routines.
- Evaluate the effectiveness of team structures frequently.

Checklist for Communication

- List and evaluate current communication formats/designs.
- Determine and understand your audience and their needs.
- Evaluate your own biases and how they relate to the biases of your audience.
- Determine the content of your communication and how/if/when it will vary.
- Design your communication.

- Evaluate the effectiveness of your communication.
- Evaluate if your process is "fair."
  - Meaningfully consider all input
  - Share the reasoning behind the ultimate decision
  - Ensure everyone affected understands the decisions and expectations are clear

Checklist for Aligning Practices with Goals

- Begin by taking inventory on all current initiatives/programs/strategies/systems used.
  - Include stakeholders across groups
  - Use a graphic organizer to display all the initiatives/programs/strategies listed
- Evaluate which initiatives/programs/strategies you will keep and eliminate the rest.
  - Determine three "must have" and three "good to have" criteria for all initiatives/programs/strategies
  - Eliminate initiatives/programs/strategies that don't align with school goals and/or that don't have at least three "must have" and two "good to have" criteria
  - Use equity protocols and/or mindset – how do these initiatives impact our under-represented students?
  - Use a rating system and/or protocol

Checklist for Aligning Roles with Practices

- Reflect on current distributive leadership.
- Detemine what knowledge and/or skills are needed to achieve your goals – write a description.
- Once these roles are created, THEN figure out who will fill those roles.
- Fill rolls with equity in mind. Representation matters.
- Don't forget community members, parents, and organizations as resources!
- Do not overextend the same small group of people.
- Find gaps in the knowledge/expertise of your stakeholders.
- Create your "who you gonna call" list (organizational chart).
- Create thorough hiring processes that help you to fill gaps when bringing on new hires.

Checklist for Using Fidelity Data

- Review current tools used to check for the participation responsiveness and engagement, efficiency and sustainability of what you are implementing, the quality of the delivery, the adherence to procedure, and the frequency/duration of prescribed implementation.
- Decide how the new fidelity data will be collected: expert rating, school community self-assessment, leadership team self-assessment, random sample of representation.
- Select a tool for collection (i.e. SurveyMonkey, observation tool, etc.).
- Develop an action plan based on the data collected.

Using Data to Monitor Systems and Target Interventions

- Create a matrix or list of all the data your school already gathers.
- Look for patterns that relate to some of the "early warning systems" of secondary schools.
- Sort your data by demographics and analyze patterns.
- Make a "big picture" plan that has actionable tasks, goals, and timelines.
- The same structure/system can be used to make smaller (individual student or smaller student groups) plans.
- Stick to deadlines. Set calendars in advance and monitor outcomes using protocols on a pre-determined schedule.
- Don't forget to check fidelity data (don't blame the intervention for not working if you aren't doing it with fidelity).
- Make adjustments based on your data reviews.

Structure for Your Setting

- Reflect on expectations established for non-classroom settings. How are these communal areas arranged, monitored, and addressed? Has a common language been defined to prevent misunderstandings and misconceptions?
- Review attendance data to determine trends that can be addressed. Assign staff to address trends as well as individual cases through tiered, evidence-based actions.
- Get students to class on time by defining what "on time" means (in your seat? In the doorway?) as well as tiered strategies for students with more frequent tardies.
- Set clear academic and behavioral expectations within classrooms with a syllabus that explicitly addresses common questions. Review and revisit

the syllabus by acting out scenarios, discussing specific components, providing models and checklists, and having the students self-rate and monitor their progress.
- Facilitate student engagement using Universal Design strategies.
  - Recruit student interest using creative methods to introduce topics, present information, and assess student knowledge and growth
  - Teach students how to sustain efforts and persevere through challenging activities
  - Teach students self-regulation strategies and provide opportunities for students to monitor and reflect on their self-regulation
- List instructional routines used within each classroom. Maximize effectiveness by utilizing a few high-leverage practices within each classroom and across multiple settings.

Being Clear on What's Expected

- Identify current expectations in your setting and how they are taught/communicated.
- Use the following principles to establish universal expectations for your setting:
  - Set a goal for identifying three to five expectations
  - Identify the typical types of issues your school needs to address with students
  - Decide on who will be involved in developing your expectations
  - Identify a process for getting input from your community
  - Organize the general expectations into three to five major themes
- Be intentional about how and where you post your expectations.
- Determine what skills need to be explicitly taught in order for students to be able to meet the expectations selected (consider all settings within the environment).
- Teach the expectations by modeling and practicing what the expectations look like in practice.
- Create a timeline for when you plan on teaching and re-teaching the expectations. This "rhythm" of instruction will help you address trends such as increases in behavior referrals before or after long breaks, etc.

Increasing Student Engagement

- Model and teach academic growth mindsets to help students value comprehension and effort as a path to achievement, scores, and grades.
- Take strides (trainings, book clubs, etc.) to ensure your instruction is culturally relevant.

- Strengthen teacher to student interactions. This can be addressed through protocols and self-reflection. Professional development around providing praise and feedback can help to improve these interactions.
- Instructional strategies can help to increase student engagement. Teachers can use thinking routines, protocols, and technology to increase opportunities for response, participation, discussion, and feedback.

Improving Academic and Behavioral Performance Through Feedback and Acknowledgement

- Remember that feedback is not always given intentionally. Our reactions, whether direct, indirect, verbal, nonverbal, etc., reinforce whether a behavior is repeated.
- Learn about how your students' families view feedback and acknowledgement from a "cultural" perspective and address this in your plans.
- Positive acknowledgement of desired behaviors is proven to be more effective than many other methods used to correct behaviors.
- Establish a strong growth mindset climate and culture to help students value and use feedback effectively.
- Consider the functions of the behaviors you want to address in order to select the feedback and/or acknowledgement that will be most effective.
- Make sure to have a 5:1 ratio of positive interactions to corrective statements.
- If you are going to use extrinsic rewards, use natural and meaningful consequences that align with the desired outcome.
- Review school, class, or lesson goals to plan ways to make feedback specific to skill development and learning targets.
- Consider the various methods in which individuals prefer acknowledgement and use accordingly.
- Feedback should be timely, specific, genuine, age appropriate, and frequent.
- Frame acknowledgement and rewards as models for life skills like self-regulation and goal setting.
- Plan strategies schoolwide to ensure consistency and familiarity with the routines.
- Use data to reflect and to establish cycles of improvement in implementation and effectiveness.
- Don't forget the adults in your setting!

Responding to Academic and Behavioral Needs

- How are you identifying students that are not responding to core curriculum?
- Evaluate the implementation and effectiveness of high-leverage tier one instructional strategies in classrooms (both academic and behavior).
- What is your instructional response cycle for groups of students that need more?
- What is your instructional response cycle for individual students that need more?
- Develop your staff's "toolbox" of strategies that can be implemented.

ACKNOWLEDGEMENTS

This book would not have been possible without the support of many people. We appreciate the support and mentoring we have received from members of the positive behavior support, response to intervention, and social and emotional learning communities. Specifically, we would like to thank Steve Goodman and JoAnne Malloy for their ongoing support and collaboration. Also, thanks to Tim Knoster for his belief that this book was possible. Thanks to Karen Berlin for reading early versions of this manuscript and providing invaluable feedback. Thanks also to Kathleen Turner, Bridget Walker, and Steve Rish for reading the first drafts of the book proposal and providing feedback. Also, we much appreciate the support from our editor at Routledge, Misha Kydd. Thank you for believing in our project. Also, we thank Olivia Powers, who provided much advice and support during our journey. Thank you to Ali Kushki who did a wonderful job of formatting our materials. We also appreciate Eleanor Smith and Tamsin Ballard for their work on editing and producing the final copy of this book.

I (Hank) would first like to thank my wife (Meng-Jia) and sons (Henry and Matthew) for their support in writing this book. Thanks for giving me the time to work on this project! Also, I would like to thank my former students in the Dallas Public schools and my mentor Andre Banks. They were wonderful teachers for me. I also appreciate the support from my university mentors Jerry Bailey, Kevin Callahan, Doug Guess, Tom Skrtic, Ann Turnbull, Rud Turnbull, and Wayne Sailor. Your wisdom, support, and guidance have helped shape my life. I would not be where I am in my professional life without you all. Thanks also to my friends in the Kansas City Kansas Schools, who taught me so much about coaching schools. I would also like to thank my colleagues at Loyola University, who have been incredible partners over the years, including students, staff, and faculty. Also, thank you to all our research partners over the years who have provided wisdom and insight into supporting schools effectively. I have learned from you all.

Finally, thanks to Kelly and Lisa. I appreciate all of the incredible contributions you have made to the lives of all of the children and adults with whom you are in contact. You both have been wonderful colleagues and friends. It was an honor to work with you on this project.

This book would not have been possible without so many inspiring people in my (Lisa's) life. To my husband Tim for his constant, unwavering support he gives me in all that I do. Your encouragement is my invigoration. Thank you for being my thought partner and my rock, and for the countless times you "took one for the team" so I could write. To my daughters Viviana and Emilia, for the patience they showed well beyond their years "working" in coffee shops while I wrote. Yes, my darlings, I will "make you a copy." To my parents Mirella and Paul who provided me the love and support I needed to reach my dreams, my sister Christina who tolerated years of "playing teacher" as a child, my grandparents Caterina, Nicola, Lucia, and Gildo, as well as Zio Andrew and Auntie Nicole who taught me perseverance, generosity, and commitment. To the rest of my family, including my in-laws June, Fran, and Julie, my Zio Claudio, Aunt Stephanie, and many cousins for their undying support. To my colleagues for all I have learned from them and for challenging me. Their feedback and insight have made me the teacher I am today and motivates me to continue to grow for tomorrow.

A special thanks to Team Yellow for keeping me sane and grounded when I needed it. Thank you to all my students who teach me something new every day and make working such a joyful and fulfilling experience. I want to thank two teacher organizations, Chicago Foundation for Education and Teacher Plus, their current leaders Sarah Hoppe Knight and Josh Kaufmann, and all those who fund the organizations through their generous donations. They have been key to my ability to implement many of the topics discussed in this book. Their opportunities strengthened my skills as an educator, elevate the profession, and have impacted countless students through the teachers they serve.

Last but certainly not least, I'd like to thank Hank and Kelly. Working with them has been an honor and privilege. Hank has been a mentor to me for over a decade. If we all had his calm demeanor, flexible mindset, and implementation methods, every school would be a model of what education should be. Thank you for believing in me. Kelly, I strive to have your depth of knowledge, ability to articulate ideas, and focus. Thank you both for your partnership and dedication to our field.

I (Kelly) would first like to thank my husband. Patrick, you took a deep breath and bit your tongue when I told you I would be co-authoring a book while expecting (and then caring for) our third child. I promise no more extra projects for a while! Special thanks to baby Calvin for sleeping more than most newborns (at least at night), and big sisters Ainslee and Matilda, for going with the flow and watching movies when I had to power through some writing or meet with my co-authors. I'd also like to thank my parents and my brother: you have loved, supported, and challenged me throughout my life. Mom and Dad, without you I never would have had the opportunities that opened so many doors for me. To my loving in-laws, I am incredibly grateful for all your help during this writing process, with everything from baby-sitting to a flooded basement!

Thank you also to my professors and mentors at Loyola University Chicago, especially Hank, Pam Fenning, and Meng-Jia Wu. My dissertation was an intense process, and I couldn't have completed it without your expertise and guidance. To the late Martie Wynne: you sat with me for hours to map out my program and talk about life lessons and education. I know I was just one of countless advisees and students you influenced, and I hope you knew how much you impacted me and my career.

To the students and staff at Foreman High School, thank you for what was probably the most impactful decade of my life. I still miss you. My former students, know that you taught me more than I ever could have hoped to teach you. And of course, thank you to the staff and students in Maine Township High School District 207. It is an amazing place to learn and work, and I am honored to be a part of the team.

Finally, Hank and Lisa, thank you for the amazing effort and wealth of information you have shared with me throughout this project. You both truly walk the walk when it comes to kindness and professionalism, and I am always inspired by our conversations. Hank, from my first year of graduate school, you offered me authentic experiences to learn about MTSS, and I can never repay you for setting me on the trajectory to an interesting and fulfilling career. I was truly honored when you asked me to be a part of this book.

PART 1

Organize Systems for Implementation

Find Your Purpose, Find Your Direction

1

WHAT MAKES AN EFFECTIVE SECONDARY SCHOOL?

In a Nutshell

- Schools have a variety of needs that should be taken into account when designing effective systems.
- Safety, physical environment, teaching and learning, and interpersonal relationships are the factors that make up an effective school culture and climate.
- Develop and maintain explicit systems that are monitored and driven by data.
- Provide tiers of support that are proactive, and then responsive according to data-identified needs.
- Tiered support systems include common academic and social-emotional/behavioral strategies that are implemented for all students, with additional supports added to benefit those who don't respond.

Introduction

While some people really enjoyed their educational experiences, not everyone has fond memories about their schooling. When Winston Churchill was told he would begin his education, he said: "I did what so many oppressed people have done in similar circumstances: I took to the woods." Much of his perception of school life did not improve over time. He was criticized for his lack of academic performance by his teachers. Later he commented that when his interests and imagination were not engaged in school, he could not or would not learn. Rather than be punished for his lack of progress in

Latin and Greek, he wished he could have done something that would have connected more with his interests.

Like Churchill, some students have similar frustrations in school. When a student demonstrates a lack of progress, sometimes they are neglected due to low expectations, criticized, or punished. Coercion and neglect are certainly not the experiences for all students, nor do all teachers respond with harshness when students are not successful. However, there are circumstances where well-meaning people unintentionally create environments where students have negative experiences. This purpose of this chapter is to help educators think about the ingredients that go into a productive environment for all students that prevents as much failure as possible.

BOX 1.1 PONDERING ON PURPOSE

- Use the Pondering on Purpose boxes to guide your thinking, deepen your understanding, and to emphasize essential information.
- Ask them in professional learning teams to drive discussion, develop consensus, and identify intrinsic biases.

Connection – Components of an Effective School

As you think back to your own secondary school experiences, what where the things that made the environment work for you? Or, perhaps you did not have a very good experience. Why was this the case? I (Lisa) went to school in a highly rated district and always considered myself a pretty good student. Surrounded by academic reputation and competitive peers, I watched as my classmates were quickly judged and sorted into classes of the "haves" and "have nots" based on their performance. The classes that were perceived as "most rigorous" were usually lecture style, and though I did fine in those classes, the teachers that I learned the most from were those that thought outside of the box in their instructional methods. They assigned us roles tapping into the strengths of each individual student and had us work together to achieve a common goal. One science teacher created an entire "Living in Space" program that taught us about project management, hydroponics, robotics, and fish farming, culminating in a "mission" that required all our efforts to succeed. Classes based on lectures, memorization of facts, and tests provided little opportunity to apply information to real life. In addition to content, classes like Living in Space focused on connections, collaboration, and problem solving with peers. Some criticized these nontraditional methods. However, the content of classes like this "stuck" with me the most. They also taught me about my learning style so that I could do a better job of accessing knowledge for the rest of my life. Sometimes we don't realize all the factors that need to be in place for instruction and learning to be effective.

Point/Principle – Components of an Effective School

Although the components of an "effective" school will vary depending on the community it serves, the State of Vermont (based on the work of the National School Climate Center) has done a nice job of describing the kinds of environments that help students be successful and feel safe. Table 1.1 provides an illustration of the key components. The four major areas include safety, the physical environment, teaching and learning, and interpersonal relationships.

Application – Components of an Effective School

BOX 1.2 PONDERING ON PURPOSE

- Take time to review the domains in Table 1.1 to establish your roadmap to a highly effective school.
- Do you have predictions as to which areas will come back as strengths? Areas of need? How do these biases impact your daily practices?
- Once you gather some evidence to help you determine where you stand in each area, that will get you one step closer to understanding your next steps. How will you gather data for this table? From who?

Connection – Multi-tiered Systems of Support and School Improvement

We should not underestimate the importance of prevention. Since you were a child, your parents have told you to wash your hands. There was a good reason for encouraging this behavior. Far more children die from hygiene-related illnesses that could have been prevented with a little soap and water (https://usa.soapaid.org/what-we-do/) than from "scary" diseases like cancer, that tend to get more attention. In a society that values "go big or go home," we often put far too much emphasis on grand gestures, and forget that the small, manageable actions that are preventative in nature can often have the biggest impact. Further, it is far easier to prevent catching a cold in the first place than attempting to make it go away once we've caught it. We can think about prevention and intervention on a continuum across tiers of support. Effective schools have a well-supported, tiered prevention and intervention system.

Table 1.1 Vermont's Domains of Safe and Successful School Climates

Safety	Physical Environment	Teaching and Learning	Interpersonal Relationships
__ Behavioral expectations __ Health & wellness __ expectations __ Sense of physical security __ Sense of social-emotional __ security	__ School connectedness & __ community engagement __ Physical surrounding	__ Support for learning __ Social skills development __ Student engagement & __ self-direction	__ Respect for diversity __ Social supports for students __ Leadership __ Professional relationships

Point/Principle – Multi-tiered Systems of Support and School Improvement

You may already be familiar with many of the components of multi-tiered systems of support (MTSS), which shares a considerable amount of overlap with school improvement efforts. You can use MTSS and school improvement approaches to analyze and meet the needs of all of your students, in the same way you address needs for individual students. For example, when we make individualized behavior plans for a specific student, we gather information about the current strengths and concerns, and define the problem in measurable, objective terms. Next, we select from a continuum of strategies for intervention that addresses the expected or problem performance, set a goal and outline how it will be measured, and create a plan that explicitly outlines what each stakeholder involved will do. Both school improvement and MTSS look at the entire school through a similar process. A key difference is that MTSS focuses on prevention and providing supports across a continuum of tiers. Table 1.2 cross-references key components of MTSS with examples from school improvement, as most schools have participated in some form of a school improvement process over the years.

Application – MTSS and School Improvement

Review a copy of your school's "school improvement plan." Consider how it connects to your current MTSS (or other tiered systems used to address student needs). The school improvement plan has goals that you would like your school to accomplish, just as in MTSS you set goals for your student(s). Neither can reach the goal without an intervention. What "interventions" have you selected to reach your schoolwide goals? Consider ways to synthesize efforts between the systems in your school. For example, what behaviors or academic issues consume the deans, administrators, or clinicians (counselors, social workers, etc.), time? What factors, strategies, or approaches do they use that could be implemented across settings such as the classrooms? How would having these supports built into their day impact all students? Developing successful systems for academics and social-emotional/behavioral needs involves identifying common practices that work well for a variety of students and using those strategies in all settings.

Connection – Systems, Practices, Data, and Outcomes

I (Hank) have a friend who is a pilot for a private jet. He was in town (Chicago) getting ready to fly one of the final guests for the Oprah Winfrey show. He let me go on board the plane as he was preparing everything for his return flight. During his preparation, he was using a checklist. He said there

Table 1.2 Comparing MTSS and School Improvement

Focus area	Multi-tiered systems of support (MTSS)	School improvement
Systems	• Systems in place to ensure interventions are implemented correctly	• Leadership roles distributed • Community and parent partners included • Staff provided sufficient resources and time • Support obtained from school staff • External support procured for technical assistance
Data	• Assessments used to determine which students need support • Student performance data collected, guides programming and improvement efforts	• Student progress monitored using data • Program evaluation conducted • Measurable goals and benchmarks identified
Practices	• Interventions organized across tiered continuum of support • Interventions selected, implemented, and monitored • Supports begin with effective core curriculum	• Programs designed comprehensively • Core instruction standardized • Research-based strategies selected

(Adapted from Goodman & Bohanon, 2018; Slavin, 2007; Sleegers, Thoonen, Oort, & Peetsma, 2014) were certain requirements that had to be met before the plane could take off. These factors included how long it had been since the plane had maintenance, and how many hours the pilot has slept the night before. He said that if the preparation requirements were not met, the plane could not take off. I told him that I wished schools had pre-flight checklists prior to taking off with a new program!

Point/Principle – Systems, Practices, Data, and Outcomes

Interestingly, if you look across MTSS approaches for academics, behavior, social and emotional learning, and school mental health, there are common components that must be in place. These features are designed to ensure that implementation will be as successful as possible. Regardless of the model, the *systems* components typically include these features:

- Administration actively supports and is involved
- Staff support is obtained prior to roll out
- The intervention is aligned with one of the top three goals for the building
- A team is established to guide the work
- An audit is conducted of current practices related to the intervention
- A self-assessment is conducted related to the key features of the intervention
- A data system related to the intervention is established
- An action plan is developed to guide the overall process and encourage accountability, which includes specific plans for staff training

According to Anna Harms and her colleagues in the State of Michigan, data systems should allow teams to accomplish four tasks:

1. Identify the problems in your setting
2. Analyze the problems in your setting
3. Develop a plan for addressing the problem
4. Implement and evaluate the plan

Application – Systems, Practices, Data, and Outcomes

Practice setting some desired outcomes and thinking about how you could measure your impact. Try choosing an academic goal and a social-emotional learning/behavioral goal for your school and determine what types of data (quantitative or qualitative information) you would use to determine if you had met that goal. For example, in the area of social and emotional learning or behavior, if you want 90% of students to consistently participate actively and respectfully during groupwork, you might create a common rating scale or rubric for teachers to use throughout the year and track each progress report along with grades. Look back at Table 1.2 (under systems). As you review these two tables, what systems are already in place that will support implementation of your schoolwide effort? What systems are needed to increase success?

Connection – Tiered Supports

A key component of MTSS is the organization of supports for students based on tiers of intervention. The idea of tiers of intervention originally comes from public health. It typically involves organizing treatment that all students (universal supports) are exposed to, some students receive (secondary supports), and those that only a few students experience (primary supports). For example, according to the prevention researcher Mark Greenberg, tiered interventions to reduce heart attacks have included banning smoking in public places (universal or tier one), daily aspirin for men over 50 (secondary or tier two), and cholesterol-lowering drugs for those most at risk (tertiary or tier three). From an MTSS perspective, universal supports (designed for all students), include ensuring access to effective instructional strategies, standards-aligned curriculum, creating an effective and engaging learning environment, mitigating systemic bias, the selection and use of social and emotional curriculum as necessary, and ensuring staff are aware of the impact of trauma on students.

Point/Principle – Tiered Supports

Tier One

A theme that goes across all MTSS approaches is to select or develop a core curriculum and common practices that can improve outcomes for all students. Next, you provide increasing intensive supports for students who do not respond to your core interventions alone. Within this logic, you would expect a least 80% of the students in your school setting to respond to the core instruction with success, if the curriculum and practices are implemented effectively. Another theme across most tier one approaches is the systematic teaching of the curriculum. Academics, behavior, and social and emotional learning all call for explicit instruction in areas of focus. This means that students are provided:

- A breakdown of the components of the skill
- A rationale for the need for the skill
- Modeling of the skill

- Guided practice (with the instructor or peers)
- Independent practice
- Feedback

Tier One Standards Aligned Core Curriculum

Most secondary teams are at least aware of the need to align curriculum to academic standards, and most educators are familiar with the academic learning standards required by their state. An MTSS lens would guide teams to ensure that common standards, objectives, skills, and competencies truly drive instruction, rather than being slapped onto the top of a lesson plan, or "retrofitted" to favored activities even though it's a stretch to see the connection. You might think that aligning your core curriculum to standards only involves academic areas, however, you can also align your core curriculum to behavioral, emotional, and social skills. Several states have begun, in some cases with the Collaborative for Academic, Social, and Emotional Learning (CASEL), to develop core standards for social and emotional learning (SEL). Illinois, for example, has developed goals, learning standards, benchmarks, and performance descriptors to help teach and assess student growth in SEL. These standards provide an opportunity to help schools identify areas that can be taught and evaluated that support academic learning (e.g., self-management, goal setting). As new federal guidelines call for states to assess areas outside of academics alone, aligning your schoolwide efforts to these standards will be useful.

Additionally, schools that have taught behavioral expectations through schoolwide approaches have sometimes aligned their expectations and lessons with Common Core State Standards. In one example, a high school aligned their behavioral expectation of being responsible with two Common Core State Standards for literacy: being able to express oneself effectively (CCSS.ELA-Literacy.SL.9–10.1) and develop and evaluate a plan (CCSS.ELA-Literacy.WHST.9–10.5).

Also, Jennifer Freeman and her colleagues at the University of Connecticut recommend that social skills, when taught through schoolwide behavioral expectations, can be aligned with College Readiness Standards. These include areas of critical thinking, academic engagement, mindsets, learning processes, interpersonal engagement, and transitions competencies. For example, critical thinking can involve giving and receiving feedback effectively. Schools are encouraged to align their expectations for students to these standards. Or in some cases, these standards can help drive the expectation that the students are directly taught.

Post-secondary planning is an area of tier one that is particularly pertinent for secondary students. Schools may design expectations, lessons, and/or experiences that all students experience. Some schools provide lessons for students help them fill out college applications or financial aid forms. Others have every student complete a personalized learning plan to weave their interests and needs into their course selection process. Others may assist all students in completing at least one career exploration activity during high school. Regardless of the area, if it is systematically provided to all students, it's tier one!

BOX 1.3 PONDERING ON PURPOSE

What are the tier one evidence-based practices you implement as a school?

- How do stakeholders know to implement these practices?
- What evidence do you have that they are implemented consistently across all classrooms?

Tier One Common Practices

While having common objectives for academics and/or behaviors is a key feature of MTSS, common practices related to instruction and response to learning needs are also a key feature. Some examples include shared graphic organizers across content areas to guide students through the writing or notetaking process, common lesson plan templates to ensure research-based features are included in plans, or universal use of an evidence-based instructional strategy (like increasing opportunities for students to respond, or cooperative learning). Universal response strategies also align well with MTSS, such as establishing clear steps for responding to common problem behaviors that all staff understand and follow.

Tiers Two and Three

When around 80% of students are successfully responding to the core curriculum and strategies that are put into place at tier one, groups of students with more intensive needs may emerge. Within MTSS, added layers of intervention and support are provided, based on needs identified with data. Often, I (Kelly) run into walls in conversations about MTSS because staff members become too focused on which tier a specific program, practice, or intervention falls into. To avoid these debates or cyclical conversations, it may initially be more helpful to think of MTSS as a continuum of increasing intensity of support, more so than discrete tiers. By intensity, we mean time, ratio of staff to students, and resources required. Tier one should require the "whole village to lighten the load" so it works efficiently, tier two should be systematic with decision rules and quick response times, and somewhat fewer staff delivering somewhat more intense support. Tier three is often one-to-one, or multiple staff members supporting one student regularly.

Three key factors to be mindful of in conversations about tiers two and three will help schools achieve a more equitable model of support. First, tier one, described above, is for everyone. Students who are provided with tier two supports should continue to have access to tier one interventions. Second, students should not need an IEP or other special label or funding to access tiers two and three supports. MTSS evolved in large part due to a need to provide more intensive interventions to students outside of special education. Even tier three is not meant to be synonymous with special education, programs for English Learners, etc. Any student, regardless of labels, should be able to access these supports if needed. Accomplishing this "access for anyone" to increasing tiers of support, and doing so without removing learners from tier one, can be very challenging due to the intersection of needs, time, staffing, schedules, legal requirements, and allocation of resources. The helpful aspect of MTSS is that there are many different ways to provide evidence-based interventions, so schools can be creative and flexible. Finally, students may have specific tier two needs in one area (such as reading fluency) but not others (such as social skills, reading comprehension, and mathematical problem solving), and not always. Added levels of support can be temporary and targeted.

So what could this look like in a secondary school? At tier one, all students regularly access a standards-based curriculum with consistent evidence-based instructional routines (such as common graphic organizers and academic vocabulary instruction). Some students may also have an added course or flex time support where they utilized a research-based reading intervention program to boost fluency and comprehension. For a few identified students who aren't responding to the program, it may be determined that they need an additional dose of reading intervention with one-on-one targeted decoding instruction.

In the behavioral realm, at tier one, all students are taught clear behavioral expectations and acknowledged regularly for meeting those expectations. Some identified students may participate in a tier two check in/check out system where they receive targeted feedback and positive attention throughout the day, and quickly touch base with a mentor at the start and end of the day. For a few students, a team may review data sources and identify whether the student likely needs a group curriculum to develop prosocial skills, an individualized behavior plan, or perhaps a wraparound-style team approach to addressing the student's social-emotional, behavioral, academic, and family/community-based needs. Regardless of the realm (academic skills, SEL

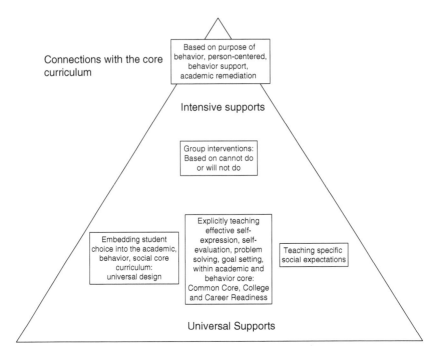

Figure 1.1 Continuum of Supports Across Tiers

Adapted from Bohanon, H., Castillo, J., & Afton, M. (2015).

needs, etc.) data are used throughout the process to determine that practices and interventions are being delivered with fidelity. If the student is not making adequate progress, a team gathers more detailed data to determine the next appropriate step. Figure 1.1 provides an example of what a continuum of tiered support can look like within a secondary setting.

Application – Tiered Supports

Think of a student who struggles with reading comprehension. What would be some logical supports that she could access in every classroom she encounters (tier one)? For example, the Main Idea Strategy from the University of Kansas Strategic Instruction Model, or the Reading for Meaning instructional routine from the *Core Six* text (Silver, Dewing, & Perini, 2012) could be implemented for all learners, across content areas. If you had a group of students you could pull together for a common intervention time outside of class, what is an intervention she could access within that group (tier two)? If she still struggled with some specific skills, or wasn't making her progress goals in reading, what could she receive one-on-one in addition to that intervention (tier three)? What are of some the evidence-based strategies/

programs/interventions you are familiar with that you could "layer up" to support this student in your setting?

Conclusion

In this chapter, we have provided an overview of some big ideas and concepts related to effective secondary schools, which will be fleshed out in more detail throughout the rest of the book. Be sure to spend time thinking about what an effective secondary school looks like to your own community, as it will drive the systems you build together. These carefully planned, data-driven systems will ensure effective practices are implemented for all learners. In the next few chapters, more attention will be paid to identifying and promoting readiness and planning of systems.

Bibliography

Alber, R. (2014). How important is teaching literacy in all content areas? Retrieved from www.edutopia.org/blog/literacy-instruction-across-curriculum-importance

Bohanon, H., & Wu, M. (2012a). Integration of social, behavioral, and academic initiatives: Part I. *Communique*, 41(2), 4–5.

Bohanon, H., & Wu, M. (2012b). Integration of social, behavioral, and academic initiatives: Part II. *Communique*, 41(3), 12–13.

Bohanon, H., Castillo, J., & Afton, M. (2015). Embedding self-determination and futures planning within a schoolwide framework. *Intervention in School and Clinic. 50*(4), 203–209. http://ecommons.luc.edu/education_facpubs/16/

Burns, M. K., & Gibbons, K. (2010). *Implementing response-to-intervention in elementary and secondary schools: Procedures to assure scientific-based practices.* New York, NY: Guilford Press.

DuFour, R., DuFour, R., Eaker, R., & Karhanek, G. (2004). *Whatever it takes: How professional learning communities respond when kids don't learn.* Bloomington, IN: Solution Tree.

The Education Alliance. (n.d.). Adolescent literacy in the content areas. In *The knowledge loom: Educators sharing and learning together.* Retrieved from www.brown.edu/academics/education-alliance/knowledge-loom

Forman, S. G., Olin, S. S., Hoagwood, K. E., Crowe, M., & Saka, N. (2009). Evidence-based intervention in schools: Developers' views of implementation barriers and facilitators. *School Mental Health, 1*(1), 26–36. doi:10.1007/s12310-008-9002-5

Freeman, J., Kern, L., Lombardi, A., Swain-Bradway, J., & Sugai, G. (2018). Stronger together: Delivering college and career readiness skills to all through a school wide positive behavior intervention and support framework. In K. B. Flannery, P. Hershfeldt, & J. Freeman (Eds.), *Lessons learned on implementation of PBIS in high schools: Current trends and future directions* (pp. 41–53). Eugene, OR: University of Oregon Press.

Gamm, S., Elliott, J., Halbert, J. W., Price-Baugh, R., Hall, R., Walston, D., … Casserly, M. (2012). *Common core state standards and diverse urban students: Using multi-tiered systems of support.* Retrieved from https://eric.ed.gov/?id=ED537476

Goodman, S., & Bohanon, H. (2018). A framework for supporting all students: One-size-fits-all no longer works in schools. *American School Board Journal*, February, 1–4, 2018. Retrieved from https://ecommons.luc.edu/education_facpubs/116/

Greenberg, M. T., & Abenavoli, R. (2017). Universal interventions: Fully exploring their impacts and potential to produce population-level impacts. *Journal of Research on Educational Effectiveness, 10*(1), 40–67.

Harms, A., Nantais, M., Tuomikoski, K., & Weaver, S. (2019). Designing educational data systems to support continuous improvement. *Association for Positive Behavior Support Newsletter, 17*(1), 2–3.

Illinois State Board of Education. (n.d.). Learning standards: Social/emotional learning standards. Retrieved from www.isbe.net/pages/social-emotional-learning-standards.aspx

Sailor, W. (2015). Advances in schoolwide inclusive school reform. *Remedial and Special Education, 36*(2), 94–99.

Sailor, W. (2017). Equity as a basis for inclusive educational systems change. *Australasian Journal of Special Education, 41*(1), 1–17. doi:10.1017/jse.2016.12

Silver, H. F., Dewing, R. T., & Perini, M. J. (2012). *The core six: Essential strategies for achieving excellence with the common core.*

Slavin, R. E. (2007). Comprehensive school reform. Retrieved from www.successforall.org/wp-content/uploads/2016/02/Comprehensive-School-Reform.pdf

Sleegers, P. J. C., Thoonen, E. E. J., Oort, F. J., & Peetsma, T. T. D. (2014). Changing classroom practices: The role of school-wide capacity for sustainable improvement. *Journal of Educational Administration, 52*(5), 617–652. doi:10.1108/JEA-11-2013-0126

The Strategic Instruction Model (SIM): Addressing the Needs of all Learners. (n.d.). Retrieved from https://sim.drupal.ku.edu/learning-strategies

VanDerHeyden, A., & Witt, J. (2008). Best practices in can't do/won't do assessment. *Best Practices in School Psychology V, 2*, 195–208.

Vermont Agency of Education. (2016). The 13 dimensions of school climate. Retrieved from http://education.vermont.gov/documents/edu-school-climate-13%20Dimensions.pdf

2

UNDERSTANDING PRINCIPLES OF PREVENTION AND SUPPORT

In a Nutshell

- Discipline means to teach. If you want a student to change a behavior or skill, you have to teach them how to do it.
- We reinforce and punish behaviors and skills, not learners. If the behavior keeps happening, it is being reinforced somehow.
- Universal and group approaches provide efficiency and incidental benefit to students who may be unidentified or at risk.

Introduction

I (Hank) first started making a conscious effort to drive the speed limit when I moved to Chicago. I wanted to obey the law (I'm a rule follower by nature), decrease the wear on my car, and save gas. So, once I am on the highway and reach the legal cruising speed, I set my cruise control. For those of you who are beginning to sweat thinking about being behind me, I make sure I am in the far right lane. Even though I moved to the slow lane, angry drivers were sometimes so close I could see the whites of their eyes, or I could see them extend their middle finger (an insult in the United States). What's the point of talking about driving in a book about schools? The climate of the larger group (the rest of the drivers) can impact, for better or worse, an individual's learning and behavior. You can have the best individual plan in the world (e.g., my driving plan), but if the climate does not encourage the new behavior, it won't be sustainable. This chapter will include an overview of some of the scientific principles related to learning and behavior as well as key systems components that will help you to implement interventions more effectively.

Connection – Reinforcement

You may never have had the need to ask a student to leave your classroom for discipline reasons, but you may have seen it happen. For example, Cedric was a 9th-grade student who read at about the 3rd-grade level. In English, when his teacher asked him to get out his book, he would begin to bang on the desk, make noises, and talk to his peers. The teacher would try to correct him, but he kept refusing to follow directions. One day the teacher had had enough, and told Cedric in front of his peers to leave the class. Cedric said, "fine with me, I don't care." He then put up his hand and said, "talk to the hand because the man does not understand." After slamming the door, Cedric walked to the chair outside the discipline dean's office, known as "Cedric's chair" due to the frequency with which he was sent to sit in it. After about a 45-minute wait, and missing his next class, Cedric met with the dean to review the events of the morning. The dean was concerned, listened to Cedric's description of the problem, and encouraged him that he had a bright future if he could keep himself out of trouble. The next day, Cedric began banging his hand on the desk when the teacher asked the students to take out their books. It is important to analyze Cedric's behavior through the lens of reinforcement.

Point/Principle – Reinforcement

In general, *reinforcement involves adding something preferred or removing something aversive following a behavior*. The end result is that the behavior is maintained at its current level or increases. What can be added or taken away following a behavior (called stimuli) can include things you can touch (e.g., food, work, objects), and things you cannot (e.g., attention from peers, attention from adults, stimulation). Seeing behavior through the lens of reinforcement allows you to understand the payoff for Cedric's behavior. If you think about your own behavior, we typically do not do anything that does not work at some level. For example, some of us shake our legs when we sit for a while (we get stimulation). Others speed to work to avoid being late.

Most behaviors, when you consider them, lead to some type of payoff (reinforcement), or we would not continue them. For academic skills, students are often given positive feedback, praise, the satisfaction of achieving the correct answer, or the "escape" of having the teacher and spotlight move on to the next student once a correct answer is given. At the secondary level, we sometimes fail to build in these consistent types of reinforcement for social-emotional learning skills and behaviors, and in fact our practices sometimes work against successful outcomes when it comes to behavior.

Let's go back to Cedric now and look at his behavior through the eyes of reinforcement. When prompted to get out his book, Cedric was about to be asked to read content at a level he could not, which would likely cause him not only frustration, but embarrassment in front of his peers. Due to his disruptive behaviors, he not only escaped these negative stimuli (frustration and embarrassment), but also received attention, albeit negative, from the teacher, and likely his peers. When Cedric was sent to the office, he was able to have one-on-one time with a caring concerned adult.

Let's recap: Cedric was able to get away from work that was not easy for him, he received attention from his peers and teacher, and had a personal counseling session with an adult. Sounds like a pretty good day to me! The point is that if we see what the payoff is for Cedric, *we might be able to help teach skills that have the same payoff as his problem behavior* (e.g., asking for help, asking for a break when frustrated, academic remediation). We do not want to make the mistake that we think we are punishing students, when in fact, we are reinforcing their behavior.

BOX 2.1 PONDERING ON PURPOSE

- How have you accidentally reinforced a student's undesired behavior in the past? Did you add something preferred or remove something aversive?
- Why is it so easy to overlook the truth behind why a behavior is happening?
- What do you think are some common examples of things that teachers and/or administrators do, thinking they are "punishments" when they are could be reinforcing students' inappropriate behavior?

Application – Reinforcement

If you were Cedric's teacher, how might you try to address his needs? Are there long-term solutions that might address his reading level and need for attention? Are there short-term skills you could teach him to handle his frustration more appropriately? Would there be any accommodations you could provide to decrease Cedric's desire to leave the class? Whatever you choose, your solutions need to work as well or better than what Cedric is already doing to obtain attention and escape frustrating work.

Connection – Correction, Feedback, and Punishment

Chris was in the 9th grade at a large urban high school. One evening his mother, his sole caretaker, left him with his baby brother alone all night. She was intoxicated when she returned the next morning as he was getting ready for school. Although Chris had taken care of his brother, he had neglected to take out the trash, which was beginning to smell. His mother called him into the kitchen. In a deafening tone, she asked him why he had not taken out the trash. When Chris said he was sorry, his mother slapped him across the face and told him to take the trash out now.

Later that morning, Chris was called in by his language arts teacher and she asked why he had not turned in his homework that week. At first, he said, he did not know he had homework to complete. When the teacher reminded him that he did have homework, he said, "If I had a dog, he would have eaten my homework." At that point, the teacher gave him a detention after school for not bringing his work. He told her that was fine, and that "my friends are in detention anyway!" Why would giving Chris a detention not be an effective punishment for being late with his homework?

Point/Principle – Correction, Feedback, and Punishment

We have to look at what punishment means in order to answer the question about Chris' punishment. Punishment is an event that follows a behavior, which should make the chances of that behavior to occur again less likely, or for the behavior to stop altogether. Punishment does not necessarily mean yelling, scolding, screaming, or taking something away. It means to **add something (typically not pleasant for that person) or take something away after a behavior, that decreases the chance that the behavior will happen again.** We actually sometimes "punish" academic mistakes when we give corrective feedback and a student stops making the same mistake. When we correct students through giving feedback, we are trying to change the problem behavior. When we attempt to punish a student's behavior, we are merely trying to make it stop.

For Chris, there is not much you could do to him that would be considered "aversive" enough to punish his behavior. He is effectively desensitized to anything you could do (yell, threaten, assign a detention). Also, thinking back to reinforcement, by giving him a detention, the teacher was actually helping him to avoid going home. The detention could increase the chances he might not bring his homework in the future. Sometimes we think we are punishing a student's behavior, but in reality, we might be rewarding it.

For academic skills, we often see similar issues with punishing errors. For example, when grading essays, teachers sometimes give such detailed and specific feedback about mistakes that the student can blindly apply the edits and not actually make changes to their thought process or writing skills on the next assignment (so the style of feedback has actually reinforced the mistakes). Or, when every type and instance of a mistake is pointed out throughout an essay, students may become desensitized to the feedback and stop reading the corrections halfway through.

Correcting students is important, but the over-reliance on corrective strategies that are intended to punish student behaviors has some side effects. In a geometry class, you would not allow a student to keep using the wrong formula (e.g., $a^2 + b^2 = c^4$) because you were afraid of hurting someone's feelings. Or, if a student was starting to run his hand toward the circular saw in a construction class, you would not say, well he just needs to experience the natural and logical consequences. In both cases, you would provide feedback in the form of some type of verbal correction, which would hopefully stop these behaviors from happening again. The key is that you would stop the mistake, and immediately add some instruction to teach the student what to do differently.

Unfortunately, in addition to the risk of accidentally reinforcing problem behaviors as described above, the overuse of traditional punishment strategies for behavioral infractions (e.g., yelling, detention, suspension) has side effects. These side effects include repetition of the same behaviors (repeat offenses) due to the fact that no skills were taught, or creating a sense of need for revenge towards the person delivering the punishment (which can lead to even more problematic behaviors). *Think about correction as a bank account. You have to make more positive deposits than you make withdrawals, or you will get an overdraft statement.*

By finding the type of feedback most valuable to the student and providing more positive than negative feedback, your corrections will be more effective. However, even though you begin to rely on strategies beyond punishment alone, you also need to remember that change takes time. Framing this concept in terms of academics, think about how difficult it would be to teach students if your only instructional method was to point out their mistakes and insist they stop (with no explanation of what they should do instead of the mistake, or feedback about the skills they are demonstrating correctly). This would not be a very efficient instructional approach!

Application – Correction, Feedback, and Punishment

Have you ever thought about the reinforcement involved in teaching an academic skill? Or the idea that what might be punishing for you could actually be reinforcing for someone else? Reflect on a time when you tried to help a student improve a skill or change a behavior and were surprised or frustrated by the outcome. Could the principles described above have come into play? If so, how?

BOX 2.2 PONDERING ON PURPOSE

- What are we doing to explicitly teach and support expectations (academic, behavioral, social)?
- How do we involve our students to encourage them to take ownership over their goal-setting?
- How do we teach students to evaluate their decisions?
- What schoolwide or classroom data do you have that could help inform you about what is working and what isn't in your school?

Connection – Incidental Benefit

Sometimes in secondary schools, people with expertise in supporting students most at risk have concerns about implementing preventative supports for all students. One of these concerns is that their time and focus really should be about helping students who have the most needs. While we understand their concern, their efforts at focusing on preventive, universal supports can help students most at risk. For example, Bailey and colleagues found that having friends exposed to an intervention around drinking and tobacco use decreased the chances of getting drunk or smoking for students even if they never attended the program. Schoolwide and classwide supports create sustainable environments for students with more intense needs, but often benefit many others.

Point/Principle – Incidental Benefit

Students without any disability or at-risk label can benefit from interventions not necessarily intended for them. In fact, some special education laws state that incidental benefit is welcomed. For, example, the Individuals with Disabilities Education Act (IDEA) in the United States says that supports can be provided to all students, "even if one or more nondisabled children benefit from such services" Sec. 1413 (a)(4)(A). This means that resources and interventions that are designed to support students with intense needs can in some cases be applied to all students, even if others who are not at risk incidentally benefit from them.

Academic vocabulary instruction is a great example of incidental benefit. As researchers Margarita Calderon and Sean Slakk suggest, for students who are English Learners (ELs), a common recommendation is to provide explicit instruction on high-impact vocabulary words (e.g., verbs from the Common Core State Standards: determine, analyze, delineate, represent, etc.). Many high school teachers assume students know what it means to explain versus analyze, and feel like it is not a valuable use of time to teach these types of words to entire classes.

I (Kelly) recall a meeting with a large group of high school administrators when they first received access to the SAT data for their buildings. They were shocked by some of the words-in-context items that 30–70% of students had missed, even at a school with high levels of academic achievement, where very few students were identified as ELs. These administrators realized that targeting academic vocabulary; as recommended by the authors Harvey Silver, Thomas Dewing, and Matthew Perini, according to the recommendations for students who are ELs, could potentially have a positive impact, even on students who were generally achieving at high levels. Providing explicit vocabulary instruction would be especially beneficial if done with instructional routines that can easily be differentiated.

Application – Incidental Benefit

Make a list of strategies you have tried or recommended for specific students who were struggling with a skill. For each one, identify another student or type of need that strategy may have supported. How could you provide this support to a larger group of students?

Connection – Schoolwide and Classwide Supports

Have you ever been to a birthday party for a four-year-old at a pizza parlor with a gaming arcade? I (Hank) have nothing against these places, but they can be a little over-stimulating for me. However, one of my favorite games there is whack-a-mole. The point of the game is to bop the heads of as many plastic marsupials (moles) as possible in a given amount of time. Bop one on the head and another one pops up. While this is an engaging way to spend about two minutes at a birthday party, it is not a great way to handle your students.

Unfortunately, schools may take a whack-a-mole approach to supporting students. Sean is having trouble with reading in his English program and gets a one-on-one tutor. Sarah is acting out in Algebra I and is given a very effective individual plan. The problem is that there are six other students who are struggling to read in Sean's class and five other students in Sarah's class that have been sent out due to disruptive behavior. These plans are working well for Sean and Sarah. However, the *interventions might be more efficient if consideration was given about what could be done classwide, or even schoolwide.*

Point/Principle – Schoolwide and Classwide Supports

Schoolwide approaches, sometimes called universal approaches, are strategies that are applied to every student in the building. These interventions can include teaching all students what is expected, using effective teaching strategies and curriculum for all students, or teaching social and emotional skill sets. Regardless of what approach your education system takes, there is typically a focus on some type of standards related to college and career readiness. While these do typically include academic outcomes, they also include literacy skills related to speaking and listening (e.g., working in groups, sharing ideas).

By thinking first about the quality of what all students are exposed to, you are saving time for the future. For instance, researchers Scott and Barrett found that every discipline action you write up takes approximately 20 minutes of the instructor's time, and about 45 minutes for the administrator to process. If you address some of the low-level problems (e.g., the student not having pencils), you would have more time to deal with more significant problems (e.g., fighting, the student who cannot read).

For example, Northfield Middle School and High School in Vermont was concerned that many of their students were having discipline problems, were not succeeding on core assessments, and were struggling socially and emotionally. They began teaching all the students in the school basic expectations for student behavior. Academically, they found that their students were struggling with the reading portion of their statewide assessment. They looked at their master schedule and created an intervention class that every student took, in addition to their English classes, that exposed them to an evidence-based reading program (Study Island). Additionally, they also began using social and emotional screening data (along with behavior and academic data), to identify students in need of more support. While this was not a short-term process, they found their teachers were eventually referring fewer of their students for discipline problems and more students were passing their standardized assessments.

BOX 2.3 PONDERING ON PURPOSE

- Brainstorm examples of ways to determine whether a student "can't" do something or "won't" do something that do not involve speculation.
- Why is it important to consider incidental benefits?
- What "whack-a-mole" situations come up in your school?

Application – Schoolwide and Classwide Supports

If you could choose one of your favorite strategies to help students succeed, that you wish every teacher in your school would implement, what would it be and why? What would be the impact if students experienced the strategy regularly in all settings throughout their day?

Conclusion

Understanding the principles of prevention and support are key, we believe, to helping people understand why taking on these initiatives are so important. The importance of understanding why schoolwide approaches are needed including talking about the principles of reinforcement, and punishment; the meaning of discipline; the purpose of prevention; and why incidental benefit is relevant will help your teams move forward with future stages of buy-in. Taking time to discuss these components with your staff ahead of implementation may lead to increased understanding, buy-in, and fidelity of implementation.

Bibliography

Alberto, P. A., & Troutman, A. C. (2012). *Applied behavior analysis for teachers*. New York, NY: Pearson Higher Ed.

Andrews, A. (2017). *The little things: Why you really should sweat the small stuff*. Nashville, TN: Thomas Nelson.

Bailey, D., Duncan, G., Odgers, C., & Yu, W. (2015). *Persistence and fadeout in the impacts of child and adolescent interventions* (Working Paper No. 2015–27). Retrieved from the Life Course Centre Working Paper Series Website: https://www.ncbi.nlm.nih.gov/pmc/articles/PMC5779101/

Bohanon, H., Castillo, J., & Afton, M. (2015). Embedding self-determination and futures planning within a schoolwide framework. *Intervention in School and Clinic, 50*(4), 203–209.

Bohanon, H., Gilman, C., Parker, B., Amell, C., & Sortino, G. (2016). Using school improvement and implementation science to integrate multi-tiered systems of support in secondary schools. *Australasian Journal of Special Education, 40*(2), 99–116. doi:10.1017/jse.2016.8

Burns, M. K., & Gibbons, K. (2010). *Implementing response-to-intervention in elementary and secondary schools: Procedures to assure scientific-based practices*. New York, NY: Guilford Press.

Calderon, M. E., & Slakk, S. (2018). *Teaching reading to English learners, grades 6-12: A framework for improving achievement in the content areas*. Thousand Oaks, CA: Corwin Press.

Cooper, J. T., & Scott, T. M. (2017). The keys to managing instruction and behavior: Considering high probability practices. *Teacher Education and Special Education, 40*(2), 102–113. doi:088840641770082

Go, A. S., Mozaffarian, D., Roger, V. L., Benjamin, E. J., Berry, J. D., Borden, W. B., ... Fox, C. S. (2013). Executive summary: Heart disease and stroke statistics: 2013 update: A report from the American Heart Association. *Circulation, 127*(1), 143–146. doi:10.1161/CIR.0b013e318282ab8f

Greenberg, M. T., & Abenavoli, R. (2017). Universal interventions: Fully exploring their impacts and potential to produce population-level impacts. *Journal of Research on Educational Effectiveness, 10*(1), 40–67.

Malloy, J. M., Sundar, V., Hagner, D., Pierias, L., & Viet, T. (2010). The efficacy of the renew model: Individualized school-to-career services for youth at risk of school dropout. *Journal of At-Risk Issues, 15*(2), 17–24.

Reinke, W. M., Herman, K. C., & Stormont, M. (2013). Classroom level positive behavior supports in schools implementing SW-PBIS: Identifying areas for enhancement. *Journal of Positive Behavior Interventions, 15*(1), 39–50. doi:10.1177/1098300712459079

Scott, T. M., & Barrett, S. B. (2004). Using staff and student time engaged in disciplinary procedures to evaluate the impact of school-wide PBS. *Journal of Positive Behavior Interventions, 6*(1), 21–27. doi:10.1177/10983007040060010401

Sidman, M. (1989). *Coercion and its fallout.* Boston, MA: Authors Cooperative.

Silver, H. F., Dewing, R. T., & Perini, M. J. (2012). *The core six: Essential strategies for achieving excellence with the Common Core.* Alexandria, VA: ASCD.

Simonsen, B., Fairbanks, S., Briesch, A., Myers, D., & Sugai, G. (2008). Evidence-based practices in classroom management: Considerations for research to practice. *Education & Treatment of Children, 31*(3), 351–380. doi:10.1353/etc.0.0007

Stephan, S., Sugai, G., Lever, N., & Connors, E. (2015). Strategies for integrating mental health into schools via a multi-tiered system of support. *Child and Adolescent Psychiatric Clinics of North America, 24*(2), 211–231.

U.S. Department of Education, What Works Clearinghouse. (2016). *Children identified with or at risk for an emotional disturbance topic area intervention report: Functional behavioral assessment-based interventions.* Retrieved from http://whatworks.ed.gov

VanDerHeyden, A. M., & Witt, J. C. (2008). Best practices in can't do/won't do assessment. *Best Practices in School Psychology V, 2*, 195–208.

Vuolo, M., Kelly, B. C., & Kadowski, J. (2016). Independent and interactive effects of smoking bans and tobacco taxes on a cohort of US young adults. *American Journal of Public Health, 106*(2), 374–380. doi:10.2105/AJPH.2015.302968

Walker, H. M. (1996). Integrated approaches to preventing antisocial behavior patterns among school-age children and youth. *Journal of Emotional and Behavioral Disorders, 4*(4), 194–209.

Wolfe, K., Pyle, D., Charlton, C. T., Sabey, C. V., Lund, E. M., & Ross, S. W. (2016). A systematic review of the empirical support for check-in check-out. *Journal of Positive Behavior Interventions, 18*(2), 74–88. doi:10.1177/1098300715595957

3

STAGES OF IMPLEMENTATION

In a Nutshell

- Schoolwide change should never be initiated "on a whim." Improvements should be based on team effort that includes a well-developed plan. Your plan should include time for establishing consensus, reviewing policies, practices, research, and data, as well as determining desired outcomes and indicators of success.
- Critical elements of "readiness for change" can be reached through six stages of implementation.
- Implementation science provides us with six steps for an effective and efficient process: Exploration and Adaptation, Program Installation, Initial Implementation, Full Operation, Innovation, and Sustainability.

Introduction

Think about the last time you or someone you know purchased a vehicle. What steps did you go through before making the purchase (e.g., research, test drive)? For some reason we forget what we would normally do in our personal lives when we try to implement an intervention in our schools. For example, I (Hank) was once invited to a high school to talk about behavior prevention with their staff. As it turns out, I had been invited there because the school had been cited for disproportionate discipline practices. Essentially, I was their consequence for their ineffective practices. Other examples include the principal simply telling their staff they are going to implement an intervention. Or, sometimes an internal school team will invite external experts to present on a model, without any preparation for their school, and then ask the staff to vote if they would be willing to implement what they just saw in the slides. While there may be some scenarios where these approaches work, in our experience they usually do not.

In this chapter we introduce an overview of phases that will help you implement change in a way that maximizes fidelity, integrity, and effectiveness. Based on the work of John Kotter (author of *Why Transformations Fail*), and Dean Fixsen and Karen Blasé at the National Implementation Research Center, these phases remind us that effective change takes time and careful planning. These phases include Exploration and Adoption, Program Installation, Initial Implementation, Full Operation, Innovation, and Sustainability. We also include Readiness for Change as a "pre-stage." The phases provide a structure that reflects the best practices recommended in implementation science. We dive deeper into some of these stages in other chapters, but a general overview is provided here.

Connection – Stages of Implementation

Have you or one of your colleagues/administrators ever returned from a one-day workshop with a shiny new binder, and then attempted to dive right into the program, only to hit roadblocks? I (Kelly) worked in a high school where we attempted to implement a tiered system of behavioral supports. We had some solid schoolwide teaching and acknowledging of expected student behaviors happening. We decided to add a second tier of support in the form of a check in/check out system.

Another teacher and I took it upon ourselves to design and implement the system, pretty much on our own. We had many detailed documents outlining the system and how it would work, we had a beautiful form for kids to carry around throughout the day to log feedback from teachers, and we had an administrator who gave his blessing to move forward. The two of us quickly found ourselves running around the building training teachers and students individually, reminding students and teachers to follow the plan, modifying plans when we had teachers who were struggling to keep it neutral (venting about the student instead), finding students who were not showing up to check in or out, slugging through data entry and analysis, and communicating with families.

We ended up with a few students who responded extremely well to the plan, but an overall failure in that we stopped trying to implement the system because "it wasn't working." In retrospect, it wasn't working because we did not take all the steps and have everything in place that we would have needed to make the system complete and effective.

BOX 3.1 PONDERING ON PURPOSE

- Reflect personally on a time you attempted to implement a strategy you learned about. It does not need to be classroom-related but could be. Perhaps it was a diet, or an exercise goal.
- What factors went into its success or failure?
- In what ways did you implement the strategy as it was intended? In what ways did you veer from the original description?

Point/Principle – Stages of Implementation

Readiness for Change

There are some general principles that you need to consider when implementing any program successfully. Susan Forman and colleagues at Rutgers University identified several components that should be in place to effectively implement an evidence-based practice in schools. Table 3.1 provides a checklist of these elements for your review. As you read through them, keep in mind that without clear, measurable steps mapped out, including data for objectivity, it is hard to establish whether the ingredients of this "recipe for readiness" are actually in place. The six stages of implementation that follow will lead to the factors in this table.

Table 3.1 What is Needed to Implement Evidenced-based Approaches

Component	In Place/ Not in Place	Result
Support from the administration for the intervention (e.g., principal)		
Support from teachers for the intervention (e.g., priority)		
Financial resources to sustain the intervention (e.g., FTE)		
Training and coaching to increase fidelity of implementation		
Alignment of the interventions with the school's goals, philosophy, policies, and programs		
Program outcomes are visible to all stakeholders		
A process is established to address the change in staff and administrators (e.g., plan, manual, specified roles)		

Stage 1: Exploration and Adoption

Stage 1 of implementation focuses on exploring the need for an intervention, building consensus around a plan, and slowly moving towards adoption of the practice. There are several steps that can be helpful to you in the first stage of exploration. Table 3.2 provides examples of activities that support your exploration and potential adoption of your schoolwide efforts. This stage can take from one to two years. Be patient, if you skip this step you may pay the price later when you have to clean up your efforts after a false start.

It may sound cliché, but "knowing your audience" in the exploration and adaption stage is really important. As you review Table 3.2, start to think about the personalities, talents, and biases of stakeholders, and how they may impact your work within this stage. Chapter 5 will guide you through the work of Stage 1. As you explore what innovations you will adopt, establish and publicize the process you will use. Transparency will prevent future roadblocks and strengthen stakeholder engagement. It will also help maximize the use of available resources and avoid "surprises" that can occur, requiring repeating or revising completed steps. Later chapters will help you consider ways to do this, including ways to share information as well as protocols for analyzing data.

BOX 3.2 PONDERING ON PURPOSE

- Who is responsible for collecting and communicating the information in Table 3.2?
- Are there existing methods your school uses to document and communicate this type of information?
- How do you determine that the information reaches all stakeholders, especially those who do not frequent school events or who have roadblocks to their ability to communicate with the school?
- How do you ensure accessibility of methods you provide for stakeholder input?
- Do you ask for input in ways that allow stakeholders to reflect honestly without fear of retribution or judgement?

Stage 2: Program Installation

Once a team has identified the desired program/practice/intervention/innovation to fit their needs, they will need to begin identifying the systems features needed for success. First, it is critical to seek training for those who will be leading the efforts. While working with an external coach or

Table 3.2 Possible Steps to Address Stage 1

Step	Purpose	Example
Identify a small group of leaders	Identifies a team that can guide the schoolwide intervention	Principal brings together five staff members, one administrator, a student, and a community member to look at adopting schoolwide social and emotional learning
Create mission and vision	Sets the priority and focus for your schoolwide team	Create a supportive community whose purpose is to maximize student learning. Students are challenged to realize the value of learning and to reach their potential in a safe, healthy, and respectful environment.
Align project with existing policies	Creates a connection to policies that schools already need to address	Crosswalk schoolwide efforts with state standards, goals for school improvement, or accountability for student growth.
Align project with existing priorities	Makes connections with existing goals or priorities for your school	One school was not making annual yearly progress according to federal law and needed to find a solution for improving reading outcomes.
Review existing data related to project	Identifies patterns and priorities that might be addressed by your schoolwide initiative	A middle school discovered that a majority of their students were not at acceptable levels for reading comprehension based on benchmark assessment data.

(Continued)

Table 3.2 (Continued)

Step	Purpose	Example
Survey readiness of staff	Identifies staff's perceptions around the need for the schoolwide intervention	Staff completed the Effective Behavior Self-Assessment Survey for positive behavior support. They identified the need for teaching expectations to students as a high priority.
Identify programs that meet your students' and community's needs	Selects programs that have evidence for addressing needs in environments similar to your own	One school reviewed the dropout prevention guide from the Institute of Educational Science, What Works Clearing House https://ies.ed.gov/ncee/wwc/PracticeGuide/24
Participate in training as a team	Creates common knowledge and language around the intervention	A secondary school team attended a statewide conference for academic- and behavior-related Multi-tiered Systems of Support (MTSS).
Connect with schools with similar examples	Finds evidence that the intervention can be effective in a setting such as yours	A district administrator set up a visit with another district that had an effective district team supporting schoolwide efforts.
Obtain support from administration	Provides the team with time and resources	A team is provided with a stipend to attend summer training and plan the development of schoolwide supports.
Complete the Hexagon Tool from SISEP (see Chapter 5)	Provides structure to accomplish many of the steps related to Stage 1	A team completed this tool and realized they needed access to external coaching.

organization is crucial, identifying the ability of stakeholders and building internal capacity is imperative for buy-in, fidelity of implementation,
and sustainability. To avoid the risk of mixed messages or ineffective leadership, the team leading the efforts must have common vision, knowledge
of content, confidence, and ability to model, teach, and give feedback on
the model.

Something that can be challenging about a tiered approach to systems
change is that it requires leaders to develop an understanding of the overall framework and critical features of the system, as well as be well-versed
in multiple specific practices and their features. For example, MTSS teams
need to know that if done correctly, tier one systems support around 80%
of students, while also freeing up time and resources need to address
more intensive needs. They need to know how to use data effectively in all
decision making. Leaders also need the ability to model and give feedback
on any specific practices chosen for implementation based on data (such
as the specific ways to teach and give feedback on behaviors, or a schoolwide style of teaching students to annotate text). The leadership team needs
to understand the micro-level of implementation (as in what the specific
interactions between adults and students should look like) and how the
macro-level of systems support implementation with fidelity (as in how
both the implementation and outcomes will be monitored and responded
to by the team). Any one practice in itself is typically easy to understand,
but learning to select, support, and sustain the implementation of practices
is more complex.

It is unlikely a team will attend one conference or workshop on a topic
such as social emotional learning (SEL), multi-tiered systems of support, or
school-based mental health and suddenly be "ready to roll" independently.
Teams should attend some initial training, then discuss and reflect to determine the type and intensity of follow-up learning and support/coaching
they will need for success. Depending on the experience and capacity of
the members on the team, the needs will vary. Keep in mind, the members of the leadership team will be minimally responsible for setting goals,
selecting practices to focus on and implement, monitoring systems, practices, and data, and providing feedback to staff and other stakeholders,
and typically providing at least some level of professional development for
other staff members. This group needs to become the expert voice for the
school, so spending some time and effort on that part of the process is a
worthy investment.

Once the team has developed a good understanding of the system as a
whole and the key practices the team will roll-out and support, they will
need to problem-solve around pertinent systems issues. These systems issues
will vary based on the context, needs, and next steps for a particular team

and school. For example, the team may determine that they need to explore scheduling options in order to carve out time for schoolwide SEL/behavioral lessons, or to add flexible time for intervention groups.

BOX 3.3 PONDERING ON PURPOSE

- Why is it important to spend time creating structural frameworks for implementation?
- What will be the major costs for implementation? What funds could be used? Are there creative solutions to defer these costs?
- How does your school define roles and responsibilities for stakeholders? Is this information accessible to all? Are there written job descriptions? How might the development of job descriptions impact your school climate and culture?

Stage 3: Initial Implementation

You may have heard the phrase, "Everyone wants change, but nobody wants to change." During the initial implementation stage, a cohort is used to help stakeholders want to change. Similar to how companies provide product samples to entice customers, a pilot group, or initial implementation cohort, can make a new innovation enticing to their colleagues. As researchers Dean Fixsen and E. Andrews Balas separately stated, developing a strong implementation cohort that follows implementation science and research significantly impacts the success of implementation. Schools that use an implementation cohort have a higher and quicker success rate (80% over three years, as opposed to a rate of 14% over 17 years for those who do not). The initial implementation cohort should be stakeholders that are ready and willing to take a risk.

Sometimes, we start with those that already have the training needed, and/or we provide additional training. They will pilot the innovation you would like to eventually see schoolwide. Selecting the initial implementation cohort should be done under careful consideration, as they model and set the expectation for fidelity to the process, integrity of implementation, and expected outcomes. They can also help provide feedback that will inform decisions as you "scale up" to the rest of the school. The State Implementation & Scaling-up of Evidence-based Practices Center provides resources that can help you think through and execute this process. Even if you do not have a cohort, you can start with an initial pilot for an intervention.

To make evidence-based decisions about what to implement and how, the cohort will need data to present back to the community. Before, during, and after implementation, the initial implementation cohort collects data, and are careful to analyze what works and what doesn't. After a pre-determined amount of time has passed or steps are taken, they communicate their results to the community. This communication is key, because their messaging can make or break the decision to proceed. A carefully constructed communication plan should be in place. While presenting their findings, it is essential to connect the data back to school improvement goals as much as possible.

After this initial implementation, as always, it is important to revisit the goals and check progress and revise your plan accordingly. Implementing something new takes time, and there are sure to be hiccups along the way while figuring out how to implement successfully in the context of your setting. Revisit your plan before launching full-scale implementation to make sure it reflects the experiences and feedback of the initial implementation cohort.

BOX 3.4 PONDERING ON PURPOSE

- What qualities or determining factors would you consider while selecting an implementation cohort?
- Being on an initial implementation team can be time consuming and bring additional stress to its members. If your school does not have the funds to provide additional stipends for these responsibilities, what are other ways you can recognize and reward teachers for their participation?
- The results of the initial implementation cohort alone should not be the only factor for determining whether to implement an innovation. What else might factor into this decision? How will you communicate this to stakeholders?

Stage 4: Full Operation

As you will see in the next two stages of implementation, a tiered schoolwide systems approach is much like school improvement in that it becomes an iterative process and is never truly complete. However, there are some established fidelity measures to determine the level of implementation of specific tiers and types of support. In order to achieve full operation, the practices roll out beyond the scope of the leadership team and/or pilot groups and become an established part of the school system and culture for all pertinent stakeholders.

At tier one, all staff members have a part to play in a system-wide strategy and it becomes a regular part of their roles. For example, all adults in the building will use the same language to teach behavioral expectations, or all teachers will teach and reinforce the same graphic organizer to support students in identifying textual evidence. At tiers two and three, the interventions become an established part of how the staff involved "do their jobs." Leadership positions are filled by staff as needed. For example, in schools that utilize a Professional Learning Communities (PLC) model, each PLC may have a lead for data analysis, or expert trainer for a specific tier one strategy, or perhaps a liaison to the tier one leadership team. All staff become familiar and accustomed to the expectations that practices are implemented with fidelity, that data are used to drive decisions, that fidelity will be monitored and coached, and that support is provided to students with increasing tiers of intervention as needed.

As the overall system evolves, practices are added and supported so that eventually all three tiers of support are implemented in response to identified needs in the various domains of student skills and outcomes (academic, SEL, career pathways, etc.). Students and parents should also be aware and familiar with the systems in place, and students in particular should begin to have an active role in monitoring their own strengths, needs, and progress related to the schoolwide vision and goals.

For full operation, a systems approach is integrated with all the work that happens across leadership and staff and is not considered a separate program that is "owned" by one particular group of staff, students, or stakeholders. Teams in a leadership capacity are aligned with each other and supporting the work of each other in an organized way, rather than operating as silos or competing with each other.

BOX 3.5 PONDERING ON PURPOSE

- How will your school measure that implementation is being done with fidelity and integrity?
- How will supports put in place during the implementation stage be phased over time?
- How will your team recognize that the new innovation has become routine?

Stage 5: Innovation

During Stage 5, the leadership team uses established credibility (based on their data) to change additional systems within the school. For example, staff roles around schoolwide efforts become codified in position descriptions. Schoolwide efforts may be included in job descriptions and become a component of the hiring process when attracting new staff. There is an expansion of the types of data the team reviews. The team is now selecting additional interventions as needed. Perhaps changes to the master schedule are made based on data and best practices of your schoolwide supports.

Stage 6: Sustainability

Within Stage 6, your team is focusing on ways to sustain your interventions and encourage ongoing improvement. The data-driven approach and iterative process of identifying needs and making adjustments accordingly becomes "how you do business." The team focuses on preparing new leadership to take over key roles for implementation of schoolwide efforts. Additionally, ongoing communication with the school staff and larger community needs to focus on the successes of the program and the next steps. The team needs to solidify the internal and external coaching support. Further, the team's approach should be a part of the master professional development schedule for the school. There are also ongoing refinements that need to occur at each tier of intervention, based on the review of your data. Connecting with sender/feeder elementary or middle schools can also help the successful transition of students. Also, as staff increase their reliable use of evidence-based practices, they can begin to consider stopping practices that are not effective in improving outcomes.

The State Implementation and Scaling-up of Evidence-based Practices Center (SISEP) provides very useful tools that teams can use to determine what stage they are in, based on implementation science. One tool is called Stages of Implementation Analysis: Where Are We? The instrument is available at the National Implementation Research Network's Active Implementation Hub (a link to the tool can be found here: https:// implementation.fpg.unc.edu). Teams can use this assessment to determine where they are in the stages of implementation, and plan for system supports they need to be successful in their next steps of the intervention.

Another tool found on the SISEP site is the District Capacity Assessment (DAC). This tool helps districts to develop the capacity to support schoolwide interventions, district-wide. The tool encourages districts to consider the systems (e.g., coaching capacity, resources) and data they will need to support effective implementation of schoolwide efforts. Specifically, the DAC is organized around what they refer to as Implementation Drivers including:

- System Interventions
- Facilitative Administrative Support
- Decision Data Support System
- Coaching

- Training
- Selection
- Performance Assessment

It is possible to implement your schoolwide efforts outside of district support. However, you will find that your ability to obtain resources to sustain your interventions in the long term can be dependent upon district support. Without a supportive district plan (DAC), your best efforts may be subject to changes in admiration and staff at the building level. Some schools have more local control than others. Finding ways to codify your schools supports for implementation will help with your long-term success. The DAC is an excellent tool to use in tandem with the Hexagon Tool from SISEP, which allows the exploration of capacity for implementation at the building level.

Application – Stage 1: Exploration and Adoption

Look back to the list from Table 3.2. It may seem overwhelming, however these steps can be very helpful to you in laying the groundwork for later rollout of schoolwide efforts. In our own experience and research, schools that took the time to follow these early stages of implementation had higher levels of implementation than those schools that did not. Look at each item in Table 3.2 and jot down some notes about each one that are pertinent to your own school.

Conclusion

Successfully implementing a new system into your school can be thought of like a transplant surgery. Just because you try it doesn't mean it is going to "take." Over the years, doctors have learned ways to maximize the chances that it will be successful, including steps before (making sure it will be a good match), to steps after (anti-rejection medicine), and patients are closely monitored throughout. When we are changing our routines in schools and classrooms, we need to take similar proactive steps to make sure the solutions we are trying to help our patients (our students) are effective. For example, if we take the time to explore our options and engage stakeholders (Stage 1), utilize needs assessments to determine what resources are required to implement successfully and establish clear expectations for outcomes and measures of how "success" is defined (Stage 2), launch in small, closely monitored cohorts (Stage 3), and then fully implement (Stage 4), we can ensure the highest chance for success for the intervention we are attempting.

Bibliography

Algozzine, B., Barrett, S., Eber, L., George, H., Horner, R., Lewis, T., Putnam, B., Swain-Bradway, J., McIntosh, K., & Sugai, G. (2014). *School-wide PBIS tiered fidelity inventory.* OSEP Technical Assistance Center on Positive Behavioral Interventions and Supports. Retrieved from www.pbis.org

Balas, E. A., & Boren, S. A. (2000). Managing clinical knowledge for health care improvement. *Yearbook of Medical Informatics, 9*(01), 65–70.

Blase, K. A., Fixsen, D. L., Sims, B. J., & Ward, C. S. (2015, April). *Implementation science: Changing hearts, minds, behavior, and systems to improve educational outcomes.* Paper presented at the Wing Institute's Ninth Annual Summit on Evidence-Based Education, Berkeley, CA. Retrieved from https://fpg.unc.edu/node/7729

Bohanon, H., Gilman, C., Parker, B., Amell, C., & Sortino, G. (2016). Using school improvement and implementation science to integrate multi-tiered systems of support in secondary schools. *Australasian Journal of Special Education, 40*(2), 99–116. doi:10.1017/jse.2016.8

Bohanon, H., & Wu, M. (2014). Developing buy-in for positive behavior support in secondary settings. *Preventing School Failure, 58*(4), 1–7. doi:10.1080/1045988X.2013.798774

Fixsen, D. L., Blase, K. A., Timbers, G. D., & Wolf, M. M. (2001). In search of program implementation: 792 replications of the teaching-family model. In G. A. Benfeld, D. P. Farrington, & A. W. Leschied (Eds.), *Offender rehabilitation in practice: Implementing and evaluating effective programs* (pp. 149–166). New York, NY: Wiley.

Forman, S. G., Olin, S. S., Hoagwood, K. E., Crowe, M., & Saka, N. (2009). Evidence-based intervention in schools: Developers' views of implementation barriers and facilitators. *School Mental Health, 1*(1), 26–36. doi:10.1007/s12310-008-9002-5

Government Alliance on Race and Equity (GARE). (n.d.). *Organizational change processes.* Retrieved from www.racialequitytools.org/act/strategies/organizational-change-processes

Government Alliance on Race and Equity (GARE) (n.d.) *Racial equity toolkit: An opportunity to operationalize equity.* Retrieved from https://www.racialequityalliance.org/2015/10/30/racial-equity-toolkit/

Kotter, J. P. (1995). Leading change: Why transformation efforts fail. *Harvard Business Review, 73*(2), 59–67.

Lenny, J. (2009). Stop the line manufacturing and continuous integration. Retrieved from https://leanbuilds.wordpress.com/tag/stop-the-line/

National Implementation Research Network Modules. (n.d.). Retrieved from https://nirn.fpg.unc.edu/

Schoolwide Integrated Framework for Transformation. (2018). *Fidelity integrity assessment 2.0.* Schoolwide Integrated Framework for Transformation, Lawrence, KS. Retrieved from www.swiftschools.org

State Implementation & Scaling-up of Evidence-based Practices Center. (n.d.). Retrieved from https://sisep.fpg.unc.edu/

Trolander, J. (1982). Social change: Settlement houses and Saul Alinsky, 1939-1965. *Social Service Review, 56*(3), 346–365. Retrieved from www.jstor.org/stable/30011558

4

SETTING THE STAGE FOR EFFECTIVE SYSTEMS

In a Nutshell

- Take your time and prepare for implementation.
- Ensure your administration supports your efforts, and if they are on the fence lead them to networks of principals and create a small "pilot" version for your school.
- The makeup of a leadership team is essential to the success of the implementation. Have a diverse team that represents the specific needs of your school and your team.
- Involve your team in the creation of a vision and mission statement, making sure that all team members can give an "elevator speech" to describe them.

Introduction

We can learn a lesson about systems from wine. During the 1980s there was a popular wine in the United States created by Paul Masson. It was neither expensive nor the best wine. Yet, it was unique in its own way. The commercials always ended with the same tagline, "We will sell no wine before its time." This statement ensured the customer that this wine was well aged. A quick disclaimer – we are not encouraging people to drink wine! Rather, this phrase appropriately highlights that *no practice should be ever put in place unless everything has already been prepared with forethought*. Being "ready" means there are systems to support your efforts.

A perfect example of the negative effects of serving a practice before "its time" is the carousel of curriculum teachers frequently complain about. When teachers are forced to implement something with little to no training over a short period of time, they are unable to implement them with success. This lack of preparation leads to the ultimate "failure" of the curriculum, with the blame falling on the curriculum rather than its incorrect or unsupported implementation. Taking the time to address misconceptions, face personal biases, and allocating the needed resources allows the intervention room for success, similar to how aging a wine brings out its finest qualities.

BOX 4.1 PONDERING ON PURPOSE

- What data does your school have to help you determine if you are "ready"?
- After reading this chapter, rate your school on these three "components" needed. Which need the most or least amount of work (e.g., time to address misconceptions, face personal biases, and allocating the needed resources)? Why?

When analyzing failures in your school's interventions consider what supporting systems were not proactively and intentionally put into place. Omissions in the development of these systems can lead to failure of the interventions. Regardless of the type of schoolwide interventions (e.g., academic, behavioral, social, emotional), you will see several key "asks" of the implementers. These "asks" are what Rob Horner and George Sugai refer to as systems. Systems that we will address in this chapter include administrative support, a clear mission and vision, and the leadership team. Additional systems that we will address in later chapters include obtaining buy-in from your community (Chapter 5), auditing what interventions you currently have in place (Chapter 8), completing a self-assessment on your intervention (Chapter 11), creating data systems to track your interventions (Chapter 12), and developing a plan of action (Chapter 6). However, without administrative support, a clear mission and vision, and a team to guide your efforts, it is difficult to put other systems components in place.

Connection – Gaining and Maintaining Administrative Support

A high school was trying to install a schoolwide approach to behavior without administrative support. They had a group of dedicated teachers who saw a need for the approach and felt they had a plan they could put in place. However, the team was in tears. They felt their principal was fighting against them by denying resources (time and money) needed to implement their plan. For example, the principal would not allow time for professional development. The team could not afford to purchase items as incentives for their students. The team also could not have anyone with time dedicated to spearheading the schoolwide initiative.

When we met with them, we talked about ways to encourage their principal's efforts. The team secretly wished the administrator would retire early. But remember, addressing reasons something "won't work" is just as important as the implementation of the parts that will. They were able to *think from a "solution oriented" approach*, and were able to keep some options on the table. They decided to create a small pilot, from their own elbow grease, to showcase the effect of their intervention. This pilot allowed them to provide data that would hopefully enlist leadership support.

Point/Principle – Administrative Support

There are several ways your administration can support your schoolwide initiatives. For example, administrators can provide support for someone's time to lead the effort. We have seen a teacher provided with a course release or someone given up to 25% of their time to guide the schoolwide effort. These individuals were identified as an internal coach. Another thing administrators can do is to encourage a fair process for implementation. According to Chan Kim and Renée Mauborgne, there are three steps for creating a fair implementation process. These are:

1. **Engage your community early** (i.e. involve people from the beginning when you make strategic decisions).
2. **Explain your thinking behind the initiative** (i.e. don't assume people know why you made a certain decision – tell them).
3. **Be clear on your expectations for staff** – (i.e. make sure everyone knows how your work will impact their roles and responsibilities).

Additionally, administrators vote with their feet if they think the innovation is instrumental. Meetings and trainings should include an administrator (or their designee) who can make key decisions without having to leave the room. There are few things worse for a team than coming up with ideas they cannot implement due to a lack of resources. *People may feel less inclined to participate in your process if they believe their efforts do not translate into actions.*

There are ways you can encourage your administration to support your schoolwide interventions. Table 4.1 lists what Kent McIntosh and his fellow researchers found as several hindering and helping factors for gaining buy-in from administrators.

BOX 4.2 PONDERING ON PURPOSE

- How can you help administrators understand the need for the approach?
- Where can you find examples of how your proposed interventions can be effective in a setting like yours?
- How can you create early successes in your schoolwide process?

Many of the principals in Kent McIntosh's study wished they could have learned about schoolwide efforts earlier in the adoption process, and attended a training or conference on planning for the implementation. There are individuals and organizations that are leading schoolwide efforts like yours. For example, your district may have a prevention officer in charge of schoolwide interventions. You also might seek regional or state support. Many states have networks in place to assist schoolwide interventions. There are also national organizations that can help your efforts. For example, the Association of Positive Behavior Support has networks all over the world that can connect you with local expertise related to schoolwide positive behavior support (see www.apbs.org/network-preview.html).

Application – Administrative Support

Review Table 4.1. Think about an idea that was rejected, or an idea you would like to get approved. Which of the elements listed in the table may have gotten in the way of approval (or potentially blocked it)? What factors did or could work in favor of approval? If you are an administrator, consider your personal bias related to the following factors. Which are your roadblocks? What can you do to overcome them? What support will you need from your staff and administration to increase buy-in for your schoolwide approach?

Connection – Developing a Clear Vision and Mission

You can pave the way for the success of your schoolwide team by having a clear mission and vision related to your end goals. Stephen Mansfield is a psychologist who traveled with United States Troops in Iraq. He provided an illustration of why being clear on your mission is so critical. He met with many soldiers before and after their missions in the field with the aim of helping them deal with Post Traumatic Stress Disorder (PTSD). The soldiers who appeared to suffer the most from PTSD were those who experienced traumatic events and were not aware of their mission and its importance.

Table 4.1 Factors that Help or Hinder Administrative Buy-in, Based on McIntosh, K., Kelm, J. L., & Canizal Delabra, A. (2016)

Addressing Buy-in Factors with Administrators	
Hindering Factors	Helping Factors
• Administrator disagrees with the philosophy behind the schoolwide approach • Administrator sees their staff as unsupportive of the approach • Administrator is unsupportive of the time commitments required for the schoolwide efforts	• Connect administrators to networks of other schools implementing schoolwide efforts so they can hear from others with similar experiences • Learn how schoolwide efforts align with their personal values • Have first-hand experience of how the intervention can work through a small pilot • See the need for the schoolwide effort through their own data • Attend informative schoolwide training • Get support from an external coach • Attend schoolwide team meetings

On the contrary, the *soldiers who were clear on the purpose of their mission seemed to come out with the best mental health*. School staff are not usually teaching in battle zones (although in some cases it's pretty close). Yet, it also may be helpful to take away any ambiguity as to the *what-ness* and *why-ness* of what the school is trying to implement and accomplish. What you are implementing is your intervention. Why you are implementing your intervention is based on your larger purpose.

Point/Principle – Developing a Clear Vision and Mission

Mission and vision statements can inoculate teams against drifting from their purpose. A mission statement provides a focus that your team will take to improve your school setting. To know if you have hit a target, you need a target. *Your school's mission statement is like a goal in a student's individualized education plan.* Chip and Dan Heath suggest using concrete language when developing your mission statement. Your statement should also include "why" your mission is so vital. For example, we were working with one school who said their mission statement was to "try to make our students feel happy." They rewrote their mission statement to say, "The purpose of our [schoolwide] team is to help our students to develop strong relationships with their peers and to become responsible citizens of our school." The team became clear on their focus (relationships) and the significance of the mission (supporting citizenship). Grant Wiggins and Jay McTighe describe mission statements in their Understanding by Design (UbD) curriculum development framework as identifying desired results you want to see for your school.

Your vision involves being clear on "how" you are going to achieve your mission. For example, the same school was working on their vision statement for their schoolwide leadership team. Their first vision statement stated they would, "be nice to all of our students." We asked them to ponder the outcomes they wanted for their students in keeping with their mission. They changed their statement to state, "We will encourage our students to have a social network of at least five friends," and "We teach our students to complete their work and self-evaluate their materials before submission." The new vision statements provided clear direction as to how to fulfill their mission goals. Moreover, due to the revised vision statement, the team was able to identify outcome data they would later need to measure success.

An example of a vision statement from a different school was, "to work with students and their families to identify core climate supports to prevent health, behavioral, attendance, social, and academic concerns." This example outlines the strategies the team would use to achieve their goals. The vision statement is similar to short-term objectives for a student's individualized education plan. Or, to use another UbD connection, your vision describes the planned experiences you want your students to have based on the evidence you want to see for success. In your vision you are focusing on the knowledge and skills you want students and teachers to know and be able to do. Again, your focus shifts from the student to the school level.

Application – Developing a Clear Vision and Mission

You should have a mission and vision statement for every working group in your school. Table 4.2 provides a guide for you to develop clear mission and vision statements. Following the completion of mission and vision statements, ask your team to take the elevator test. For now, focus on the group of people you would like to guide your schoolwide initiative. Have the members pair up with another colleague from the group. Give them 30 seconds (the same time as a short elevator ride) to see if they can explain the mission and vision. There are two reasons for this test. First, sharing the mission and vision in their own words helps them internalize the message. Second, your colleagues are going to ask your team about their approach. To spread a consistent message, your team needs to be clear on what you are trying to accomplish and why it is important.

BOX 4.3 PONDERING ON PURPOSE

- What approach can you use to help determine what to include in your team's vision and mission?
- Why is it important for stakeholders to be able to give the "elevator speech" version of your vision and mission?
- How can you include students and community members in the development of the vision and mission of your team?
- How will you make the vision and mission accessible to students?
- How often will you revisit the vision and mission?

Table 4.2 Describing Your Mission and Vision

What is your team's mission and vison? (Example: *The mission of the schoolwide team is to increase the likelihood of positive behavior, social, emotional, and academic achievement of our students*). If needed, think about what your team will not do. This will help you to think about the limits of your work.
Your mission statement:
What is your team's vision? (e.g., what are your outcomes – related to what do you want all students to know and be able to do?) Examples: • To work with students and their families to identify core climate supports to prevent health/behavioral/attendance/social/academic concerns. • To identify reliable predictors of students' performance. • To determine likely source of problem and recommend changes to core interventions based on needs. • To assist and support teachers, students, and parents in achieving efficient and effective schoolwide interventions.
Your vision statement:

Connection – Creating a Leadership Team

Elves can actually teach us a lot about team development. Perhaps you have read or watched J. R. R. Tolkien's *The Lord of the Rings*, a wonderful story about a band of unique individuals on a quest to bring order back to their world. The composition of this band of travelers teaches us an important lesson about team formation. First, they had their leader, Frodo. Frodo was the primary person responsible for returning the ring to its proper place.

Second, there was Gandalf the wizard. Gandalf explained the mission to Frodo, and provided support throughout the journey. He was not always with Frodo, but he provided coaching and wisdom to help he and his fellow travelers to overcome obstacles. Third, there was the fellowship of the ring. These "team members" had unique skills that helped Frodo return the ring. No one member of the group could have completed their purpose without the backing of the others. While you are not on a journey to restore lost mystical jewelry, you are trying to bring order to your school community, which sometimes could feel like even more of a difficult mission.

Point/Principle – Creating a Leadership Team

Back here on Earth, you too will need at least three types of team members. Each team member will fulfill a very specific role and is interdependent to the other. One member should be an external guide or coach (think Gandalf but without the walking stick). This person will be external to your school and guide you along the schoolwide journey. Coaches work with your team leader to assist with your schoolwide process. They can also meet with the team to give feedback on their work. They should understand how to aid you in utilizing data to guide your process. This person can bring in knowledge and ideas that may not exist in your current team, and provide a new perspective. They also may have less internal bias or attachment to current "routines" that can block the flow of new ideas or solutions that may be "hidden" in plain sight.

The second person you need is an internal coach or team leader (think Frodo, but with smaller feet). This person should be someone who has the trust of the staff. The internal coach should be able to rely on the goodwill of the team and faculty. The internal coach oversees and makes sure the schoolwide process is implemented as designed. This work should be built into their responsibilities and not a peripheral component simply added to their current role. For example, the internal coach might have one class release to have time to be able to organize the work. This person can serve as the internal "compass" of the team, ensuring that the team is always on the right course, and helping to steer the team in the right direction.

When determining the amount of time this person will need to have dedicated to schoolwide systems, think about the scope of the needs, the capacity/expertise/readiness of other team members and the staff at large, and the timeline/pace at which you expect to see change. For example, you might have a large high school with many academic and social-emotional behavioral needs, a leadership team and staff with minimal knowledge of tier one practices and effective systems of support, little to no systems currently in place, and you wish to see both academic and behavioral tier one strategies implemented within two years in 80% of classrooms. If so, you are going to need heavy support at first from your external coach, and your internal coordinator may need to have a full-time position dedicated to the work. You may even need two people to share the leadership. The bigger the ship, the longer it takes to turn it, and the more preparation required with all hands on deck.

The third group of people you need are those who will distribute or carry out much of the work (think the fellowship of the ring minus swords). Normally, the entire team is composed of eight to ten people, however the larger the school and the wider the variety of types and tiers of support you wish to tackle, the more hands you may need on deck. Just be careful to organize teams (and possibly subcommittees) so that you don't run into giant meetings where there are too many voices at the table to efficiently make decisions and plans. When deciding the makeup of your team, you are looking for a gamut of skill sets.

For instance, if your plan features social and emotional support, you need someone (e.g., special education teacher, social worker, school counselor) who knows how to teach social skills. If your work involves changes to the school's academic schedule or professional development calendar, you will need someone (e.g., school counselor, curriculum director) with know-how in the school schedule. The team will not be carrying out every task of your schoolwide plan. It is responsible for key tasks on the action plan for your work as well as the division of labor among colleagues. Each person also needs a job description that guides their work (to be described in Chapter 6). The position description includes the amount of time required for tasks assigned to team members. The configurations of your team will depend on your school's size and mission and vision. Some examples are listed below.

A large urban high school team could include:

- Vice Principal (administrator)
- Discipline dean (administrator)
- A department chair or division head
- Two special education teachers (one serving as the internal coach)
- University partner (external coach)
- A reading specialist, literacy specialist, or instructional coach
- School psychologist
- Three general education teachers
- Parent
- Student

A smaller middle school's team could include:

- Vice Principal (administrator)
- State or district provided technical assistance provider (external coach)
- Two special education teachers (one serving as an internal coach)

- Three general education teachers
- School counselor
- Parent
- Student

The skills you need for your mission and vision should drive the recruiting of your team. For example, a school recruited math teachers to help with data analysis. In another school, members of the community joined the team to provide assistance with student mental health. The team also included a curriculum coordinator in charge of the professional development calendar. One team benefited from a physical education teacher who knew how to teach social skills to students. External coaches have come from local school districts, statewide initiatives, regional cooperatives, and university partners.

Application – Creating a Leadership Team

Create your dream team. List eight to ten respected, proactive people in your building who each have a unique set of skills and type of expertise. Try not to have too much overlap in the specific strengths of each person. Then review the roles and examples described above. How well did you cover your bases to build a schoolwide team based on your mission and vision?

Conclusion

There are other systems components that are essential that we will address in the coming chapters, but we focused on three system components that can help you prevent some of the common errors people make when starting initiatives:

- Developing administrative support
- Establishing a clear mission and vision
- Forming a leadership team

Irrespective of the focus of the intervention type (e.g., social and emotional, academic), these systems are necessary. Most schoolwide interventions require these elements because they need to be in place before you take up your project. To paraphrase Paul Masson, you should never serve any practices until you have systems to support them.

Bibliography

Bohanon, H., Gilman, C., Parker, B., Amell, C., & Sortino, G. (2016). Using school improvement and implementation science to integrate multi-tiered systems of support in secondary schools. *Australasian Journal of Special Education*, *40*(2), 99–116. doi:10.1017/jse.2016.8

Forman, S. G., & Crystal, C. D. (2015). Systems consultation for multi-tiered systems of supports (MTSS): Implementation issues. *Journal of Educational & Psychological Consultation, 25*(2/3), 276–285. doi:10.1080/10474412.2014.963226

Heath, C., & Heath, D. (2007). *Made to stick: Why some ideas survive and others die.* Crawfordsville, IN: Random House.

Kim, W. C., & Mauborgne, R. (2017). *Blue ocean shift: Beyond competing.* New York, NY: Hachette Books.

Mansfield, S. (Date not available). #218: Stephen—Avoiding the Fall [Audio podcast]. Retrieved from https://www.entreleadership.com/blog/podcasts/stephen-mansfield-avoiding-leadership-fall

McIntosh, K., Kelm, J. L., & Canizal Delabra, A. (2016). In search of how principals change: A qualitative study of events that help and hinder administrator support for school-wide PBIS. *Journal of Positive Behavior Interventions, 18*(2), 100–110. doi:10.1177/1098300715599960

Sugai, G., Horner, R., Fixsen, D., & Blase, K. (2010). Developing systems-level capacity for RtI implementation: Current efforts and future directions. In T. A. Glover & S. Vaughn (Eds.), *The promise of response to intervention: Evaluating current science and practice* (pp. 286–309). New York, NY: Guilford Press.

Sugai, G., Horner, R. H., Algozzine, R., Barrett, S., Lewis, T., Anderson, C., & Simonsen, B. (2010). *School-wide positive behavior support: Implementers' blueprint and self-assessment.* Retrieved from https://osepideasthatwork.org/sites/default/files/SchoolwideBehavior Support.pdf

Wiggins, G., & McTighe, J. (1998). *Understanding by design.* Alexandria, VA: Association for Supervision and Curriculum Development.

5

EXPLORATION, READINESS, AND BUY-IN

Asking Before You Tell

In a Nutshell

- Listen before you speak. Provide stakeholders opportunities to share what they feel they need rather than telling them.
- Leadership and teams should use concrete data (qualitative or quantitative) to determine the readiness of their stakeholders. Think of it as a "temperature check" for change.
- Know your audience. Personalities and prior experiences influence how different stakeholders perceive the needs of your school and how to address those needs.
- Be intentional about how you organize and share the data you collect. It will impact the swiftness and openness your stakeholders accept and act on the need for change.

Introduction

In sales, buy-in is referred to as qualifying the customer. Through establishing buy-in, you are trying to see if the end user needs what you are offering, and if they can commit to your product. In our school community, when we talk about buy-in we are "selling" a new idea. Like a good salesperson, you believe that your product (or intervention) will have benefits for the user. We have found that schools that took more time to address buy-in realized significant improvements in student outcomes and improved their overall implementation for their schoolwide approach. In one study Hank completed with colleagues, comparison schools that did not address this step noticed decreases in the level of their implementation of schoolwide supports over time. While there were certainly other factors that led to these outcomes for the schools, establishing buy-in appears to be an important part of the overall intervention process. In this chapter we are going to focus on the exploration stage related to buy-in. Our goal is to highlight the urgency that will create the buy-in needed to effect change in your community.

If you want to demonstrate urgency, you will first need to help stakeholders see there is a need for your approach (e.g., MTSS). Next, you will need to highlight why it is important for your school or district to act on that need. In organizations, people tend to live in smaller, tight-knit circles that often echo the same perspectives. These perspectives perpetuate biases, whether positive or negative, of the current system. In order to facilitate a productive conversation around current trends and desired outcomes, it is important to start with gathering information and data around existing practices. Having this information to look at together will help you to develop consensus around the needs of your current systems.

Connection – Alignment with School Needs

I (Hank) was working with four high schools as a part of a project to implement schoolwide academic and behavior support within their settings. We had conducted a needs assessment. We identified several themes that we could perhaps address. These included:

- The need for effective communication with staff
- High staff turnover
- Inconsistency in defined practices, polices, and procedures
- Negative outside community perception of school
- School climate concerns
- Lack of use of data for decision making
- Lack of buy-in for staff to address concerns

Table 5.1 demonstrates how we were able to connect the needs of the schools with schoolwide interventions. As you can see in this table, we were able to align the concerns of the school with strengths of the schoolwide intervention we were proposing.

Point/Principle – Alignment with School Needs

To assess readiness, begin by looking for connections between your initiative and what the school or district is already doing that is related to your schoolwide approach. You can start with looking at existing plans and documents to see if there are any related goals or approaches. For example, create a list of current initiatives in your setting. Be sure to look at the school or district

Table 5.1 Example of Aligning School Concerns with Schoolwide
Intervention Strengths

Priorities/Next Steps	Connections with Schoolwide Initiative
Improve communication	Develop a leadership team that can effectively communicate with the school community
Define responses for students who struggle academically and behaviorally	Develop a continuum of supports for all students
Improve school climate	Develop, teach, acknowledge, and redirect students to expected behaviors
Use data for decision making	Identify problems and needed data sets for decision making using MTSS framework

improvement plan, identify internal personnel who are doing work that is similar to what you are proposing (or have the skill sets needed to carry out the work), identify community partners, connections to state/district/professional standards, mission and visions, and review the current professional development plan and schedule. This is an opportunity to address equity issues within the school community by reviewing evidence of needs and/or existing initiatives related to areas such as race, gender, socioeconomic status, and ability.

In the interest of transparency and stakeholder buy-in, it is essential to conduct surveys, interviews, and/or focus groups with people from your community. Your first goal here is to look for strengths, in terms of what the community is already doing right in terms of addressing your goal. Your second purpose is to identify "pain points," or barriers to effectiveness for your school, that you can connect between your intervention and the community. Table 5.1 provides an example of how you can match the needs of the setting with your intervention.

BOX 5.1 PONDERING ON PURPOSE

- How can you ensure that lists you create with current practices are exhaustive?
- Why is transparency important?
- What will be the roadblocks/limitations of collecting information via surveys, interviews, and focus groups?

Application – Alignment with School Needs

In our own work, we have used structured interview guides, adapted from the work of Jim Knight, to conduct focus groups with administrators, teachers, and non-certified staff. We have used the interview guide to structure conversations during the focus groups. They typically run between 30–45 minutes. Table 5.2 provides examples of questions that can be used to guide an interview. These interviews help to parse out the qualitative data needed to make informed decisions about your school.

As you report these data back to stakeholder groups, try to organize the responses into at least two columns; strengths (areas where the school/district is already doing well), and next steps (areas where the school/district can improve). If you can, try to use bullet points to fit all of your report onto one page. It can be hard to get busy educators to read more than one page, particularly if buy-in has yet to be established. Table 5.3 provides an example of what a reporting format can look like.

Table 5.2 Needs Assessment Questions (Based on the Work of Jim Knight)

Question	Response
What is going well in your department/school/district for students academically, behaviorally (e.g., discipline), socially/emotionally, and/or in mental health?	
What are some of the barriers to teaching related to academics, behavior (e.g., discipline), social and emotional learning, and/or mental health?	
What would you like to change about your job around academics, behavior (e.g., discipline), social and emotional learning, and/or mental health?	
Can you say anything about who, when, where, what, and why problems occur (or what is going well) for students in terms of academics, behavior (e.g., discipline), social and emotional learning, and/or mental health in your building?	
What have you liked/disliked about professional development and/or implementing initiatives in the past?	

Table 5.3 Summary of Strengths and Next Steps from Needs Assessment

Strengths	Next Steps

Connection – Quantitative Data: Surveys and Self-Assessments

I (Kelly) once facilitated an MTSS fidelity self-assessment in a high school where there were some really great pieces of systems and practices in place, which had led to a sense among leaders that "all was well" and they were "doing response to intervention (RtI)" pretty much as designed. As I gently asked probing questions to include evidence for the high initial ratings, leaders around the table began to identify their own misconceptions or oversimplifications. One moment in particular stands out, when several administrators exclaimed a bit of surprise when I asked what tier three interventions were available for students regardless of whether or not they had Individual Education Plans (IEPs). They had been under the impression that tier three was synonymous with special education, when the state RtI guidelines had defined it otherwise.

Point/Principle – Self-Assess

Structured self-assessment utilizing a vetted tool (questionnaire, checklist, survey, or protocol) is a crucial step in developing strong systems of support. Further, it helps your staff to identify priorities based on important components of your schoolwide model. They are also very useful for later development of action plans. One concern around self-assessment is that these tools are based on the perceptions of the staff. In this case, your goal is to determine the perceptions of the staff related to your MTSS intervention. Using a vetted tool should help reduce concerns about inflated or deflated perceptions, and many self-assessment tools include clear descriptors to help make decisions about ratings that are tied to evidence. Some tools are best conducted (at least initially) with an external coach to help facilitate and explain nuances of certain items, especially if the staff members participating do not have extensive understanding of MTSS. However, if this is not possible, teams can rest assured that most vetted tools will give them good information, and that developing systems is a process that happens over time, so it is okay if the information is not perfect every time. Never give up on better just because it isn't perfect!

One example of a helpful tool (listed in Table 5.4) is the Seven Stages of Concern Survey. Using a survey like this one helps leaders/leadership teams get a snapshot of concerns stakeholders have around the implementation of an innovation/program/strategy, allowing for targeted support and professional development. The results can also provide the stakeholders with a self-reflection tool that allows them to understand their perceptions and attitude towards the topic being evaluated. When you use self-assessment and other surveys, you can identify needs for a schoolwide model, you can see how much of something is in place, you can develop action plans, and you can track fidelity of implementation over time. Table 5.4 provides a list of tools than can be used to self-assess components of your implementation of MTSS.

Table 5.4 Tools You Can Use to Get a Sense of What is in Place around MTSS

Tool	Focus areas	Developer	Link
Measuring the 7 Stages of Concern	Determining stakeholders' concerns about an innovation	American Institutes for Research	https://www.sedl.org/cbam/stages_of_concern.html
The Hexagon: An Exploration Tool	Evaluate new and existing initiatives – focuses on the program and its fit	State Implementation and Scale-Up of Evidenced-Based Practices	https://sisep.fpg.unc.edu/
North Carolina Self-Assessment of MTSS	Academic and behavior supports	North Carolina Department of Education	www.livebinders.com/play/play?id=2052295#anchor
Fidelity Integrity Assessment	MTSS, including all students at risk of failure	SWIFT Center	www.swiftschools.org/shelf
Schoolwide Positive Behavior Support Implementation and Planning Self-Assessment	School climate and positive behavior support	Center on Positive Behavioral Interventions and Supports, Schoolwide Positive Behavior Support	https://www.pbis.org/resource-type/assessments
PBIS Action and Commitment Tool	PBIS	Kevin Filter, University of Minnesota, Mankato	http://sbs.mnsu.edu/psych/psyd/people/filter/
Tiered-Fidelity Inventory	PBIS	Center on Positive Behavioral Interventions and Supports, Schoolwide Positive Behavior Support	https://www.pbis.org/resource-type/assessments
School-Based Mental Health Capacity Instrument	School-Based Mental Health	Feigenberg, Watts, and Buckner (2010)	https://link.springer.com/article/10.1007/s12310-010-9041-6
Collaborative for Academic, Social, and Emotional Learning Self-Assessment Rubric	Social and Emotional Learning	Collaborative for Academic, Social, and Emotional Learning	https://casel.org/guide/

Application – Self-Assess

In conversation, many stakeholders will be quick to speak in generalities and say that something (MTSS, positive behavior interventions and supports (PBIS), etc.) is already being done. As Kelly mentioned before, an important question to ask is "How do we know?" The tools in Table 5.4 break down best practices into specific "look fors" that will help teams analyze components that exist, those that need development, and those that do not exist. It is not enough for just one person or team to complete the surveys. This will not account for bias or implementation "bubbles," where one or a few teachers or departments are implementing, but not others. Including a variety of stakeholders will give a more accurate picture of what is happening across the board, especially in secondary schools where silos perpetuate practices and echo perspectives. Review the tools and select the one that is most aligned with your focus area. Determine how the survey will be formatted, who will distribute them, and how the information will be collected and shared. Encourage participants to be detailed in their responses, providing specific evidence for their responses to help you to determine your next steps.

BOX 5.2 PONDERING ON PURPOSE

- In what ways do you already self-assess your MTSS practices?
- Why do we tend to over-generalize when we reflect on our practice? How does this impact our ability to change?
- Do you feel the climate/culture at your school lends itself to productive self-assessment? Why or why not? If not, what can your team do to address this?

Connection – Organize Existing Data

It is important to take time to consider what data you have and how you can organize it in a way that makes it useful. My math team (Lisa) gave a mid-chapter quiz in the middle of each chapter and a test at the end. Being a high-achieving school, it is common for our class to only get one or two problems wrong, and when this happened, we typically would just enter the grades and return the quiz to our students. When reviewing standardized test data, we noticed that though our achievement scores were high, we'd like to see more individual student growth. We decided to track which problems students were getting wrong across a few assessments and found patterns that lead us to address gaps. Thankfully, we rectified a missed opportunity to use the data we had more effectively, helping us to increase growth scores.

Point/Principle – Organize Existing Data

For purposes of readiness and buy-in, start with data you have rather than seeking new ways of gathering information. Most secondary schools enter massive amounts of information into the student information system (attendance, grades, standardized test scores, discipline infractions, demographics, courses, transcripts, etc.), and often some sort of perception data are often collected via climate surveys or social-emotional screener. So, the data are typically available, but may not be organized in a way that makes it easy to answer questions or share with staff.

Organize the information visually, and as simply as possible to give an aggregate view of how things are going in your school. Graphs and charts tend to be better received than tables or narrative reports. If you want to share information from a survey, for example, in table format, visually highlight just a few key areas of strength or need that you want to draw attention to. Share the information in a presentation, meeting, or groups rather than via email and include some accompanying details to highlight the importance for staff. For example, if you show a bar chart that indicates higher numbers of discipline referrals each year and current numbers over 1,000, it can be helpful to point out that according to Terry Scott and Susan Barrett (2004), each referral costs students about 20 minutes of lost instructional time and 45 minutes for the staff member to process the referral. Table 5.5 lists some examples of common data representations to share with staff to establish the need for a systems approach to change.

Application – Organize Existing Data

Just to get started, take a few minutes to brainstorm data you already have access to into Table 5.6. This can help you document all that you have available to you in one place. This activity will also give you an idea of areas that you are not currently collecting data in and may need to. Once completed, you can begin to look deeper into each set of data in a chart similar to the one in Table 5.4 to analyze what information the data are able to give you. Chapter 12, "Using Data to Monitor Systems and Target Interventions," will provide even more information about how to use and organize the data to make progress on your goals.

BOX 5.3 PONDERING ON PURPOSE

- What areas do you have the most/least data related to MTSS?
- What data might you need to collect before moving forward?
- Why will it be important to reflect on how the data are represented and the pertinence of the data?

Table 5.5 List of Options for Data Presentations

Type of Data	Representation Example	Pertinence
Grade distributions	Stacked bar charts showing counts and percentages of students achieving each type of grade (A, B, C, D, F), with differences in demographic groups represented by colors within the bars	Shows number and percentage of students who are unsuccessful, and disproportionality between demographic groups
Standardized test scores	Bar chart showing average test scores over multiple years with line indicating "target" or "college readiness"	Shows trends over time and average scores falling below target
Discipline referrals	Graphs showing numbers of referrals by time of day, location, type, major vs. minor, gender, ethnicity, grade level, and total number across years (per 100 students to normalize), triangle chart showing the percentage of students in each category: 0–1 referral, 2–5 referrals, 6 or more referrals.	Shows patterns of concern, number being processed, disproportionality
Climate survey results	Table showing items with low (or high) average scores of note highlighted	Gives perceptions of staff, students, families that show areas of strength and concern within school climate
SEL data	Graphs showing numbers of hospitalizations, students receiving regular support from clinicians in school, drop in support requests from clinicians, etc.	Shows numbers of students receiving extra support, indicates need for more preventative support (because numbers too high to address solely with clinicians)
Early Warning System data	Shows count and percentage of students flagged for risk factors related to delayed graduation or drop out in areas such as attendance percentage, earned credits, grades, and discipline referrals	Demonstrates the numbers of students at risk of drop out or delayed graduation

Table 5.6 What Data already Exists in Each of the Four Domains of Schools

Safety	Teaching and Learning
Physical Environment	Interpersonal Relationships

Consider how you will consolidate your existing data to share. Using spreadsheets makes it easy to organize the data and to enter data points from across classrooms and departments. It can then be used to make charts and graphs that can be put into a PowerPoint highlighting essential information to the community.

Using protocols to discuss the data you share will help you assess stakeholder readiness and buy-in and what work you need to do to engage and prepare them for change. Chapter 12, "Using Data to Monitor Systems and Target Interventions," will provide more information about how to use and organize the data to make progress on your goals.

Connection – Present Your Data, Make Connections

Being concise, clear, and connected to priorities is important when presenting data to establish buy-in. I (Kelly) was eventually given a new tool to visualize data (which solved many of my woes described in a previous section of this chapter). Early on in the process of learning to use this software, I was working with a couple of others to plan a "data dig" where we hoped to share the current state of the district and spur some action planning. We were so excited about our new tool, that we presented many different interactive visualizations. Unfortunately, we did not follow the suggestions described in the previous section, and thus we lacked guiding questions, and we were not concise, clear, and connected to established priorities. We basically threw out a lot of "food for thought" via cool data visualizations. Stakeholders came away interested, but overwhelmed and uncertain of what to focus on or what steps to take next.

Point/Principle – Present Your Data, Make Connections

Before doing any work with teams or stakeholders, take some time exploring this chapter and yourself. When presenting data, it is important that you start by being aware of your own personality and bias. Chapter 6 on creating effective teams provides a more "in-depth" discussion on sharing data. There are tools that you can use to determine how your personality and biases can impact how others perceive the information you are sharing. There are a few recommendations we have in summary that can help you more effectively share your information with your school team.

- Be careful what you communicate implicitly to your school (e.g., write discipline referrals if needed, but the hope is you have fewer reasons to do so)
- Present qualitative themes as strengths and next steps
- Connect your intervention with school/district improvement priorities
- Present self-assessment data graphically by major components of the schoolwide approach
- Present outcome data graphically, listen for questions
- As Charles Duhigg points out in his book *Smarter Faster Better*, avoid data snow blindness (presenting too much data that is not well organized)
- In his book *Buy-In*, John Kotter recommends preparing for possible attacks ahead of time by considering questions people will have and prepare your responses

Application – Present Your Data, Make Connections

There are many protocols you can use to help you frame your presentations in a way that will increase productivity and buy-in. Each protocol provides structure to achieve different outcomes. Protocols keep the conversation focused and productive, ensures equal contribution among participants, defines parameters for feedback, and helps to keep the conversation objective which can help participants feel more comfortable rather than vulnerable. Considering the perspectives of all stakeholders, including students and families, is an important part of the buy-in process. Look up Harvard Project Zero Visible Thinking "True for Who?" protocol linked in the resources. With a colleague, practice using this protocol (see Box 5.4) to deepen your conversation around the current state of data usage at your school.

BOX 5.4 PONDERING ON PURPOSE

- Select from your school to discuss.
- Use "True for Who?" protocol from Harvard's Project Zero to consider the various perspectives related to the data you are presenting (Adapted version below).

    - Discuss – what are the factors influencing those impacted?
    - Brainstorm – list all possible viewpoints
    - Stand back – How does considering these viewpoints effect your approach?

- Talk about using the protocol. How did it impact your contributions to the conversation? How did it influence the way you thought about the data/topic/issue?

Conclusion

Assessing the readiness of your stakeholders and fostering buy-in is no small task. It will take time and a considerable amount of resources. However, it is an essential component to effectively creating change. Engaging stakeholders to understand what they need will ensure you have the buy-in you will need for successfully implementing new practices. It is easy to get caught up in the day-to-day and generalize what we think we are implementing. Using data and protocols forces us to provide evidence for our thinking. Using protocols and cycles of practice as a part of the school's culture will enhance your ability to make changes more quickly and effectively. Presenting the data to stakeholders also builds accountability and institutes a level of transparency that builds trust and consensus within the community. For additional resources on buy-in, please see this collection of blogs at www.hankbohanon.net/tag/buy-in/.

Bibliography

Bohanon, H., Fenning, P., Hicks, K., Weber, S., Their, K., Akins, B., ... Irvin, L. (2012). Case example of the implementation of schoolwide positive behavior support in a high school setting. *Preventing School Failure, 56*(2), 91–103.

Bohanon, H., & Wu, M. (2014). Developing buy-in for positive behavior support in secondary settings. *Preventing School Failure, 58*(4), 223–229. doi:10.1080/1045988X.2013.798774

Duhigg, C. (2016). *Smarter faster better: The secrets of being productive.* Crawfordsville, IN: Random House.

Feigenberg, L. F., Watts, C. L., & Buckner, J. C. (2010). The school mental health capacity instrument: Development of an assessment and consultation tool. *School Mental Health, 2*(3), 142–154.

Knight, J. (2004). Progress through partnership. *Journal of Staff Development, 25*(2), 32–37.

Kotter, J. P. (2010). *Buy-in: Saving your good idea from getting shot down.* Watertown, MA: Harvard Business Press.

McCauley, C., & Cashman, J. (2018). *The engagement playbook: A toolkit for engaging stakeholders around the four domains of rapid school improvement.* San Francisco, CA: WestEd.

Scott, T. M., & Barrett, S. B. (2004). Using staff and student time engaged in disciplinary procedures to evaluate the impact of school-wide PBS. *Journal of Positive Behavior Interventions, 6*(1), 21–27. doi:10.1177/10983007040060010401

Visible Thinking. (n.d.). *True for who? A routine for exploring truth claims from different perspectives.* Retrieved from www.visiblethinkingpz.org/VisibleThinking_html_files/03_ThinkingRoutines/03f_TruthRoutines/TrueForWho/TrueForWho_Routine.html

PART 2

Encouraging Teams to Be More Effective

6

WHAT DOES AN EFFECTIVE TEAM LOOK LIKE?

In a Nutshell

- Effective team leaders build and maintain psychological safety for their team.
- Effective teams have a mission and vision that drives their work.
- Develop clearly defined roles for team members.
- Collaborate on team ground rules (norms) and expectations that are revisited and assessed.
- Use data in decision making.
- Use strategically built meeting procedures (agendas, notetaking, action plans).

Introduction

Saturday Night Live (SNL) is one of the most successful and longest running comedy shows on United States television. The success of the show is largely dependent on the team of comedians and writers who develop their material. You might think that the success of the show depends on like-minded people who always agree with each other. This is not the case. According to Charles Duhigg, who interviewed directors and cast, there is a different formula for their achievements. The SNL team has set norms where **everyone** talks during a meeting and they all feel safe when speaking. For example, when someone suggests an idea that may not work, the director always says "Yes! And what else?" Rather than saying someone's idea will not work, the team keeps putting out ideas and builds on them until one sticks. They create what researchers such as Amy Edmondson described as psychological safety.

Creating effective teams is not just about having good team members. Without structures even the most talented team cannot reach their maximum potential. These team structures include creating a safe environment; creating written team roles; having a clear mission, vision, and strategy; ground rules and expectations for working together; use of data; and effective meeting procedures. While there are certainly more parts to a healthy team, we have found these to be helpful in creating communities where people want to contribute to the goals of the group.

Before we jump into the effective structures for teams, it is important to note an overarching structure for success. Teams must be able to meet regularly! This can be one of the greatest challenges in large secondary schools, as schedules are complicated. It can be difficult to get various stakeholders in the same place at the same time. Administrator support via after school stipends, planning the master schedule, or providing release time are all common approaches to solving this issue.

BOX 6.1 PONDERING ON PURPOSE

- What are the biggest complaints about meetings in your school? How do you know?
- Does your school subscribe to the "yes and" approach or are ideas quickly dismissed, ignored, or not shared at all?
- When considering teams, what does "effective" mean to you?
- Are your current teams effective? How do you know?

Connection – Creating a Safe Space for Your Team

I (Kelly) once worked as an external coach with a tier one high school team. Team problem behaviors included arguing, raising voices when disputes arose, venting sessions, interrupting with negative statements such as, "That's a bad idea," and even literal finger pointing. Some members were ready to quit the group. Meetings were running hours past the scheduled ending time, often with no concrete decisions or plans to show for it. I sat down with the internal coach and made a plan to establish some formal meeting norms. At the next meeting, we discussed the fact that our meetings needed to become more efficient and worked as a team to determine a chart of "please do" and "please don't" behaviors (see Table 6.1). Whenever

Table 6.1 "Please Don't/Please Do" Team Meeting Expectations

Please Don't	Please Do
• Discouraging participation of others (in and out of meetings) • Eye rolling, finger pointing, loud or aggressive tone of voice, "snapping" • Dominance of one voice when discussing an item • Sarcasm • Straying from the agenda • "Venting" or storytelling • Bringing up individual names when discussing a negative example (students or staff) • Acting as a spectator (no real participation) • Making judgemental or intimidating comments (e.g., "That's a bad idea") • Allowing a disagreement to escalate or take up more than five minutes of meeting time	• Leave each meeting with a task to do and report back on the next time • Stick to the agenda • Start and end on time • Be aware of paralanguage (facial expressions, tone of voice, etc.) and its impact on meeting climate • State any barriers or concerns respectfully, and accompany them with a suggestion for improvement • Be sure multiple voices are heard ("share the mic" and ask for input) • Limit discussion to task completion • Designate a note-taker • Honor the direction of the facilitator (name) • When giving feedback, acknowledge the idea without negative adjectives, then offer an alternative (e.g., "I see where you are going with this, but could we do _____ instead?") • Recommendations/decisions are made by majority vote of present members • Disagreements should be voiced with respect, noted in the meeting minutes, and resolved by majority vote

someone began to vent, escalate, dominate, finger point, stray from the agenda, etc., the internal coordinator would gently lift the sheet of paper with the norms and tap it, with a pleasant smile on her face. We would all chuckle, including the person who was heading astray, and then get back on track.

Point/Principle – Creating a Safe Space for Your Team

The term "safe spaces" has been thrown around a lot lately, and we want to be deliberate in defining our use of the phrase. During meetings, the loudest voices are sometimes taken as the majority, even when they are not. When few members speak, a small group will leave the meeting feeling "right" and the rest feel overlooked or disgruntled. Those who speak out in unproductive ways dismiss the needs of those who are silent, obstruct progress on goals, prevent meeting spaces from feeling "safe," and interfere with organizational trust. Trust breaks down when frustrations build without outlets. In his research, Frédérique Six details the importance of implementing intentional trust-building structures and polices. You may even see trust within question items on culture and climate surveys. Safe spaces balance voices, allowing members to feel heard and valued as they contribute to the solution seeking process. When safe places exist, trust follows, building the positive culture and climate needed within school communities.

Google is a company that is well-known for their effective teams. In order to create an environment that allows their teams to be effective, they not only encourage, but also *recognize and reward* those that take risks, ask for help, disclose and celebrate failures, and have healthy disagreements. Building trust takes leaders who both explicitly model and actively encourage this type of vulnerability.

BOX 6.2 PONDERING ON PURPOSE

- What topics in your school incite the most debate?
- What factors contribute to the "safe spaces" for that debate? Which factors hinder that safety?
- Do colleagues trust each other to share freely? How do you know?
- How do you structure meetings/conversations to limit negative interactions and foster and reinforce positive interactions?

Application – Creating a Safe Space for Your Team

Reflect on what structures you currently have that foster safe spaces, build psychological trust, and guide participants to share opposing opinions. Do you provide an outlet that is respected, or are opposing ideas left to be shared sporadically and haphazardly? We recommend reviewing the instrument, "Team Learning and Psychological Safety Survey," created by Amy Edmondson at Harvard University (see www.midss.org/content/team-learning-and-psychological-safety-survey). This instrument can help to inform your team about the strengths and weaknesses of the trust climate among your team. Some additional tools we have seen used effectively to help teams learn about how to work together include the Enneagram, Myers Briggs, and the DiSC (Dominance (D), influence (i), Steadiness (S), and Conscientiousness (C)).

Connection – Clear Mission, Vision, and Strategy

When we were writing this book, we wanted to make sure we stayed on track with the overall goal for the project. So, we developed a mission statement. One component of the mission statement related to the fact that many educational resources are geared toward elementary schools. These resources sometimes lack middle and high school examples. The second part of the mission included our intent that this book be written in a "user-friendly" format for guiding school staff through stages of implementation of schoolwide approaches. We wanted to bridge the gap between research and practical application. Our vision for the book included helping the reader to (1) successfully organize their systems for implementation of schoolwide intervention strategies, and (2) implement effective strategies that could improve the academic and behavioral climate of their school. We had four strategies we used to accomplish this aim, including:

- Provide a user-friendly structure for guiding secondary-level school staff through stages of implementation of schoolwide approaches
- Use examples from other fields when possible to make connections to what would be familiar to secondary school readers (e.g., interacting with service industries)
- Help staff members prevent common mistakes of implementation and ensure implementation fidelity
- Serve as a catalyst for high school and middle school staff who are already in the process of implementing an approach to school improvement by identifying clear goals and aligning school staff and resources to these priorities.

The mission, vision, and strategies helped us stay on track with the original intentions we had for this book.

Point/Principle – Clear Mission, Vision, and Strategy

To stay on course, teams need to clearly identify what they are trying to accomplish and why (mission), the envisioned outcomes they are seeking (vision), and the approach utilized to reach goals (strategy). Each of these steps becomes a map you can use to guide your overall implementation of your schoolwide efforts. Much of this work may already be a part of your school's current operational or school improvement plan. If your school already has a mission, vision, and strategy for their work, then you need to align your schoolwide efforts with these components. If your school does not have these components, then your team needs to spend some

Table 6.2 Creating a Mission, Vision, and Strategy for Your Teams

Focus of Team (Tier One, Tier Two, Tier Three, District Level)	Team members' response
Mission (What are we doing and why is it important?):	
Vision (What are our team's intended outcomes?):	
Strategy (What are we going to do, and not do, to reach our goals?):	

time focusing on developing them. We have found having clear purposes for every major task or team you are working with helps teams prevent what Jesse Lyn Stoner describes in the *Harvard Business Review* as "mission drift."

Application – Clear Mission, Vision, and Strategy

Use Table 6.2 to help your team develop a clear mission, vision, and strategy for your team. To determine your team's strategy, it may help to reflect on what your team will **NOT** do. For example, a tier one team should not be talking about individual students. They should be focusing on data that are aggregated at the school level to look for themes and patterns. The opposite would be true for tier two and three teams, who will be looking for patterns in small groups or for individual students.

Connection – Creating Written Team Roles

I (Hank) once heard someone speak who was trained in providing triage at emergency scenes. He said that one of the first rules he learned during a sudden emergency is the right and the wrong way to ask for help. The wrong way is to generally say to bystanders, "Someone call an ambulance." By using this method, everyone assumes someone else has called. He said the correct way (that will lead to a greater chance of someone acting immediately) is to point to someone specifically in the crowd. Then, you state, "You, call an ambulance." The person is identified, and their specific role is delineated. This ensures that someone will follow up with the task.

Point/Principle – Creating Written Team Roles

Just like with triage, we need to provide specific roles and actions that are needed for our teams to be successful. Chapter 9 will provide greater detail about the specifics for this step. Key components of organizing teams would include:

- Knowing where your schoolwide team (for example, MTSS) fits into the larger structure of the school or within school improvement in general
- Have a structural flow chart that provides a visual representation of where your team and team members fit into your school's organization
- Have written position descriptions of the roles of your team members, and the amount of time needed to successfully complete the role

Application – Creating Written Team Roles

While Chapter 9 will provide specific examples and tools you can use to help prepare the organization of your team, you can start with some preparation now. We ask you to consider the following questions as you consider the structure of your schoolwide teams:

- How does your schoolwide team (e.g., MTSS) fit into the larger structure of the school?
- What does your school's current organizational structure look like? Is there a current version of your organizational chart you can use to see where your schoolwide work might fit into the structure of the school?
- What kinds of written procedures or positions descriptions currently exist for other committees or task groups in your school? For example, are there position descriptions for members of your school's current leadership or school improvement team?

Connection – Ground Rules and Expectations

Another component to building an effective team is setting ground rules and expectations (norms). My husband and I (Lisa) occasionally host game nights at our house. We enjoy finding new and obscure games to switch things up. Informal observations we have made over the years have helped us develop a sense of which games our guests will enjoy playing. One such factor is learning the rules to a new game. When the rules are too long, unclear, or complicated, we've had players become frustrated and give up before we even begin playing. The rules and expectations of the game can make or break our guests' interest in participating.

Point/Principle – Ground Rules and Expectations

Just as setting ground rules and expectations is essential when playing a game, it is a crucial step in creating effective teams. Setting operational norms can help teams better collaborate around their work. As mentioned above in the section about creating safe spaces, and with Kelly's team example from Table 6.1, clear expectations can help create a team where people feel secure in sharing ideas and participating. In addition, these norms will help to keep your team focused on the mission and vision you have created. One way to set these ground rules and expectations is to use a variety of available norm-setting protocols. Once agreed upon, the norms should be revisited at the start of each meeting and referred to in order to keep teams on track.

Application – Ground Rules and Expectations

Aside from the example provided in Table 6.1, there are many norm-setting protocols available for use. Some of the tools we recommend you consider are the Harvard Graduate School of Education's Datawise Project protocols that help with setting the groundwork and expectations for teams. The "Norm Setting Protocol" tool is great for teams coming together in just one session. The "Hopes and Fears Protocol," also from the Datawise Project, gives teammates the ability to have context behind others' thinking, as well as information that will help the leader navigate possible roadblocks. Additionally, I (Lisa) once had team members write their norm suggestions on post-its. We then sorted them and rewrote the norms in three to five phrases/sentences that summarized the input of the team. If you would like to see a non-example of a team meeting that went completely off the rails, we suggest you see the resource "Meeting Notes from a Schoolwide Meeting" on the website associated with this book. This would be a great resource for teams to review to develop an objective sense of what healthy teams do and do not look like.

Connection – Agendas, Notetaking, and Action Planning

Another structure that contributes to the development of effective teams includes the creation of agendas, methods for notetaking, and action plans. I (Kelly) worked on a committee once where each agenda and set of notes was created as a separate Google Doc. After working for a large portion of the school year, we realized that finding links to embedded docs or pulling up details about a decision we made was extremely tedious. It was unlikely that we would recall the specific meeting date of when we created a document or made a decision. We would have to click through each agenda document and scan the narrative notes for the information we wanted. This method drew our focus and our time away from our work. A different group I worked with created one long running document in which we used a continuous action plan in table format that lived at the top of the document. The action plan items can be moved to the bottom of the table or moved to an "Archived Action Items" table (see Table 6.4) at the very bottom of the doc as they are completed or no longer pertinent. Within this format, the narrative notes were listed below the table, organized by date, with the most recent meeting at the top. I found this format to be much more effective!

Point/Principle – Agendas, Notetaking, and Action Planning

BOX 6.3 PONDERING ON PURPOSE

- What does your current agenda look like?
- How do you ensure all team members have the opportunity to contribute and agree upon the agenda?
- What are your meeting timelines? Time constraints? Deadlines?
- How do you document what was discussed and achieved at the meeting?

Start with a well-constructed agenda. There is a plethora of suggested meeting agenda formats available. My favorite (Lisa) is a modified version of one I found on *Harvard Business Review* (Table 6.3). They suggest stating the topics in the form of a question rather than a statement, as well as list whether the purpose is to share information, seek input or information, or to make a decision. I have also used a three-column version that combines the topic column with the activities and materials column. Once you have an agenda structure selected, you can begin planning the activities within the meetings. I try to remember that even adults have limits to their attention spans. To counter this, I "chunk" activities to allow for natural breaks and transitions that will maintain focus and engagement.

Setting up the notetaking process and assigning the role of note-taker proactively will help the notes to be useful. Meeting minutes document the team's journey and should reflect the people, process, and discussions that lead to decisions made in a succinct, objective manner. If you have a well-constructed agenda and a pre-created note format, taking meeting minutes will be much easier and the notes themselves will be more useful. Each team

Table 6.3 Modified Version of the Harvard Business Review's Meeting Agenda

Topic & Time	Activity & Materials	Notes	Actions/Due Data
-State as a question. (Time) (Name) (Share/Seek/ Decision)	*List protocol or activity that will be used with link to material(s).	*List important information that attendees need to "take away" from discussion, particularly information that answers the question posed.	-List next steps (person responsible, date action is due)

agenda and notetaking process requires that teams identify the specific tasks that will be completed and by when.

Attending a meeting should not be a spectator sport! We have noticed that people who typically cause the most problems during meetings are those who do not have any accountability for participation. An action column distinguishes between ideas/topics discussed and the actions that need to be taken. It is essential to identify who specifically will be responsible for the action and by when. An action plan table could include the following columns:

Table 6.4 Template of Archived Action Items Notetaking

Date Added	Goal or Problem Statement	Data sources (to measure fidelity and outcomes)	Actions/ Tasks	Deadline or check-in date	Committee and/or Person(s) Responsible	Status (In progress, Not started, Completed, Tabled for later)	Key Notes/ Updates

The document "Sample Bad Action Plan" on the companion website shows an example of what it looks like when teams do not have a very clear process for guiding the next steps of their work.

Application – Agendas, Notetaking, and Action Planning

Think about an upcoming meeting you will participate in. Use some of the tips or tools described above to plan your agenda and notetaking formats. If you can, implement your plan and reflect on how "successful" the meeting was, compared to prior meetings. Would you try the same format again? Would you make changes?

Connection – Data Routines of Effective Teams

Take a moment to think about the way that families (ideally) look at financial data. The best approach would be routines for weekly, monthly, and annual checks. It would not be effective to sit down together and stare at every piece of financial data you have every time all at once. If you reviewed your data all at once, you might have to sort through IRA and 401K statements for the past ten years, three years' worth of individual credit card and checking account transactions and utility bills, and every mortgage statement from the past five years. You need to develop focused routines to review your data.

Point/Principle – Data Routines of Effective Teams

Data routines for schoolwide teams should work similarly to a healthy household plan for financial management. Later chapters will include a more detailed overview of some recommended methods for utilizing data effectively, but in general, healthy, effective teams follow a few guiding data principles: look at data with a clear purpose, use a balanced and efficient amount of data to make decisions, establish routines for how and when data are reviewed, and plan ways to access data efficiently.

First, data should be looked at with a **clear purpose**. Rather than looking at every piece of data, the team should first identify specific goals related to their mission and vision, and then determine the precise views of data that would help them either answer specific questions about how well goals are or are not being met.

Second, teams need to work to establish a "Goldilocks" **balanced amount of the types and views of data** they use. Teams should identify data sources to help them determine fidelity of implementation (did we actually do what we said we would at the level we meant to?), the social validity of the practices (do stakeholders such as parents, teachers, students, and other staff feel that the thing we did is useful, appropriate, effective, and reasonable?), and the outcomes of the efforts (did the thing we did have the impact we hoped for?).

Table 6.5 Goal/Problem to Address

Purpose (specific information needed from data – only one per row!)	Data type (fidelity, perception, outcome)	Data source (discipline referrals, walk-through tallies, grades, test scores, survey data, etc.)	Routine (when would we look at this source? Frequency/ time of year?)	What are two questions we would ask and what action or decision would be made based on possible answers?

Third, teams need **established routines** for when and how each data source is utilized. Some data sources may need to be reviewed monthly, and others might be reviewed less frequently, but the team should map out a calendar of data sources to review, and the timeline for decision making should drive the calendar. For example, the Team Initiated Problem Solving (TIPS) protocol and materials available at www.pbis.org can be used by teams to help guide their use of data for decision making and action planning.

Fourth, once a team has decided the various data sources needed to serve each purpose and the schedule for reviewing each source, they should determine the **most efficient way to access those data sources** in a useful and timely format. Customizable data dashboards and automated reports or exports are both helpful options for teams, if available.

Application – Data Routines of Effective Teams

Using the headers with guiding questions in Table 6.5, select one goal or problem you would like to address. Try to fill in a row or two of the table to begin thinking about effectively using data to help drive and monitor your work (Table 6.5).

Conclusion

Healthy, functional, effective teams do not happen by magic or chance, even with a group of highly professional members who get along together. Taking time to establish parameters and planning for how a team will function is time well spent. The work it takes to systematically and consistently intervene in a secondary school setting to evoke positive changes is complex. Change efforts involve many steps and stakeholders, which can put a lot of pressure on the team leading such efforts. Team members must plan carefully and establish clear norms in order to function effectively. The better organized a team is in terms of delineating roles and responsibilities, establishing data routines, and running safe and efficient meetings, the better able team members will be to accomplish the myriad of tasks necessary to move the work forward in a timely manner. When a school is healthy, stakeholders can be vocal about their disagreements, respect each other, and value one another's contributions as a vital part of the decision-making process. For more information on how to assess the effectiveness of your teams, see the companion website for this book. Look for the document "Assessing Your Team".

Bibliography

Allen, D., & Blythe, T. (2004). *The facilitator's book of questions: Tools for looking together at student and teacher work*. New York, NY: Teachers College Press.

Blythe, T., Allen, D., & Powell, B. S. (2008). *Looking together at student work*. New York, NY: Teachers College Press.

Boudett, K. P. & City, E. A., (n.d.) *Meeting Wise Checklist – Full Version*. Retrieved from https://datawise.gse.harvard.edu/files/datawise/files/meeting_wise_checklist_1.pdf

Delizonna, L. (2017). High-performing teams need psychological safety: Here's how to create it. *Harvard Business Review*. Retrieved from https://hbr.org/2017/08/high-performing-teams-need-psychological-safety-heres-how-to-create-it

Easton, L. B. (2009). Protocols for professional learning. Retrieved from http://static1.squarespace.com/static/55560e1ae4b0cf3d98431253/t/5666742c0e4c1145da0f1f78/

Edmondson, A. (1999). Psychological safety and learning behavior in work teams. *Administrative Science Quarterly, 44*, 350–383. Retrieved from www.midss.org/content/team-learning-and-psychological-safety-survey

Glaude, C. (2004). *Protocols for professional learning conversations: Cultivating the art and discipline*. Courtenay, BC: Connections Pub.

Harvey, J.-F., Johnson, K. J., Roloff, K. S., & Edmondson, A. C. (2019). From orientation to behavior: The interplay between learning orientation, open-mindedness, and psychological safety in team learning. *Human Relations*, 1–26. doi:10.1177/0018726718817812

Hopes and Fears Protocol Instructions. (n.d.). Retrieved from https://datawise.gse.harvard.edu/files/datawise/files/hopes_and_fears_protocol_instructions.pdf

Martin, N. R. M. (2005). *A guide to collaboration for IEP teams*. Baltimore, MD: Brookes Publishing Company.

McDonald, J. P., Mohr, N., Dichter, A., & McDonald, E. C. (2007). *The power of protocols: An educator's guide to better practice*. New York, NY: Teachers College Press.

National School Reform Faculty. (n.d.). *NSRF Protocols and Activities… from A to Z*. Retrieved from https://nsrfharmony.org/protocols/

Schwarz, R. (2015). *How to design an agenda for an effective meeting. Harvard Business Review*. Retrieved from https://hbr.org/2015/03/how-to-design-an-agenda-for-an-effective-meeting

Six, F. E. (2007). Building interpersonal trust within organizations: A relational signaling perspective. *Journal of Management and Governance, 11,* 285–309. Retrieved from doi:10.1007/s10997-007-9030-9

Stoner, J. L. (2011). Diagnose and cure team drift. *Harvard Business Review.* Retrieved from https://hbr.org/2011/10/diagnose-and-cure-team-drift

The President and Fellows of Harvard College (n.d.) *Norm Setting Protocol Instructions.* (n.d.). Retrieved from https://datawise.gse.harvard.edu/files/datawise/files/norm_setting_protocol_instructions.pdf

7

COMMUNICATION

In a Nutshell

- When communicating, remember to be strategic with your ABCDs: Audience, Bias, Content, and Design.
- The flow of communication between stakeholders should be open, timely, and intentional.
- Communication flows to, within, and out from the team, and communication from the team to the community.
- Using data in communication can be a powerful tool or a hindrance to progress.

Introduction

Sometimes our best attempts at marketing fall flat. One famous example is from the 1980s, when Coca-Cola attempted to release a new re-formulated version of their soda they called "New Coke." They underestimated their consumers' brand loyalty, setting their sales into a tailspin. Even though blind taste tests had determined that most preferred the new version, the company had to go back to the original version after they poorly communicated the change to the public. The whole fiasco damaged their name and their bottom line. The lesson? Communication is key. It can make or break your campaign. Even the best intentioned, researched decisions can backfire if you are not intentional in how they are communicated to your stakeholders.

When we think about communication between stakeholder groups within our school, the obvious forms of communication come to mind such as emails, verbal announcements, surveys, meetings, and forums. These are not the only way we communicate. Our actions and inactions, the methods we use, who we communicate with, and what we share or don't share delivers messages, many times unintentionally. Sometimes in the hustle and bustle of the day to day, we are ignorant to the subtleties behind our communication, and can inadvertently cause harm through our messaging.

There are three major areas of stakeholder communication to consider when implementing systemic change in schools: communication from the community to the team, internal team communication, and communication from the team to the community. The flow between these groups will either help or hinder your progress towards school goals. We need to be purposeful when we focus on creating communication structures and processes to facilitate effective communication among these groups. Teams that see communication as a strategy for their overall schoolwide effort will potentially see more success.

Connection – Assessing Your Communication Structures and Process

The need for effective communication structures is not limited to schools. The Space Shuttle Columbia disaster cost the lives of seven astronauts. Insulation from the fuel tank broke off during takeoff, hit the left wing, and struck a hole in the heat resistant tile causing the shuttle to break into pieces upon re-entry. According to authors Chris Clearfield and András Tilcsik, the National Aeronautics and Space Administration (NASA) had been aware of the problem with the insulation from previous missions, but managers saw the issue as an acceptable level of risk. The Accident Review Board who investigated the crash later said that the organizational structures (e.g., communication) within NASA were just as important to address as the insulting foam. Lack of effective communication processes may not cost the lives of your stakeholders, but it could cost the health of your schoolwide effort.

Point/Principle – Assessing Your Communication Structures and Process

Evaluating the structure of your communication practices will make your organization's communication more effective and productive. A miscommunication in your organization could put your students at risk, or at the very least cause unrest, confusion, and frustration among the community. However, miscommunication is preventable.

To begin, communication should flow freely and frequently between stakeholder groups. The communication may vary in content, structure, or even purpose. However, all stakeholders including staff, students, parents, and community members should be provided some form of communication and input procedure in matters that impact them. There are various components that keep the circulation of information moving effectively. They can be remembered as the "ABCDs" of communication: Audiences, Biases, Content, and Design.

Your audience may vary, even breaking into multiple subgroups. For example, you may have "parents" as an audience, but then have subgroups for things like each of the languages spoken or methods of transportation the family uses. In addition, people have different preferences in how they receive communication. Some might prefer an email or newsletter while others may prefer verbal options like recorded phone messages or podcasts. Communication is an equity issue. It is important to ensure your stakeholders receive information in a format that is accessible to them, and that all stakeholders' opinions are heard.

Our life experiences and backgrounds formed our personal biases that impact the content and design of our communication. Biases also influence how we perceive information, develop opinions about that information, and react to the content received. For example, someone who personally benefited from the availability of technology in the classroom as a student may feel differently about its use as a teacher. Abstract concepts like perception and tone can also play a big part in your audience's interpretation of your communication and contribute to biases. Being more aware of our personal biases help us to balance these when sending and receiving communication.

Carefully consider the content and purpose in any form of communication. What data or information are you sharing? For what purpose? How will it be received? When creating content, our biases shape what we decide to share, how much or little we include in our message, the point of view, tone, complexity of language, level of detail, and the format we use to share the content. Content should be clear, factual, and thorough. Explicitly state your purpose for sharing, and what you intend the recipients to do with the information. Unless intentional in the constructs of a formal activity, you don't want your content to raise more questions than answers.

There are seemingly infinite ways communication can be formatted. It can happen verbally, in written form, between individuals, groups, visually, through body language and tone, and can be intentional or unintentional. Spend time evaluating the formats you use and their effectiveness. Data shared via written communication should be visualized in a way that is clearly labeled, simple to interpret, and without too many different visualizations at once. A few charts with clear labels that contain data most of the stakeholder group are familiar with work well in this type of format. An overview of aggregate data points that show the current "state of the school" may make the most sense to share via a presentation or gallery walk at a staff meeting. A video presentation is another option that may make sense for some school teams. The communication should be designed in a way that makes it easy for the recipient to address the purpose. Proactively addressing the ABCDs of communication will keep the conversation productive and give empathy and insight to those involved.

BOX 7.1 PONDERING ON PURPOSE

- What are ways your school addresses the different receptive communication needs of your community?
- How do you ensure consistency of messaging when multiple people are communicating the same information?
- Do you use a variety of formats for your communications? How do you track your communication processes?
- What personal biases do you bring to your work?
- How do you balance the need to provide timely updates without overwhelming people with too much information at once?

Application – Assessing Your Communication Structures and Process

Before diving into assessing the biases and content of your communication structures, use the checklist in Table 7.1 to assess the variety of the communication formats you use. Place an "x" in the column that best represents how often you engage in communication in each format listed.

Table 7.1 Types of Communication Formats Used By Your Team

Format	Couple times a year	Monthly	Weekly	Daily
Face to Face (1:1)				
Face to Face (Group)				
Email (1:1)				
Email (Group)				
Newsletter(s)				
Phone Call (1:1)				

Phone Call (Group)				
Video Call (1:1)				
Video (Group)				
Text Messaging/ Phone Blast				
Social Media				
Pamphlet/Flyer				
Presentation				
Panel(s)				
Workshop				
Forum				
Blog/Online Publication				
Study Group				
Banner/Poster				
Surveys				
Other:				

After considering the various formats you use to communicate, begin to evaluate the content and effectiveness of that communication. Use Table 7.2 below to reflect on the ABCDs of current (or future) communication.

Using tools to reflect on your communication is important because the methods, frequency, tone, and content of your communication can impact stakeholders' satisfaction and buy-in with the work done in your school.

Table 7.2 Reflecting on Your Team's Communication Style

Audience	Biases	Content (Purpose)	Design
Who is providing the communication to the audience?	What are their biases?	What is the purpose of sharing? How will this impact *what* information is given?	How will this impact *how* the communication is provided?
Who is receiving the communication?	What are their biases?	How will this impact how the information is *received*?	How will this impact how the recipient *responds*?
Are there multiple communicators?	How do their biases impact the consistency of the messaging?	How do we keep our message consistent across multiple communicators?	Will all the communicators use the same structure/method?
Are there multiple audience subgroups?	How do the subgroups' biases differ? How are they the same?	Do we need to change the content we provide based on the subgroups? What portion of the content needs to remain the same?	Do we need to change the structure/design of how we communicate based on the different subgroups?

Connection – CAIRO Plan

I (Kelly) had been hired in a district to work with several schools and had a meeting with two assistant principals in one of the buildings to discuss some academic interventions. At some point, they asked for some ideas for the reading intervention classes. Toward the end of the discussion, it seemed we had come up with a plan we all liked and decided to move forward. The English Department Chair's name brought up, but no one mentioned needing to ask his opinion, so I assumed that the assistant principals were the authority for this decision. Later, I sent a follow up email and copied the Department Chair to loop him in. I quickly discovered that he was not in favor of the suggestion I had made, and that the assistant principals deferred to him on the decision. On top of that, he was quite displeased that I appeared to be attempting to make changes in his department without his knowledge or consent! Secondary schools tend to have more complex hierarchies of leadership, larger groups of stakeholders, and a wider variety of stakeholder groups (due to divisions or departments by content areas), so communication about decision making can be a major challenge. Had we used CAIRO, discussed below, or a similar strategy protocol, we could have avoided this mishap.

Point/Principle – CAIRO Plan

Sometimes communication problems can be the result of crimes of commission (intentional) or omission (inadvertent). Kelly's example above is a crime of omission. She (and the vice principals) did not intend to leave out the Department Chair, however this error caused a loss in time, trust, and progress. An example of a crime of commission would be when a team intentionally does not include a group that is resistant to their project out of fear that they will attempt to prevent the project before it begins. Once that group does find out, it will only make their reluctance stronger. In both cases, people were left out of the communication process and may become more resistant to the change as a result of the ineffective communication. We need a structure that will help teams to prevent commission and omission errors in communication.

One of the processes we have found to be most useful in preventing communication issues is a framework developed by Lee Bolman and Terrence Deal. The acronym for their communication approach is called CAIRO. Each letter stands for a step in the communication process team needs to consider when making decisions that impact their community. These steps include:

- Who is consulted?
- Who has ultimate approval?

- Who should be **i**nformed?
- Who should be **r**esponsible for carrying it out?
- Who can be **o**ut of the loop?

Application – CAIRO Plan

Table 7.3 includes a blank communication plan that teams can use to prevent problems with their communication processes. We recommend using this form during the early stages of your team's formation and then refer to it as needed once the steps become second nature. You can also use the key areas of the CAIRO process and include them on your action planning or notetaking processes. Include this form and process in your training of new team members.

Identify a task for any group that you have worked with in the past. Was each component considered? How well did the task go? Which, if any, CAIRO components caused roadblocks for successful task completion? How could it have been avoided by considering each CAIRO component proactively? Reflecting on our past can help us to learn to apply new strategies. Team leaders should emphasize that it is okay to make mistakes, and that they should be used to determine new strategies for moving forward.

Table 7.3 CAIRO Communication Plan

Task	Who is Consulted?	Who has ultimate Approval?	Who should be Informed?	Who is Responsible for carrying it out?	Who can be Out of the loop?

BOX 7.2 PONDERING ON PURPOSE

- What are the ways that your team has welcomed the community to communicate with the team?
- Why is it important to have an open line of communication from the community to the team?
- How do you evaluate the effectiveness of the communication?

Connection – Ways to Gather Input

Giving a survey can be a powerful tool. It can dispel assumptions regarding the opinions, practices, and perceptions of the school community. However, if not used carefully, they can cause more harm than good. This can be for a few different reasons. Surveys themselves are a form of communication. Depending on how the survey is worded, it could influence the participants responses, cause misinterpretation of responses, or miscommunicate the creator's intent.

I (Lisa) was attending an action planning summit with a team tasked with strengthening the use of assessments in our school. I found what I thought was a great assessment use survey for the team to get some input from the staff. Upon initial review, the questions all seemed well worded and relevant. I shared the survey with a few team members who quickly reviewed the questions and out of deference to me agreed. After sending it out to the school, I sat in my grade band meeting with my colleagues and took the survey. While taking it I realized that it was repetitive and, in some cases, confusing. Teachers questioned how to interpret the prompts, and I was embarrassed. In the end, there were two questions that were most significant to our work. With a little more work on the front end, I could have saved my colleagues a lot of time and frustration by being more intentional with how I reviewed the survey myself and the way I asked for feedback from my peers.

Point/Principle – Ways to Gather Input

When gathering information from others, it is important to think about the most appropriate format for gathering the information, and how many ways you plan to utilize it. Once chosen, design the experiences for community members carefully to avoid pitfalls such as the survey issue described above. There are not hard, fast rules about whether you should start with a focus group or a survey, but there are some tips that will help you achieve more valid information. The following bullets highlight some survey design tips:

- Each item only asks one question at a time.
- A variety of options exist to fit the opinions of all respondents.
- Items are clear and concise. (Surveys that are too long can become less reliable as respondents progress.)
- Try to avoid "and" items because respondents might feel different about each part. For example, "Rated on a scale of 1 to 5, I frequently share my opinions at meetings and in one-on-one conversations with the principal of my school."
- Consider the nature of the information being collected. What do you need to know to move forward with a decision?

- Provide response options for responses as much as possible. When surveying a large number of people, too many type-in responses can become meaningless when you have hundreds of responses to sift through.

I (Kelly) took a graduate-level course on survey design, and still find it challenging to design the "perfect" survey! It is a great idea for team members to read up or complete some tutorials on survey design, but in addition to that, schoolwide team members should always pilot surveys among themselves and then a few volunteers who don't have all the "behind the scenes" information to get feedback on items. Next, do a quick check to see how actionable and informative the responses are to avoid problems like in the scenario above.

Focus groups can be helpful when you want to provide more flexibility in responses and can provide some powerful examples to share with others. When hosting focus groups, be sure to select participants carefully as to not perpetuate false assumptions. Carefully word questions objectively as to not "lead" responses. Our school (Kelly) used focus groups to find out more information from a subgroup of students who were failing only certain classes. Students were asked about what helped them to be successful in the classes they passed, and what challenges they faced in classes where they had failed. The four different groups provided similar themes in their responses, which helped to guide the leadership team toward important focal areas as tier one plans were developed.

Focus groups are time intensive, and require thoughtful questioning, filming, and, objective notetaking to identify themes. They can be a great way to "flesh out" some general patterns identified in survey responses or other data, or a great place to start in order to identify what types of information ought to be gathered from a larger group.

There are plenty of other ways schoolwide teams can gather input from the community as well. Some teams use "suggestion boxes," or agendas for staff meetings that include time for people to share opinions on what is going well and what could be improved, preferably related to specific topics. Many schools have advisory councils for students, staff, and/or parents where representatives meet regularly with an administrator and share feedback. Gathering information from a variety of sources is a good idea, so long as it is carefully planned, and shared back with the community in a way that indicates how the information will impact the team's decisions and plans.

Application – Ways to Gather Input

Pick a topic you would like to gather information about, related to schoolwide efforts. Write three survey items or three focus group items related to the topic. Ask at least five people from your community for feedback on your questions before you use them. Share your questions with five other people. Immediately afterward, ask your respondents for feedback. Were the questions clear? Did they feel like they would be able to answer in a way that communicates their opinions effectively? Was there anything else they wish you had asked about the topic?

Connection – Specific Strategies to Improve Communication

We each have our own personalities that impact our communication with others, both in the messages we send and how we interpret the messages others send us. I (Lisa) spend a lot of time analyzing things in my head. I am constantly thinking about the "best" way something can be done, and how to improve upon the systems and structures around me. I like to create order around me because it makes me feel more comfortable when there are explicit expectations. Of course, I have a lot of opinions of what that should look like. Also, when I hear about a new concept that I am excited about, I'm all in. I enjoy being the leader in innovation and feel excited about sharing my findings with the people around me.

Imagine how my approach to innovation may be interpreted by some of my colleagues. For the longest time I would get comments referring to me as critical, bossy, dismissive, and impatient. I felt sad, frustrated, and misjudged, because I did not understand why. My excitement and passion were met with pushback and isolation. Then I took the Enneagram. The Enneagram is a personality test that helps to frame actions and perspectives based on core motivations. I read and learned about my Enneagram Type, and how my type is interpreted and received by other types. It significantly changed how I approached interactions with my colleagues. This is an example of using specific strategies to improve communication.

Point/Principle – Specific Strategies to Improve Communication

Communication can be improved by using strategies that focus on both getting to know the person you are communicating with and improving the methods of communication. Each person has individual communication styles and experiences that influence their reactions during communication. Whether you are leading or participating in a team, learning about communication styles can help you to improve your communication experiences, especially when used proactively. In Chapter 5 we mentioned the Stages of Concern. This process is an example of how knowing the person you are communicating with will help you to set the stage for a productive conversation. Someone who is in the "collaboration stage" will be able to have a very different conversation than someone in the "unconcerned stage."

BOX 7.3 PONDERING ON PURPOSE

- Pull up the American Institute for Research's Stages of Concern as well as the Enneagram Institute's relationships page. How might a "type 1" person who is in the "informational stage of concern" communicate different than a "type 9"? Compare and discuss a few pairs.

Application – Specific Strategies to Improve Communication

I (Lisa) find the book *A Guide to Collaboration for IEP Teams* by Nicholas Martin to be a good resource for learning to mediate tension during difficult meetings of all kinds, including steps for safeguarding a collaborative process. Leading meetings can put you in the position to become a mediator or negotiator. Martin includes steps to take when there is a momentary impasse (disagreement but coming to an agreement at the meeting is still possible), versus a fatal impasse (agreement not currently possible). Take a moment to try his Fourfold Model by recalling a meeting that was particularly contentious. Think about the people (Who are they? What are their experiences?), their interests (What do they want?), options (What are some possible ways to give them what they want?), and criteria (How is the decision made?) who attended the meeting. In retrospect, had you thought about these four areas, how could you have changed your approach to make the meeting go more smoothly?

Another way to prevent or address breakdowns in communication is to look for one of the four feelings that precede anger (The Four Pillars) which are fear, hurt, frustration, and injustice. If the team identifies that these feelings are being triggered, it is important to address them right away. Martin suggests using diagrams called "behavior trains" to help analyze the behaviors triggered by these feelings, consequences for the behaviors, and identify good behavioral alternatives that help address the issue in a productive way.

Probing questions can be useful. I (Lisa) have used them in study groups, and as a tool when I find myself over-telling instead of listening during a meeting. Schoolreforminitiative.org has a guide that walks you through how to use probing questions. We recommend you check out their site for more details. In general probing questions are intended to dive deep into a topic, help you to avoid asking leading questions, and require the responder to avoid yes or no answers.

BOX 7.4 PONDERING ON PURPOSE

- How do you recognize the difference between a momentary impasse and a fatal impasse during a meeting?
- Imagine the last time you were angry during a meeting. Which of The Four Pillars emotions triggered that anger? What could have prevented you from escalating from that emotion to anger?
- Brainstorm scenarios where using probing questions as a protocol would be helpful for your team's work.

Connection – Communication Through Meeting Notes

I (Kelly) once participated in a planning meeting. There had been a series of meetings leading up to this final session, and we ran into a frustrating phenomenon. We had made decisions at a previous meeting, but had failed to take detailed notes, share them, or to follow any sort of notetaking protocol (as described in the previous chapter). One person had taken handwritten notes but did not have them handy. We could all remember making a decision, but none of us could recall the details of the decision. We ended up having to rediscuss and jog each other's memories, which was not an efficient use of time!

Point/Principle – Communication Through Meeting Notes

The first step in having effective notes is to have a structure to keep them consistent and organized. In Chapter 6 we talked about having a column in the agenda to track essential information next to the corresponding agenda item. However, there is more to effective notes than scribing what was said during each portion of a meeting. It may or may not be important to document everything said. There may be visual representations that need to be documented or transcribed. In some cases, the notes may have to be published, emailed, or shared with people outside of the team. Other times notes serve as documentation and reference for an internal team. What you document and share serves as a vital bridge between the work you have done, and the work that you need to do.

Application – Communication Through Meeting Notes

If you can, pull up some meeting notes that your team has taken. Use the chart below to review your notes. What parts do your notes include? What is missing? How can you structure your notes to ensure that no matter who is in the note-taker role, these components will be included? (See Table 7.4.) The Team Initiated Problem Solving (TIPS) process, found at PBIS.org, also has templates and tools to help guide your note-taking approach.

Table 7.4 Relevant Features Included in Effective Meeting Notes

Feature	Description	Rationale
Meeting Demographics	The "who, where, when" of the meeting. • Who was in attendance? • Where did the meeting occur? • When did the meeting occur? • When did each topic/task begin/end?	Provides context to the meeting. It provides the basic facts about who was in attendance, timelines, and location.
Topics	The "what" of the meeting is broken down into a few different components of the notes, because it is the "meat" of your notes. • What topics did the meeting cover? • What was the intent of including each topic (to share information, seek input for a decision, or to make a decision)?	Provides an overview of what will be covered and why so that participants can adequately prepare in advance.
Meeting Tasks	Reflects the method used to drive the discussion and outcomes of the meeting. • What did participation look like? • What materials were used? • How were participants expected to prepare for the meeting? • How were tasks delegated?	Helps the facilitator be intentional with how they will engage participants.

Feature	Description	Rationale
Discussion/Outcomes	Reflects answers to the question "What happened?" Reader should be able to determine why action items and decisions were made based on what is documented. • What was discussed? • What roles did members play?	Provides documentation to participants' contribution and context for final decisions.
Action Items	Reflects "how" your team will take action based on the outcomes of the meeting.	Defines next steps, who will be responsible for them, and by when.
Meeting Evaluation	Small checks for each meeting, more in-depth opportunities for reflection and evaluation every few weeks/year.	Allows participants to provide facilitators feedback as well as input in the meeting's structure and effectiveness.

Connection – Fair Process – Sharing Decisions with Stakeholders

There will be times that after you have gathered input from your stakeholders, you will have to go a different route than they might expect. I (Kelly) have witnessed several major decisions in school districts where pilot groups shared major concerns about a curriculum or technology tool, but the district went forward with the purchase. In these cases, stakeholders were left feeling angry, frustrated, and unheard. The staff were given the impression that the decision had already been made before the pilot, and the time spent studying the effects and giving feedback had been wasted. This outcome may make staff reluctant to **take on** responsibility **in the future.**

In in the case just mentioned, there may have been other factors that weighed more heavily for the administrators, or other pilot groups that found positive results, or a completely different logical explanation for the decision. However, the administration's rationale for purchasing the software was not shared with the teachers or students in the pilot groups. Communicating the reasoning behind a decision helps those involved feel as though there was a "fair process," even if the decision was contradictory to their stance. If your stakeholders typically complain about policies but shrug at taking accountability or steps to effect change, it is possible that your stakeholders do not believe your district or school follows a "fair process" for its decision making.

Point/Principle – Fair Process – Sharing Decisions with Stakeholders

The concept of fair process comes from Kim and Mauborgne and evolved in the business world but is helpful to keep in mind when communicating decisions with any group. First, individuals who will be affected by a decision should be engaged at some level in the process of making the decision. This step is about providing meaningful, reasonable voice. This does not mean that everyone (or even all groups) will be happy with a decision, but it should be clear that their opinions, ideas, and concerns are to be *meaningfully considered* in the process.

Second, the *reasoning behind the ultimate decision should be shared* with everyone involved and affected. This step should reinforce the fact that voices were heard and considered, and explanations should be provided for concerns that could not be resolved or addressed. Finally, the process should include a way to *ensure that everyone affected understands the decision*, and their role in next steps. This third step will be especially important for those who disagree with the decision that has been made. They will need extra support to help them "get on board" with the execution of the decision.

BOX 7.5 PONDERING ON PURPOSE

- How have you helped stakeholders feel their opinions, ideas, and concerns were meaningfully considered?
- How have you shared the reasoning behind final decisions?
- How have you ensured that everyone affected understands the decision?

Table 7.5 Reflecting on Past Decisions

Decision	Outcome/ Reaction from Stakeholders	Missing step(s) or areas to be strengthened?	How could the outcome be different had the steps been addressed?

Application – Fair Process

Think back to a decision you were involved with that was unpopular. Use the chart above to reflect on what evidence you have that each "Fair Process" step was completed, missing or weak areas, and how the outcome could have been different (Table 7.5).

Conclusion

In some cases, a well-designed and very expensive plan does not work as a result of issues around communication. It does not matter if you are dealing with a leading soft drink company, flying a million-dollar spacecraft, or trying to guide the resources of a school. Effective communication can be the secret sauce that can make or break your plans. As a rule, you can never really over communicate your intentions and actions to your stakeholders. Try to find ways to provide information about what you are doing, and why, to all members of your community. Communicate early and often. Communication does not mean to broadcast your ideas, it means that we listen to and engage others. Communication, as we have tried to highlight, involves a process of authentically engaging your community towards a common goal.

Bibliography

Bolman, L. G., & Deal, T. E. (2002). *Reframing the path to school leadership: A guide for teachers and principals*. Thousand Oaks, CA: Corwin Press.

Clearfield, C., & Tilcsik, A. (2018). *Meltdown: Why our systems fail and what we can do about it*. London, England: Penguin.

Kim, W. C., & Mauborgne, R. (2005). Blue ocean strategy: From theory to practice. (marketing strategy). *California Management Review, 47*(3), 105–121. doi:10.2307/41166308

Kim, W. C., & Mauborgne, R. (2017). *Blue ocean shift: Beyond competing*. New York, NY: Hachette Books.

Kim, W. C., & Mauborgne, R. (2005). *Blue ocean strategy: How to create uncontested market space and Make competition irrelevant*. Brighton, MA: Harvard Business Review Press.

Martin, N. R. M. (2005). *A guide to collaboration for IEP teams*. Baltimore, MD: Brookes Publishing Company.

School Reform Initiative. (n.d.). *Pocket guide to probing questions*. Retrieved from http://schoolreforminitiative.org/doc/probing_questions_guide.pdf

8

ALIGNING PRACTICES WITH GOALS
Working Smarter

In a Nutshell

- No matter the focus of your team, the connection to your school's mission and vision should be clear.
- Use strategies to ensure your team's tasks align to your goals.
- Make sure EVERYONE knows your goals and strategies – test this out – don't assume!
- Use graphic organizers to ensure your team is working "smarter, not harder."
- Clean out your closet. Don't waste limited time and resources on programming that does not help you work towards your goals.

Introduction

According to researcher Pauli Alin and colleagues, building designers in Finland use a system called Building Information Modeling (BIM). The BIM provides a three-dimensional computer-generated model of an entire building before it is completed. The BIM includes things like structures, electrical plans, networks of pipes for plumbing, and hearing and air conditioning. This makes is possible to for contractors across a variety of fields to work together more effectively. For example, if a window needs to be moved before construction, the electricians, plumbers, and heating and air conditioning team members can see how each of their focus areas would be impacted. The visual model helps these contracts to collaborate and align their tasks (e.g., moving a pipe, running electrical conduit) that lead to a common goal (e.g., moving a window).

While we are not creating buildings, we are constructing environments that we hope will support all learners. If team members have a clear sense of the district or school's goals (e.g., mission and vision), they can align their tasks and workflow for the greater good. By developing tiered intervention plans that align with the school or district improvement plan, these school-wide supports become more relevant to the school's needs.

Connection – Connecting to the Mission and Vision for School Improvement

I (Kelly) once spent time working on discipline policies related to attendance with a group of deans. During the same span of time, I was working at the district level to develop cohesive statements about the mission, vision, and goals for the district. My district work related to our main focus areas for all school improvement efforts. Many of the ideas that some of the deans were proposing were aligning with previous practices, or the policies and proce-dures we had heard about from other districts, such as denying course credit to students who had missed more than a certain number of classes. I was able to point out that our new mission, vision, and goals for the district included building systems for proactive and restorative interventions, and reducing disproportionality in disciplinary outcomes. Highlighting the district's new mission, vision, and goals changed the course of conversation to focus on more proactive strategies. Sometimes educators view mission and vision state-ments as "catch phrases" or simply public relations material to post on the website. But if they are well-written and truly reflect the values and priorities of the school community, your mission and vision can be useful tools that help guide efforts and push people to plan more cohesively.

Point/Principle – Connecting to the Mission and Vision for School Improvement

As we have previously mentioned, there is a considerable overlap between various MTSS-related approaches (positive behavior interventions and sup-port (PBIS), social and emotional learning (SEL), and response to intervention (RtI)) and the process of school improvement. Connecting to the mission and vision of the school and/or district and integrating MTSS planning with the school improvement efforts and strategies will help teams be more cohesive and effective. This integration will assist teams in avoiding the redundancy and "competition" that can arise when these are siloed instead of aligned. Look back to Table 1.2 in Chapter 1. Using this table, consider ways teams can integrate their schoolwide efforts (e.g., multi-tiered systems of supports (MTSS)) with school improvement plans (SIP). For example, they could look at integrating:

- MTSS/SIP Teams
- MTSS/SIP Goals
- MTSS/SIP Data/Evaluation

- MTSS/SIP Practices
- MTSS/SIP Systems

Application – Connecting to the Mission and Vision for School Improvement

One way to see if your tasks for your schoolwide approach are aligned with your SIP goals is to reflect with your team. Psychologist and change coach Henry Cloud and authors Chip and Dan Heath offer a list of reflective questions to use to see how clearly your team is aligning your approach with the mission and vision of your setting. Take a few moments on your own or as a team to reflect on the questions provided in Figure 8.1

---

1. Have we defined success in all areas where we have specific problems to address?
    Your response: _____

2. Is our mission and vision clear and communicated in a way that allows everyone in our organization to attend, exhibit, and move toward it? (e.g., did we use concrete language)
    Your response: _____

3. Does our community know what our mission and vision are? (stop 10 people at random, as them)
    Your response: _____

4. Do they know what are part of your mission and vision?
    Your response: _____

5. Do we state clearly why our goals are important?
    Your response: _____

6. Can your community members take actionable steps towards your mission and vision?
    Your response: _____

7. Do they know what activities belong to the mission and vision and which do not?
    Your response: _____

8. Do they know how what they control directly contributes to the mission and vision?
    Your response: _____

Figure 8.1 Mission and Task Alignment Reflection Questions

BOX 8.1 PONDERING ON PURPOSE

How does your current school improvement plan align with your MTSS efforts?

Connection – Strategies for Aligning Tasks to Goals

REI is a successful sporting goods store that is continuously named one of the top 100 places to work in the United States. At the same time, may of REI's competitors are closing their doors due to loss of business. REI closes on "Black Friday" and Thanksgiving, even refusing to process online sales, yet their profits continue to soar. REI is successful because they align their tasks to their goals. Their website states, "For us, success means running a healthy business and making a positive impact on our employees, members and society." Their mission is to "inspire, educate and outfit for a lifetime of outdoor adventure and stewardship." From tasks such as interview processes, how they treat their employees, and to how they spend their profits, all decisions are made with their mission in mind. They give their employees a paid day off on Black Friday and Thanksgiving and suggest spending time outdoors, sell and rent used gear (to limit what goes into the landfill and increase access to the outdoors for those on budgets), and invest in "rewilding" urban and suburban communities to provide more space for outdoor recreation. While some might think these actions would lead to a decrease in their profits, it does the opposite. Their tasks align with their goals, and they are rewarded because of it. Not only do their employees work harder, but their consumers spend more too. Because of their tasks align with their mission and vision, REI is consistently able to make an impact on providing access to the outdoors.

Point/Principle – Strategies for Aligning Tasks to Goals

As you think about your school's current and future tasks, do you work from a plan that aligns with your school vision and mission? As you begin work related to your goals, we encourage your team to think about the following three areas.

First, do you know if every strategy or program your school is implementing is related to the school's goals (e.g., school improvement goals, MTSS action plan)? How do you know? Do you have a document to track and communicate this information?

Next, what is your process for selecting interventions and practices? The interventions should be selected based on evidence that they will work in your setting. The Clearinghouse that can help you with this process such as the What Works Clearing House sponsored by the United States Department of Education or the National Center for Intensive Intervention. A selection process should have universally known and documented criteria that are specific to your setting to help you meet your goals within your context. This can be particularly challenging for secondary schools, as many empirical studies are conducted in elementary settings.

Secondary schools may also find that they need to utilize interventions that involve specific evidence-based strategies or routines (for example the Collaborative Strategic Reading process developed by Janette Klingner and SharonVaughn), rather than selecting a "packaged" program. Schoolwide teams should not use this as an excuse to "throw things against the wall to see if they stick" or pull together bits and pieces of evidence-based strategies. Whatever is implemented should have some key characteristics or fidelity measures that can be monitored. In Chapter 16 we provide resources on where to find helpful interventions.

Finally, your tasks should have some alignment with the budget for the school. If your administration is not willing to work with your team on aligning budget line items with your goals, then you have a larger issue to deal with as a group. If you do not have alignment with the school's budget, then we recommend going back to the chapter on buy-in and obtaining support.

Application – Strategies for Aligning Tasks to Goals

The author Greg McKeon developed a useful approach for selecting strategies based on alignment with your goals. This strategy can be adapted to help you select a new car, job, or schoolwide approach. We refer to this strategy as the "You Gotta Love It." If you only like the intervention, then do not marry it! Your school needs criteria to determine if the intervention is a good match. Use Table 8.1 to help you create criteria to select practices that will address your school improvement plan. Start by selecting three criteria that the practice you end up choosing "must have" and three that would be "good to have." In order to select/support the practice you will implement, it must meet the standard for all three "must haves" and at least two of the "good to have" criteria. For example, possible criteria for selecting an intervention might be:

- Use data to monitor their efforts (must have)
- Are related to the school improvement plan (must have)
- Are based on evidence the approach can work in our setting (must have)
- Are politically important
- Can be implemented efficiently by teachers
- Includes training for staff
- Provides access to some type of coaching for staff

Table 8.1 Criteria for Selecting Interventions

1. List out your criteria for selecting practices below (you can create your own – three "must have," and three "good to have" components)

Must Have	Good to Have
1.	1.
2.	2.
3.	3.

2. List one schoolwide practice you are implementing here:_____
3. How many "must have" criteria does it meet? _____
4. How many "good to have" criteria does it meet? _____

If your intervention does not meet all three of the "must have," and at least two of the "good to have" criteria then we recommend considering whether or not the intervention is a good match for your school.

Connection – Working Smarter

In his *New York Times* best-selling book, *Essentialism: The Disciplined Pursuit of Less*, Greg McKeon encourages his reader to pressure fewer, but better, tasks. In his book, he tells the story of the nineteenth century economist Vilfredo Pareto. Pareto studied the economy of Italy during his time. He noticed that for business, 20% of their efforts lead to 80% of their profits. The point that Greg McKeon makes is that very few of our tasks actually have an impact on the goals we are trying to achieve. The key to being successful at reaching goals is to focus on the few things that have the ultimate impact on your outcomes. I (Hank) used to think that when people asked how I was doing I needed to say, "I'm so busy." Now, my hope is to be able to say, "I have been so effective."

Point/Principle – Working Smarter

In this section, we define working smarter as starting the right projects, and ending the ones that no longer serve your mission. In order to make sure your team is only focusing on tasks and strategies that address the mission of your school, you need to know what you are already doing. We once worked with an urban high school. By the time we had them list out all of their interventions, at every tier, they had over 75 different programs that were being attempted at the same time. We are not sure they were all being effectively implemented. However, the staff were shocked, and then somewhat relieved, to know why they felt so overwhelmed. We recommend that you also have your team take an audit of every practice that your school is implementing at this time.

Application – Working Smarter

As you think about your school or classroom, what are the practices or interventions that have seemed to have the greatest impact? Can you identify one practice that, based on your data and observations, has had the most impact on your students? We are not asking you to select anything yet. We just want to you think start thinking about what is essential.

What intervention has had the greatest impact on your students in the last year? _____

Next, think about your own focus area. What is one practice that has been the most useful to you in your own personal or professional growth? You do not have to limit this to school-based activities. This essential activity could include behaviors such as reading books about your profession, exercising more, or getting more sleep.

What activity, or intervention, has had the greatest impact on you in the last year?_____

Reflecting our your own experiences can help you practice for reflecting corporately with your team.

Connection – Working Smarter in Selecting Practices

I (Kelly) have guided several high school leadership teams through the process of mapping out all the academic and social and emotional learning and behavior (SELB) strategies/practices/interventions that were in place at each tier of support. I gave the team some guiding questions to determine whether a practice was fully in place or partially in place, and we made a diagram on a large dry-erase board of all the ideas that were shared. The activity was incredibly eye-opening for the teams. Often administrators were shocked to learn about initiatives happening that they had no idea existed. We saw redundancies and overlapping initiatives. We saw great interventions happening for only specific pockets of students that would make sense to offer to larger groups. There were "things" that people had heard of and knew existed, but that no leaders in the room could describe with confidence because they "belonged" to specific teachers or counselors who ran them autonomously (and without much communication with or support from the building leaders). Every time we complete this diagramming process the group has been overwhelmed by how much "stuff" goes on the board, and how many gaps they still see. And thus the planning began!

Point/Principle – Working Smarter in Selecting Practices

A great way to get started on working smarter is to create a visual representation of all the current efforts in place at a school, based on a triangle of support. Several organizations offer templates and examples for this type of visual mapping. An actual example from a school can be found in Figure 8.2. The example uses the triangle as a visual model of each tier of support, with academic supports on one side and behavioral supports on another. Another method involves setting up a "visual graph" where the y axis is an arrow pointing up that says "intensity" or "tier" and the x axis has "academic" on the left and SELB on the right. Teams can place practices in the middle that overlap academic and SELB realms. Describing both axes as a continuum can help teams avoid becoming bogged down in debates over what "counts" as a tier two versus a tier three support, or whether an executive function support group should fall on the academic or behavioral side of the triangle. A third possibility would be to list the practices in a table format as seen in Table 8.2.

Whichever format a team chooses, the key is to get members thinking about all of the practices in their schools that kids have access to, and getting them mapped out in one place. The goal of this process is to identify redundancies and/or gaps in the supports needed to achieve the vision and mission of your school. When facilitating this type of activity, it is important to keep reminding teams that it doesn't have to be perfect to be helpful. It is

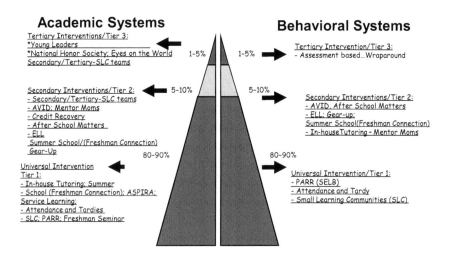

Figure 8.2 Example of Visual Auditing Current Supports

also a great opportunity to gently review the differences between systems, practices, and data, and/or the different tiers of support. Teams can add symbols such as dotted lines around items that are considered partially in place, and solid lines around items that are fully in place. There are lots of ways to modify this activity, so long as the result is an overview of all the "stuff" done for students in a school.

Once you have your interventions listed, another task can include looking at the alignment of the interventions with the school's goals. Table 8.2, originally developed by George Sugai, asks teams to list crosswalk their schoolwide strategies with the intervention's purpose, the intervention's outcomes, the target group, the staff involved, and the link to the school's overall goals (e.g., school improvement goals). You will start to see some patterns once you begin your process. If the intervention is not linked to outcomes or goals, you might be getting some hint that this might be a strategy that needs to be reconsidered.

Application – Working Smarter in Selecting Practices

Use Figure 8.3 to complete a visual audit of the tasks/strategies/interventions your school implements. Do not get stuck in debates on whether something belongs to a particular tier as long as it is represented on the chart. Every strategy, practice, or program you implement can be placed on the chart and should be reflected here.

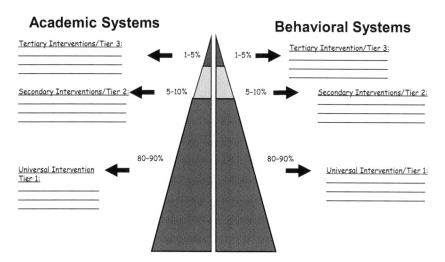

ACTIVITY
Designing Schoolwide Systems for Student Success
A Response to Intervention Model

Figure 8.3 Blank Version of Visual Auditing Current Supports Triangle

Table 8.2 Example of Matrix Crosswalk – Goals and Interventions

Working Smarter

Initiative, Project, Committee	Purpose	Outcome	Target Group	Staff Involved	SIP
Tier One: Behavioral and Academic Systems					
Core Math Curriculum and Assessment	Raise math scores, provide unified core, improve critical thinking skills	Measures of Academic Progress (MAP) data, ISAT, Unit tests, check-ups (quiz)	All students	Math department, KLN, MC2	Goal 2
ACHIEVE	Raise reading levels, provide differentiated instruction in informational text	MAP, ISAT, AHIEVE report, Explore	All students	Reading, science, social studies, MAB	Goal 1
ST Math	Basic skills for all students	MAP data, ISAT, ST math reports, pre- and post-tests	All students	Math department, KLN, MC2, Tech coordinator	Goal 2
Extension Time	Targeted improvement for specific skills and differentiation	MAP data, ISAT, pre- and post-tests (specific skill test)	All students	All content area teachers and special education	Goals 1 and 2
Schoolwide Positive Behavior Support	Improve student behavior through positive supports; improve school climate for everyone	Office discipline referral rates, my voice my school	All students and staff	DES, SNB, ZPCD, RAM, RFW, KLN, PJF	Goal 3

Olweus (e.g., class meetings)	Decrease bullying at schools	Office discipline referrals	All students and staff	MC2, MAB, BB, VB, DS, EN, RR, EM, ED, MM	Goal 3
CHAMPS	Improve classroom management	Office discipline referrals	All students and staff	DB, WB, KP, ZPCD, MAB, EM,	Goal 3
Gear Up (e.g. Teaming)	Get students to be college ready – summer program – transition to high school, professional development	Gear up number of students who go to college (see data?)	All students and staff	Outside support	Goals 1 and 2
Daily oral reminders	To improve school climate – pre-teach and re-teach expectations	Office discipline referrals	All staff and administration	Staff and administration	Goal 3
Team discipline plans	Create consistent rewards and consequences to improve climate, communicate with parents	Office discipline referrals, number of goals, detentions, decrease in phone calls	All teams and all students	All staff	Goals 1, 2, and 3
MAP Goal Setting	Increase student accountability and motivation	MAP scores, number of goals met, number of students meeting expected growth	All students	All teachers	Goals 1, 2, and 3

(Continued)

Table 8.2 (continued)

Tier One: Behavioral and Academic Systems			
All Stars	Provide after school enrichment activities for students at-risk	Provide a safe place to learn new skills after school and develop positive relationships between students and teachers	Students who apply	Ms. M, Ms. G and selected teachers	Goal 3

Tier Two: Behavioral and Academic Systems			
SES	Raise reading and math test scores	Increase scores	Students selected based on low reading and math test scores if they qualify for free/reduced lunch	SES of Illinois Providers, school coordinator, teachers	Goals 1 and 2
Gear Up Tutors	Academic support for low-achieving students	Higher report card grades, higher test scores	Teacher selection	Gear Up Tutors, classroom teachers	Goals 1 and 2
Morning ST Math and Achieve (AM/PM)	Raise test scores	Higher test scores	Students on the bubble between low/meets or meets/exceeds	Teachers, tech coordinators	Goals 1 and 2
Extension (differentiation)	Improve targeted areas of weakness based on MAP data	MAP Test Scores improve	Students placed in groups based on data	All students and teachers	Goals 1 and 2
Morning Math Tutoring	Academic support for students struggling with math curriculum	Higher math grades	Teacher selected and student self-selection	Math team	Goal 2

All Stars	Provide enrichment activities for at-risk students	Positive relationships between students and teachers	Students and parents sign up	Teachers, security, school coordinator	Goal 3
Algebra Class	Provide advanced class for capable students, differentiated curriculum	Students prepared for high school	Students selected by teacher recommendation based on report card grades and test scores	Math department	Goal 2
Youth Guidance Social Work	To help students identify why they behave inappropriately so that they can change their behavior	Positive changes in a student's emotional and academic success	Students referred through IEPs, parents, teachers, or self	Youth guidance and social workers	Goal 3
Check In and Check Out	A formal way to track a student's behavior and academic performance	Improve behavior and academic progress	Students referred by teachers based on behavior	Classroom teachers	Goal 3
Children's Memorial Partnership	Anger management instructions	Student accountability for behavior	Students referred by teachers	Children's hospital	Goal 3

(Continued)

Table 8.2 (continued)

Tier Three: Behavioral and Academic Systems				
Academic Contract and Remediation Plans	To identify problem areas and create a plan to solve those problems	Better grades and test scores	Students with low grades	All teachers	Goals 1 and 2
Awards Assemblies	To reward students experiencing success in school	Students maintain focus and motivate others	Achieving and excelling students	All teachers	Goals 1 and 2
Reading Lab	Provide additional literacy instruction to the low-achieving students in reading	Help students improve their literacy skills and increase test scores	Students identified by test data	Ms. B	Goal 1
Behavioral contract and remediation plan	To identify problem behaviors and create a plan to solve those problems	Improve behavior	Students identified through misconduct reports and teacher referrals	All teachers	Goal 3
Youth Guidance Social Work	Individual counseling sessions to help students identify why they behave inappropriately so that they can change their behavior	Positive changes in a student's emotional and academic success	Students referred through IEPs, parents, teachers, or self	Youth guidance and social workers	Goal 3

Connection – Eliminating Non-Essential Programs

When was the last time you cleaned out your closet? What impact did it have on how you used the clothes that you have? Many report feeling weighed down when they have neglected their closets. Perfectly good outfits sit buried with the tags still on them while you wear an old standby that you don't actually like very much because it is comfortable and you know it well. There have been many different methods published by expert organizers to help you tackle this feat, but they all boil down to taking note of what you have, thinking about how you have used each piece, how often, and how it makes you feel. The final step of purging includes separating clothes into keep, donate, and throw away piles.

Thinking about your current programs and eliminating non-essentials can be thought of in the same way. You may find programs that you have been meaning to use and want to keep in rotation, some that are great but just not a good fit for you anymore and would be useful for someone else, and some that are outdated or ineffective that you can let go completely.

BOX 8.2 PONDERING ON PURPOSE

- How does letting programs/strategies go unused without intentionally cleaning them out impact your school? (Think about what leaving unused clothes does to your closet.)
- How often should you "clean out" your programs? Why?

Point/Principle – Eliminating Non-Essential Programs

Letting go of practices can be a difficult thing for school teams to do, for many different reasons. It can be particularly difficult when you see redundancies and have to make a choice between two good practices. For example, a school may offer two reading intervention programs and both are yielding good results for groups of learners with similar needs. Choosing one reading intervention program would free up money, time, and training resources to put toward an area where a different type of intervention is needed.

In other cases, there is a fear that even though a program is ineffective or misaligned with goals, losing it would be worse. For example, a school might decide to close an in-school suspension room in order to use the personnel and space to deliver a behavioral intervention for groups of students with multiple discipline referrals. Often these types of decisions are laden with fears that the new approach will be seen as too lax by students, staff, and/

or parents, and the students will take advantage of that change and behave worse than the status quo. All too often, when we ask why we do something a certain way, the response is "because that's how we have always done it." Making decisions based on research and clear criteria can help guide these conversations, along with reassurances that there is no such thing as "set in stone" in schools beyond state and federal regulations. Continuous reminders may be needed that systems change is an ongoing process, and adjustments can always be made down the road if data show a decision had a negative impact.

Application – Eliminating Non-Essential Programs

If you haven't already, create a list of all of your current interventions/programs and rate them on a scale from one to ten. A ten means it is aligned with your goals, (see criteria from above). A rating of one means there is little alignment with the goals for MTSS/school improvement and other criteria you developed. If the intervention is not ranked as a nine or ten, consider stopping that practice. As George Sugai has said, we should consider eliminating practices that are no longer needed or are not effective to make room for interventions that have good evidence, that will meet your students' needs.

In order to systematically audit, begin by reviewing the criteria for an effective practice that aligns with school goals. Use the guidelines from below for this, and possibly add some other criteria as well. For example, a well-functioning tier one practice would have a "yes" for each question in Table 8.3.

Table 8.3 Questions to Ask When Reviewing Tasks/Strategies/Interventions

Question	Yes	No	Potentially
Is it provided schoolwide to all students?			
Is it based on research/evidence?			
Is there a system to ensure all staff are trained?			
Is there a system to measure fidelity/ frequency?			
Is there a system to ensure frequent feedback/coaching/follow-up PD for staff?			

Is there a system to routinely make adjustments (as needed) based on fidelity and outcome measures?			
Is information about implementation and outcomes routinely shared with staff, students, parents, etc.?			

Once team members all understand/agree upon the criteria, examine each practice listed on the visual map. As a team, rate each item based on the established criteria. In addition, determine whether the practice overlaps with other practices. Once you have rated each practice within a tier, decide as a team which practices could be eliminated or merged with others in order to free up resources to better implement others. Next, identify gaps where additional practices are needed.

Conclusion

Sometimes we hear that schools or organizations need to tear down their silos to become more efficient. Farmers, however, would never tear down their grain silos and mix their grain into one place. Bakers need to pull the raw materials from separate grain silos to make fantastic bread. Like farmers and bakers, we think we should spend less time thinking about how we can tear down silos between groups within an organization. Instead, like the baker who is using an excellent recipe for cooking, we need a clear school improvement plan that can guide different staff and practices towards a common goal. Secondary schools are full of people who feel extremely busy and overwhelmed. There is always "a lot going on" and often staff members feel pulled in too many directions and overwhelmed by many initiatives without cohesiveness. For systems of support to be effective, they must align clearly to overarching goals, and be delivered in the most efficient manner possible. It should be clear to all stakeholder groups how various practices implemented in a school fit into the overall vision of how students are supported. If the team leading the efforts struggles to visualize and articulate this cohesiveness, it will be difficult to work effectively or establish buy-in from other stakeholder groups. Mapping out practices and auditing to "work smarter" is a crucial step toward success.

Bibliography

Bohanon, H., Wu, M., Kushki, A., Vera, E., Carlson-Sanei, J., LeVesseu, C., ... Harms, A. (2019). *The role of school improvement planning in the implementation of schoolwide supports.* Manuscript submitted for publication.

Cloud, H. (2013). *Boundaries for leaders: Results, relationships, and being ridiculously in charge.* LA Porte, IN: Harper Collins.

Heath, C., & Heath, D. (2007). *Made to stick: Why some ideas survive and others die.* Crawfordsville, IN: Random House.

Klingner, J. K., & Vaughn, S. (1998). Using collaborative strategic reading. *Teaching Exceptional Children, 30*(6), 32–37. Retrieved from http://www.ldonline.org/ld_indepth/teaching_techniques/collab_reading.html

Klingner, J. K., & Vaughn, S. (1999). Promoting reading comprehension, content learning, and English acquisition through Collaborative Strategic Reading (CSR). *The Reading Teacher, 52*(7), 738–747.

McKeon, G. (2014). *Essentialism: The disciplined pursuit of less.* New York, NY: Crown Business.

Slavin, R. E. (2007). Comprehensive school reform. Retrieved from www.successforall.org/wp-content/uploads/2016/02/Comprehensive-School-Reform.pdf

Sleegers, P. J. C., Thoonen, E. E. J., Oort, F. J., & Peetsma, T. T. D. (2014). Changing classroom practices: The role of school-wide capacity for sustainable improvement. *Journal of Educational Administration, 52*(5), 617–652. doi:10.1108/JEA-11-2013-0126

Sugai, G. (2010). Working smarter matrix committee/group self-assessment & action planning. Retrieved from https://www.mayinstitute.org/pdfs/presentations/PBIS2018-B3-E-PBIS-Working-Smarter-Matrix.pdf

Sugai, G., Horner, R., & Lewis, T. (2020, March 25). Moment to moment and year to year: Preventing contemporary problem behavior in schools. Office of Special Education and Rehabilitative Services Blog, U.S. Department of Education. Retrieved from https://sites.ed.gov/osers/?guest_author_name=George+Sugai%2C+Rob+Horner%2C+and+Tim+Lewis#_ftn1

Data Wise Improvement Process. (n.d.). Retrieved from http://datawise.gse.harvard.edu/files/datawise/files/stoplight-system-leaders.pdf

9

ALIGNMENT OF PROFESSIONAL ROLES WITH PRACTICES

In a Nutshell

- Know and understand the strengths and weaknesses of your community.
- Delegate tasks to others to foster buy-in, improve efficiency, and develop the competencies of your team.
- Take the time to write out descriptions of roles, so that those agreeing to and fulfilling the roles know the expectations tied to them.
- Identify the needs of the task and then select the person/team with the knowledge that matches those needs.
- Use visual models to identify roles, including hierarchal structures for those responsible for leading/approving tasks.
- Keep equity and representation in mind while creating teams.
- When you have gaps of competencies within your teams, use behavior-based interviewing to find "good matches" when hiring new staff.

Introduction

There is a financial planning company in Nashville lead by Dave Ramsey that has grown exponentially over the last few years. One of the reasons for their success is what they call key responsibility areas (KRAs). Every employee has a KRA that guides their work. These plans help the team member determine the best use of their time. The KRAs also help other team members understand how their work relates to that of other team members. Finally, KRAs help with transitions when an employee moves to a new role.

Like in business, the success of your schoolwide efforts depends on the ability to harness the strengths of your community. Organizations can work more effectively when its members know how their work aligns with important tasks and they have clearly defined roles. This chapter will focus on the ways you can align your roles with tasks that make the work more efficient for everyone, including ways to distribute leadership, identify areas of expertise needed for the work, assigning staff to roles, preventing burnout, and creating role descriptions.

Connection – Distributive Leadership

During World War II, two generals led efforts on the opposing sides of the war. According to historian Stephen Ambrose, General Erwin Rommel of the German army was a brilliant tactician who could think quickly in the field. His leadership style was to rely on his own abilities rather than trust his subordinates. General Dwight D. Eisenhower was the talented leader for the Allied forces. He made decisions after seeking input from his staff. By working with his team on the development and implementation of his operations, he was building both buy-in and the capacity of his team. Since he relied on himself, success for General Rommel depended on his presence in the field. General Eisenhower was able to delegate and distribute responsibilities that did not require his actual presence during campaigns. One leader built his reputation, while the other won a war.

Point/Principle – Distributive Leadership

According to researchers Kris Bosworth, Rafael Garcia, Maryann Judkins, and Mark Saliba, distributing leadership may be an important part of improving your setting, not just battlefields. These researchers studied the connection in high schools between leadership, school climate, and reducing school bullying. They found that the involvement of leadership in the change process, including distributed leadership, was related to lower levels of bullying. Distributive leadership reflects a model closer to what General Eisenhower used in his leadership style. According to researchers Vicki Park and Amanda Datnow, distributive leadership can include these actions:

- Include leaders from all levels and teams in the development of the vision for the school
- Build trust by engaging in protocols that encourage data-driven decision making and focus on learning and improvement rather than blame

- Give relevance to data by dispensing decision-making authority, empowering team members to use their collective knowledge to problem solve
- Develop team members' capacity through modeling and sharing knowledge

Application – Distributive Leadership

Reflection on the current leadership style of your team can help you find ways to distribute leadership and prevent burnout for team members. Use the following reflection questions in Table 9.1 to consider the efforts of your own team to empower your staff and distribute leadership. The first column proposes a question for your team's consideration. Use the second column to reflect on your current style of distributive leadership. In the third column, consider ways to improve your approach to distributive leadership.

Connection – Knowledge Areas Needed for Your Tasks

Once, I (Hank) was on my way with a colleague to give a presentation on high school positive behavior support. We were sitting on the airplane during the final approach. As the plane descended, a child began to cry in her mother's arms. My colleague and I watched and felt bad for the mother and child. Suddenly, a young girl reached over from across the aisle and handed

Table 9.1 Reflecting on Approaches to Distributive Leadership

Question	Reflection	Possible Improvements
In what ways are we including leadership at every level in developing vision for the school, and data-driven decision making? Does our team focus on learning and improvement rather than blame?		
How do we give relevance to data by dispensing decision-making authority that empowers team members to use their knowledge?		
How is our team doing at focusing our resources on developing leaders at all level's capacity through modeling and sharing knowledge?		

the mother her keys. The child grabbed the keys and began to play with them, and amazingly, stopped crying. We wondered how the girl (about 13 years old) knew the keys might work. She said, "It's no problem, I've babysat before." The girl was a stranger to the child and wasn't a parent, so we were surprised when she knew how to solve the problem. This happens in the workplace when we make assumptions of what people know based on titles or education. This causes missed opportunities to bring those with knowledge to the table, ultimately leading to delay or undermining possible solutions.

Point/Principle – Knowledge Areas Needed for Your Tasks

Researchers Susan Forman and Chana Crystal have identified several areas that help teams to implement evidence-based practices in schools. We think these areas relate to any type of implementation approach – including multi-tiered systems of supports (MTSS) and school improvement. When we think about the knowledge needed for teams, we may limit ourselves to the current skill base of the group. Accomplishing a goal as a team goes beyond content knowledge. According to Forman, the knowledge and skill domains team members need for successfully supporting MTSS implementation include:

1. Leadership (not necessarily a title, e.g., change agents, guiding efforts, setting goals, conflict resolution, providing resources, adjusting the organization's policies and procedures).
2. Selecting interventions that focus on fit and effectiveness (e.g., knowledge of the setting, working smarter, knowledge of domain-specific practices).
3. Data-based decision making (e.g., testing the effectiveness of interventions and implementation strategies).
4. Developing stakeholder support (e.g., establishing buy-in).
5. Developing the competency of the implementors (e.g., skills-based training and coaching).
6. Developing organizational supports (e.g., systems).
7. Obtaining facilitation from external supports (e.g., obtaining support from districts, universities, regional cooperatives, state technical assistant agencies).

Application – Knowledge Areas Needed for Your Task's Application

Table 9.2 provides you with space to reflect on the areas of knowledge you may need for your setting in order to accomplish your ultimate goal. It also asks that you begin to think about the people in your community who might possess

Table 9.2 Knowledge and Skills for Schoolwide Implementation

Knowledge Area	Specific Skills Needed	Potential Stakeholder Matches
Leadership		
Data-based decision making		
Selecting interventions		
Developing stakeholder support		
Developing competency		
Developing organizational supports		
Obtaining external supports		

some of the knowledge and skills you need. These individuals may or may not be a part of your formal team. If you cannot identify specific people for your team, then you can think about the roles people play that might include the skills you need (e.g., community member, counselor, math teacher). Proactively identifying knowledge gaps in current staff allows you to actively seek candidates with these skills as your school undertakes future hiring.

Connection – Strategically Selecting Team Members

Sometimes the people you need for your teams do not necessarily have formal titles or roles. For example, one high school was beginning to implement MTSS. They had an in-school suspension room. The room was being supervised by a staff member who did not have a teaching degree, but he did have a strong math background. Over time, the school administration realized that they would be better served in their long-term mission by having this staff member support their data efforts related to MTSS. At first, this person supported the MTSS team by developing basic reports. The data he generated were so helpful that he was moved into a full-time role for supporting data for the school. The data he provided were a key component of what we referred to in Table 9.2 around decision making. To develop an effective team, keep an open mind and match people to tasks based on skills, rather than titles alone.

Point/Principle – Strategically Selecting Team Members

In order to harness the strengths of your community, you need to know they exist. If a stakeholder has a knowledge set you don't utilize, they may feel disengaged or slighted when they are not asked to contribute. Other times, stakeholders don't recognize a strength within themselves, and if not discovered by others, it can go untapped. Sometimes the environment causes a person to be hesitant to step forward and share their skills because they are afraid of the criticism or pushback they may receive. Others may not even know their expertise is needed. In any case, these reasons all lead to a waste of rich resources within an arm's reach of the school. When strategically selecting members for you team, consider how you will keep apprised of the skills within your reach.

Equitable representation should be one of the major factors weighed when creating a team. It is ideal to have staff and student members that represent the demographics of the building. A healthy, balanced team will include a variety of professional roles, expertise, and years of service. Teams should represent groups who traditionally report feeling less safe or supported (people of color, religious groups, or those who identify as gay/lesbian, trans, gender fluid, etc.). The team is responsible for creating systems that support ALL members of the community. Without representation, teams can become echo chambers where members only reinforce their own perspectives instead of hearing other points of view. When that happens, teams are less likely to consider the various needs of stakeholder groups.

When selecting members of your team, think about both varied perspectives and abilities to accomplish the specific tasks you will need for success. Here are some stakeholders to consider including:

- An *internal and/or external coach or coordinator* (preferably with expertise in MTSS).
- At least one *administrator or authorized decision-maker* related to the team's focal strategies and tasks.
- One or more *teachers* for perspective on classroom implementation.
- Those in *support staff* roles (such as custodians, security staff members, or administrative assistants). Often overlooked when teams are formed, these adults frequently have more interactions with students than all the administrators put together!
- *Students as active members of the team*, and not just students who typically experience success. Some teams "ease into" student participation by having a student committee or panel, which is a great starting point, but there is a powerful message sent to adolescents about the importance of their voices in their own school community when they are invited to participate as full members of the schoolwide team.
- *Parents and community members* should be represented as well. High school staff members sometimes assume that parents do not wish to be involved now that their children are older, which is often not the case.

- *Community agencies*, such as local mental health organizations, community centers, nonprofit tutoring organizations, etc., are potentially helpful partners for schoolwide teams. Having representatives from local restaurants, coffee shops, and other types of shops become part of the team can help reinforce strategies, communication, and even the mission of the school community.
- A person with *data analysis experience* and the ability to access school-wide data.

In addition to a variety of perspectives, general areas of expertise outlined in Table 9.2 must be represented, if not already included in the team members described above. Team members with expertise in current best practices and interventions related to *reading/literacy, mathematics, social emotional learning and behavior, key populations of students* (such as those who are English Learners or who have Individualized Education Plans), and *post-secondary planning* will be needed.

In order to find the balance between representing the needed perspectives, expertise, and roles, and keeping the team to a manageable size for discussion and decision making, team members can serve two roles (for example, a counselor who has knowledge of post-secondary planning and is also able to pull data and create the needed graphs). Often teams are divided up into committees, and only committee chairs come together for the overall schoolwide team meetings, or sometimes members only attend meetings or portions of meetings where their role or expertise is needed.

Application – Strategically Selecting Team Members

As you think about your schoolwide team, reflect on the current membership of the group. Consider the makeup of the group first by official title (e.g., roles, positions). Next, we will ask you to consider your team based on the knowledge base of the group. To begin, use the checklist below to identify the members of your team by role or title.

What are the titles of those who oversee your school improvement planning? Check all that apply.

- ☐ Administrator
- ☐ Community member
- ☐ External coach (person outside the building who regularly provides feedback)
- ☐ General education teacher
- ☐ Parent/family member
- ☐ School counselor
- ☐ School psychologist

- ☐ Social worker
- ☐ Special education teacher
- ☐ Support staff
- ☐ Student
- ☐ Other: _____

Now that you have identified the members of your group based on titles and roles, identify the makeup of your group based on areas of knowledge. Remember, knowledge may not only be based on title or role alone. For example, you might have a parent who is also a psychologist who understands childhood trauma. What areas of professional knowledge are represented on your team? (This could be broader than professional role.) Check all that apply.

- ☐ Assessing student learning
- ☐ Behavior intervention
- ☐ College and career readiness
- ☐ Community
- ☐ Culturally relevant instruction
- ☐ Curriculum development
- ☐ Families
- ☐ Limited English proficiency
- ☐ Safety/school crisis planning
- ☐ Special education
- ☐ Student learning
- ☐ Student mental health
- ☐ Data analysis
- ☐ Other _____

While our lists are not exhaustive, it does give you a place to start your discussion. Looking at your mission and vision, what additional areas of expertise do you need to ensure the success of your team? Take time to reflect who might bring in additional knowledge (See Table 9.2) to support the development of your group. The auxiliary website for this book provides a tool called the **Tiered Inventory of Effective Resources in Schools (TIERS)**, which you can use to further consider your alignment between mission and vision, tasks, and people.

Connection – Organizational Chart of Roles

A few years ago, Zappos shoe company in the United States tried a new management style. The CEO Tony Hsieh decided he wanted to try an approach called holacracy. Essentially, holacracy meant that there would no longer be any organizational hierarchy and/or structures. In this model, there were no more titles or bosses. The spirit of this approach was to encourage collaboration and self-management. Bourree Lam of *The Atlantic* reported that this new approach led to confusion for many employees. According to the report, over 30% of the employees left the company during 2015. There may be a place for flat organizational structures, however, knowledge of how your efforts align with the larger organization may help you operate more effectively as a group.

Point/Principle – Organizational Chart of Roles

Having a visual organizational structure can help your team in several ways.

1. Your team can see how their efforts fit into overall school leadership structures.
2. The organizational chart can help team members develop specific roles for their work.
3. Organizational charts can help your team determine if they have appropriate representation of the needed skills, and authority for carrying out tasks.
4. The chart can help your team develop an effective communication plan like the CAIRO plan that we discussed in Chapter 7. As researchers, Eric Knight and Sotirios Paroutis explain, using visuals is an important part of developing an effective strategy.

Schools we have worked with used the two visual organizational structures in Figure 9.1 and Figure 9.2. The first example comes from a large high school. The "system" that the group was primarily focusing on was positive behavior interventions and supports (PBIS). The layers for this chart include district-wide support, external coaching, administrative support, tier one and tier two teams, and subcommittees. The subcommittees supported the work of the teams but did not attend every leadership meeting.

The second example (see Figure 9.2) of an organizational chart is from a large suburban school. This school was implementing both academic and behavior supports for their students. The chart includes the principal, administrative team, internal coach for schoolwide behavior support interventions, and four chairs that directed their schoolwide efforts (i.e., data, lesson plans – teaching expectations, community outreach chair, professional development chair). Intensive supports fell under the chair for their Instructional Decision-Making Model, a formal process for using data for decision making in schools.

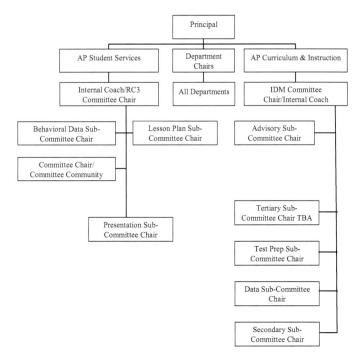

Figure 9.1 Organizational Chart for One School Implementing PBIS

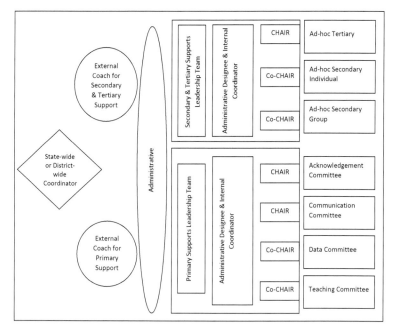

Figure 9.2 Example of Organizational Chart for Academic and Behavior Support

Application – Organizational Chart of Roles

Before jumping into creating a new organization chart of roles, we recommend you start with what you have. Take time to see if your school has an organizational chart. If your school does not, connect with an administrator to see if you can develop one. The end goal is to see how your efforts align with the mission and vision of the school. Having an organizational chart will help you to develop specific roles and position descriptions that can help you when recruiting for those positions to be filled. No matter how you design your chart, remember that you are trying to create a visual representation for how communication, responsibility, authority, and collaboration can be best harnessed in your setting.

Connection – Position Descriptions for Roles

Have you ever had a friend who was dating someone for a while? Things may have been going very well, and the two enjoy each other's company. At some point one of them may start to ask, "Where are we going with this relationship?" Essentially, the question the person is asking is, can we define the relationship. Knowing the expectations for a role is helpful to us. This is true in our roles at work just as it is true in friendships and romantic relationships. When all sides have clearly communicated their expectations, it prevents uncomfortable, unproductive, or destructive situations from occurring.

Point/Principle – Position Descriptions for Roles

At this point we hope that you have a draft organizational chart which means you have some idea of the types of roles needed for schoolwide work. Use that chart to detail what it means to serve in the role. With written descriptions, current team members know what to expect when they serve in a certain role. Also, new team members are aware of what they are committing to when they join your team. With written team roles, it is easier to sort out communication and assign action steps. We have encouraged teams to consider the following when developing position descriptions (not exhaustive):

- Address every area of your organizational chart
- The title of the role (not the person's title at the school)
- A description of the major tasks involved with the role
- The number of hours per month required to carry out the role
- Include a space for the name of the person (or persons) who are serving in this role

Including the number of hours per week will help new team members know if they have the capacity to carry out the role and administrators will know what kind of support they need to provide to team members in terms of release time as needed and if possible. Table 9.3 includes an example of what a position description chart looked like for part of the organizational chart in Figure 9.1. We have included an example of a graphic organizer and

Table 9.3 Example of a Team Chart

Building Based Staff			
Position Title	**Description**	**Hours per month**	**Names**
School Liaison	Administrator who oversees functioning and makes administrative decisions for all tiers of MTSS within the building (e.g., attends meetings, allocates resources)	ten hours a month	Sara
Internal Coordinator (Primary Support Leader Team)	Internal staff who can lead staff, with support from the External Coach, in implementing MTSS schoolwide academics and behavior practices, run meetings and oversee subcommittees	ten hours a month	Sara
Acknowledgement CHAIR	Lead the acknowledgement of student and staff behavior for schoolwide efforts, subcommittee in planning for celebrations and reinforcement systems within the school, meet with internal coordinator two times a month	eight hours a month	Terry
Acknowledgement Subcommittee	Facilitate schoolwide acknowledgment activities, including design and implementation.	four hours a month	Janet

possible roll descriptions for your school's team. You do not have to follow this format exactly, however, you need a graphic organizer that shows the roles of people on your team and their role descriptions. The organizer can include roles for district level and school level teams. Through his study of schoolwide approaches, Kent McIntosh has found that having teams that use data effectively and district level support can help with the sustainability of your efforts. However, if you are starting with school level support, use the school level roles provided.

Application – Position Descriptions for Roles

For your next step, take time to clearly define the roles you have for your team. Your organizational chart is a good tool to use to help you describe what you need. If you do not have an organizational chart, start with the key roles you need on your team (see Table 9.2). Make sure the roles are specific to your setting and the needs of your school. You can use Table 9.4 as a template to help you get started with defining your roles.

Table 9.4 Blank Team Chart

Position Title	Description	Hours per month	Names

Connection – Review Working Smarter Matrix

Once we were working with a high school that was implementing a schoolwide intervention. They had completed a working smarter matrix (see Chapter 8). The team listed the names of people who were associated with each of the programs. They found that the same names continued to appear throughout the matrix. For example, Mrs. Jones was on a credit recovery program, an attendance program, a schoolwide behavior team, and several other intervention teams. While it is great that she was so involved in the school, she was close to burnout. There were other community members who could have been involved.

Point/Principle – Review Working Smarter Matrix

It can be easy to rely on the same people who "get things done" in your school. To prevent this lack of distribution of tasks, look at your team organizational chart to see patterns. If you are seeing the same names repeating, consider a process for identifying new people to take on roles. If you have trouble recruiting participation, you will need to revisit buy-in and the systems needed to engage your stakeholders in this work. There also might be things you can stop doing. If you have a smaller staff there may not be many people to do the work in the first place, which makes auditing your practices and removing non-essential programs even more critical.

BOX 9.1 PONDERING ON PURPOSE

- Does your team have a distributive model in place? How do you know?
- If people already have roles assigned to them, how will you prepare them for possible changes in those roles?
- How does the school make role assignments and descriptions clear to everyone?

In reviewing your charts, you may notice that there are gaps in your school's needs and/or the expertise/experiences of your team. Before engaging in the interview process, make sure to write a job description that reflects those needs and strategically fill gaps when hiring new staff.

Application – Review Working Smarter Matrix

There is a famous science fiction movie called *Ghostbusters*. In the movie, people who are afraid of paranormal activity are encouraged to call the Ghostbusters for help. Marla Israel, an assistant superintendent at Stevenson High School in Illinois, developed a model for identifying new team members loosely based off this movie. She refers to it as, "Who Are You Going to Call?" In this process you identify (1) the overall initiative you are focusing on, (2) the specific committee related to the initiatives, (3) the role or title of the team member who is overtaxed in terms of time, (4) the responsibilities of the team member, (5) who they work with in their current role on this team, and (6) a list of up to three other people who could potentially fill this role who are not already overtaxed. Table 9.5 provides a tool to help you identify new potential team members using the "Who Are You Going

Table 9.5 Who Should You Call?

Initiative	Committee	Role/Title	Responsibility	Work w/ whom	Bring to the table

to Call?" model. By looking at the areas we just listed, you are more likely to identify people with the skills you need to make progress with less burnout.

When hiring to fill the gaps, do not rely on a "likeability" model or the candidate's word on whether they have the skill set you need. Studies have shown this leads to a mismatch and a quick turnover. Use Behavior-based Interviewing to determine the candidate's specific competencies as well as defining the school's expectations for the candidate. The Society for Human Resource Management put out a toolkit on Behavior-based Interviewing that uses the STAR Model (Situation, Tasks, Action, Results) to create questions. Asking candidates to describe actions they have taken in the past is a good predictor of how they will contribute to your school and fill the needs of your teams.

BOX 9.2 PONDERING ON PURPOSE

Using Behavior-based Interviewing:

- Who participates in our interviews?
- What questions do we ask?
- How do we rate responses?
- How do we ensure candidates have the competencies and qualities we need to balance our teams?

Conclusion

Aligning roles with practices goes beyond listing job titles. Sometimes knowledge of a topic can come from an unexpected source. It is important to find ways to continue to discover information about the knowledge, expertise, and experiences of your community. This makes delegation of tasks more efficient and effective, and makes more informed hiring practices, as search committees are able to identify gaps in the community's knowledge base. Once roles are aligned, take the time to create visual representations of the role structures along with detailed description. This will ensure that members know who to go to with questions, limit the duplication of work, and establish expectations. Using the tools in this chapter can help teams see who is overworked, what areas need to be redistributed, and where there are disparities between needs and people to meet them.

Bibliography

Ambrose, S. E. (1991). *Eisenhower: Soldier and president (The renowned one-volume life)*. New York, NY: Simon & Schuster.

Bosworth, K., Garcia, R., Judkins, M., & Saliba, M. (2018). The impact of leadership involvement in enhancing high school climate and reducing bullying: An exploratory study. *Journal of School Violence, 17*(3), 354–366.

Ch., M., Allensworth, E., & Ponisciak, S. M. (2009). The schools teachers leave: Teacher mobility in Chicago public schools. Retrieved from https://consortium.uchicago.edu/publications/schools-teachers-leave-teacher-mobility-chicago-public-schools

Forman, S. G., & Crystal, C. D. (2015). Systems consultation for multitiered systems of supports (MTSS): Implementation issues. *Journal of Educational & Psychological Consultation, 25*(2/3), 276–285. doi:10.1080/10474412.2014.963226

Jacobson, L. (2018). Hiring teachers based on 'likeability' is not the best practice. Retrieved from www.educationdive.com/news/hiring-teachers-based-on-likability-is-not-the-best-practice/514534/

Knight, E., & Paroutis, S. (2019). How visual methods can enhance our understanding of strategy and management. In B. Boyd, R. Crook, J. K. Le, & A. D. Smith (Eds.), *Standing on the shoulders of giants: Traditions and innovations in research methodology* (pp. 77–90). West Yorkshire, England: Emerald Publishing Limited.

Lam, B. (2016, January 15). Why are so many Zappos employees leaving? *The Atlantic*. Retrieved from www.theatlantic.com/business/archive/2016/01/zappos-holacracy-hierarchy/424173/

McIntosh, K., Mercer, S. H., Nese, R. N. T., Strickland-Cohen, M. K., Kittelman, A., Hoselton, R., & Horner, R. H. (2018). Factors predicting sustained implementation of a universal behavior support framework. *Educational Researcher*, 0013189X18776975.

Park, V., & Datnow, A. (2009). Co-constructing distributed leadership: District and school connections in data-driven decision-making. *School leadership and Management, 29*(5), 477–494.

Ramsey, D. (2011). *EntreLeadership: 20 years of practical business wisdom from the trenches*. Simon and Schuster. New York: NY

Society for Human Resource Management. (2016). *A guide to conducting behavioral interviews with early career job candidates*. Retrieved from www.shrm.org/Learning AndCareer/learning/Documents/Behavioral%20Interviewing%20Guide%20for%20 Early%20Career%20Candidates.pdf

10

USING FIDELITY DATA TO DEVELOP A PLAN

In a Nutshell

- Using fidelity data helps to eliminate human error.
- Components of MTSS fidelity tools can typically be categorized as systems, practices, or data.
- There are various types of fidelity data, including reviewing participant responsiveness and engagement, efficiency and sustainability of the intervention, quality of delivery adherence, frequency, and duration.
- Approaches to collect fidelity data of overall systems can include using an expert rating, a school community self-assessment, a leadership team self-assessment, or a stratified random sample of a representative group.
- Fidelity data can also be collected about individual practices, which sometimes requires creating methods to assess.
- Use an action plan to establish goals, the resources and activities you need, a timeline for your progress, and the outcomes you desire.

Introduction

I (Kelly) have watched my mother make apple pie at least a dozen times over the course of my life. However, whenever I try to make one, it never comes out exactly the same. Baking is a science and changing or omitting one small ingredient or step can ruin an entire pastry. It is important to stick to the plan, exactly, or you cannot expect good results.

Just like baking, schoolwide systems require sticking to the plan in order to achieve success. Perhaps you have seen an intervention that was only partially put into place, and people in your community said, "See, we tried it, and it did not work." Measuring fidelity is simply checking to see how well you implemented what you committed to do. Fidelity data ensures that your efforts are consistent with the prescribed components designed to ensure intended outcomes, can help your team determine what steps are needed for improvement, and document components as they are done. They can also be used to evaluate the accuracy and quality of your implementation. Fidelity data provide evidence as to whether the implementation or execution of the intervention impacted the intended outcomes.

Connection – Why Fidelity?

According to Atul Gawande, a surgeon and author of *The Checklist Manifesto*, fidelity checks are important in many settings, including hospitals. He reports that one study found that each intensive care unit (ICU) patient required, on average, 178 treatment steps (e.g., administrating medication, suction) to be carried out on any single day. He shares that the average survival rate in an ICU is about 86%. Many of those who do not survive are a result of errors (e.g., leaving surgical instruments in the body, forgetting to wash hands) made by medical professionals who are under considerable pressure. Gawande suggests that many problems in any setting can be prevented if teams follow a checklist or "fidelity checks" for a procedure, to remind people of the minimum steps that are needed.

Point/Principle – Why Fidelity?

Some may scoff at the idea of using a checklist or ignore its importance when completing tasks that they see as "routine." As in the case above in the ICU, not using checklists can lead to errors (in some cases fatal) that impact the final outcomes of the work. Think about a time where you questioned yourself or missed a step in your routine. For example, have you ever left the house and then turned around because you couldn't remember if you turned off the coffee maker?

Gawande says there are two problems people have when they complete any process. First, our *memory and attention can fail us*, particularly when we are under stress, disrupting the quality and detail of our work. Even a little bit of stress or a bad night of sleep can cause disruptions in the pre-frontal cortex's processes. This stress impacts our attention, ability to think clearly, and the execution of even basic steps or procedures we do every day.

The second problem we face is *error of omission*. We might convince ourselves that a certain step is not important and skip it. We are also more likely to skip smaller tasks at the end of procedures out of excitement of being "done." Other times we omit steps when a task is repeated, or very similar to another task, we are distracted while following the steps, or when there is a planned variance in a series of steps that are followed out of habit. Teachers often "feel" like they are doing something regularly (such as giving feedback) and are then shocked by the actual observation data from their classes.

Checklists help because they remind us of the minimum steps needed and make them explicit. They prevent us from these "errors of omission" or memory failures and increase the accuracy, integrity, and fidelity of the task at hand. As Lauren Molloy and her fellow researchers have found, tracking what needs to be implemented can become even more important in larger settings, like secondary schools. These schools typically include more staff and students. Heather George and Karen Childs also suggest that monitoring implementation steps can help district and state agencies determine school's needs for support and technical assistance. Higher ratings in fidelity are also associated with more supports for students. Lucille Eber and colleagues in Illinois found that schools that implemented schoolwide positive behavior support with better fidelity had more tier two and three interventions to offer students, indicating that fidelity with tier one can build capacity to provide more intense support as needed.

Application – Why Fidelity?

With a partner, choose a practice you think you implement well. Decide what to measure: frequency (e.g. number of different students you give feedback to in a class period) or quality (did I include all key characteristics of the peace circle?). Observe each other. Before sharing your observations, predict what your rating will be. Afterwards, discuss. Were the results surprising?

BOX 10.1 PONDERING ON PURPOSE

Reflect on an intervention that people considered to be "not working."

- Did the implementation include a checklist?
- If there was a checklist, was it reviewed regularly?
- Based on what you know about how the intervention was intended, do you think the approach simply did not work in your setting? Or, do you think that the intervention did not work in your setting because important steps were left out?

Connection – Common Components of MTSS Fidelity Tools

If you have ever taken different types of fitness classes, you many have noticed that the personal trainers or instructors followed some common elements or patterns, despite differences in classes. For example, a kickboxing class at the gym often begins with a light warm-up, then intervals of intense punching and kicking exercises interspersed with some strengthening exercises, like push-ups. Circuit-style workouts often begin with a light warm-up, followed by intervals of high and/or low intensity cardio work interspersed with strength building activities. Research on fitness has yielded some common elements or characteristics that lead to effective results. Though they can be accomplished through a variety of activities, classes often have some similar structures. The same can be said about systems of support in schools, which is why fidelity measures contain some common components.

Point/Principle – Common Components of MTSS Fidelity Tools

As your team works to select or develop fidelity measures for the systems and practices you put in place, it may be helpful to become familiar with the common components of fidelity tools that are typically utilized by teams leading multi-tiered systems of supports (MTSS). Each schoolwide approach (e.g., social and emotional learning (SEL), positive behavioral interventions and supports (PBIS)) usually comes with its own check for fidelity of implementation.

I (Hank) at one time served as the statewide evaluator for our state's approaches to SWPBIS, SEL, RtI (response to intervention), and school-based mental health. Each approach had its own protocol for checking fidelity. I noticed that there was considerable overlap across the protocols. Each could be categorized into systems (e.g., administrative support), data (e.g., identifying relevant data for decision making), and practices (e.g., specific interventions). The following list provides some of the features we find on many of the schoolwide fidelity of implementation tools:

- Systems
  - Administrative commitments
  - Coaching (external/internal)
  - Representative teams
  - Audit of practices
  - Level of priority for the intervention
- Practices
  - Evidence-based interventions
  - Explicit instruction and practice of skills

- Data
  - Fidelity measures
  - General outcome measures (e.g., student outcomes)

Application – Common Components of MTSS Fidelity Tools

Review the current tool(s) or instruments used to track the fidelity of implementation for your schoolwide approach or one you are considering (e.g., the PBIS Tiered Fidelity Inventory). Use the bulleted list we just provided to scan the instrument. Does the instrument seem to follow an order of items that move from systems components (e.g., administrative support) to practices and data? Does it appear that the developers of the instruments are implicitly suggesting an order of action based on the way the items are listed on the instrument? In our experience, many of the developers do provide an order of implementation based on the organization of the fidelity tool.

Connection – Types of Fidelity Data

To add onto our baking metaphor from the start of the chapter, I (Lisa) am just not a very good baker no matter how hard I try. The running joke with my friends and family is that my attempts make the best "Pinterest fails." My problem is that I usually start "winging it" at some point. If I wanted to retrace my steps, there would be many areas for me to review. Did I use the proper tools? Was my flour a bit stale? Did I only let the dough rise for 30 minutes instead of an hour? The same is the case for reviewing intervention implementation. There are many types of fidelity data to consider collecting.

Point/Principle – Types of Fidelity Data

According to Ann Lendrum, Neil Humphrey, and Mark Greenberg, there are a variety of areas of fidelity that can be assessed. Areas for fidelity checks can include:

- **Participant responsiveness and engagement** (i.e., are the participants ready and willing to complete the intervention?)
- **Efficiency and sustainability of the intervention** (i.e., how big is the reach of the intervention? How many people participated in the intervention from the group you are focusing on? Were you able to implement the intervention? Do the outcomes justify the amount of resources put into the intervention?)
- **Quality of delivery** (i.e., how well were the strategies carried out?)

- **Adherence** (i.e., has the intervention been implemented following the explicit procedures?)
- **Frequency and duration** (i.e., was the intervention given on schedule, both in how many times it should be delivered and for how long?)

For the purpose of this book, we used Todd Glover and Sharon Vaughn's definition of fidelity implementation: the adherence to the factors that are associated with effectively carrying out an intervention based on its design. As Gregory McHugo and his colleagues explain, fidelity of implementation based on adherence is typically measured using scales, created by researchers. These scales, or instruments, which look much like a checklist, can help your teams navigate the steps for implementation for your approach.

BOX 10.2 PONDERING ON PURPOSE

Why might your team consider measuring fidelity of each of the following areas? What might that look like, and how could it benefit your efforts?

- Participant engagement (staff and students)
- Efficiency and sustainability
- Quality of delivery
- Adherence
- Frequency and duration

The tools mentioned in previous chapters, which contain the common elements described above (e.g., the North Carolina Self-Assessment of MTSS, or the Tiered Fidelity Inventory) are primarily used by teams to monitor the implementation of the overarching systems, sometimes with the inclusion of measures of specific practices. However, there is a wide variety of evidence-based practices that a schoolwide team may implement, based on needs and context. Teams should monitor their overall system utilizing the protocol or tool that best matches their approach (e.g., SEL or PBIS), but they may also need to choose or design fidelity checks for specific practices being utilized within the schoolwide system (e.g., teaching and reinforcing Cornell style notes).

For example, a team may use the PBIS Tiered Fidelity Inventory (TFI) annually to determine how well their tiered system of behavior support is functioning. But they may also determine that they need to monitor the implementation of a specific classroom practice, such as providing students frequent opportunities to respond. The team will need to locate or develop some method to track how often and how well that strategy is being utilized. This can be challenging in large schools with many teachers, but there are a variety of ways to approach this challenge, which we will look at in a later section.

Application – Types of Fidelity Data

Reflect on a specific practice you or your team have attempted to implement (either in your own classroom(s), or as a group or school). Did you measure fidelity? If so, what types of fidelity did you choose to measure or not? What were the outcomes, and how may they have been related to your assessment of fidelity of implementation (or lack thereof)?

Connection – Ways to Collect Fidelity Data

I (Kelly) worked with a school that prioritized a specific tier one approach to academic vocabulary instruction. They conducted frequent, brief walk-throughs, where team members popped in and out of classrooms and checked off various types of evidence of academic vocabulary instruction. Data were compiled and shared with staff in a newsletter, celebrating the evidence observed. For example, if 80% of classes utilized word walls, that would be cause for celebration. A general "challenge to grow" was also included in the newsletter when few instructors demonstrated evidence of teaching roots and affixes. This is just one example of how to creatively collect and share fidelity data in a way that does not feel like a "gotcha" for staff members.

Point/Principle – Ways to Collect Fidelity Data

Fidelity of Overall Systems

There are several approaches to collecting data on the fidelity of implementation of your overall schoolwide system. The tools mentioned above and in previous chapters typically include some of these methods. Table 10.1 provides example data collection strategies. Some fidelity tools use combined approaches in their data collection process (e.g., expert rating and leadership team self-assessment).

These approaches often triangulate well, so choose the method that is most efficient and is recommended to be used with your tool. In a study I (Hank) conducted with colleagues, we compared a self-assessment of the community, a self-assessment of the leadership team, and a stratified random sample with an expert rater. The expert rater only disagreed with the

Table 10.1 Methods of Gathering Fidelity Data

Method	Advantages	Procedure	Example Instrument
Expert Rating	Requires limited intrusion on staff time. Expert rater is typically highly trained on data collection process.	External expert rates implementation based on observations, interviews, and examining school products	Schoolwide Evaluation Tool
School Community Self-Assessment	Provides insight on perspectives that are intended to represent the staff. Also useful for obtaining data on priorities for buy-in. Can provide additional insight on class-level implementation.	Survey is provided to the entire school *obtain at least a 30–40% response rate	Effective Behavior Support Self-Assessment
Leadership Team Self-Assessment	Less intrusive of time for the entire staff. Leaderships team is highly knowledgeable of the overall practice.	Members of the leadership team self-assess implementation	Team Implementation Checklist
Stratified Random Sample of the Team's Representation	Ensures representation from a variety of groups for input. Has the least impact on time for the entire staff and the leadership team.	Usually five to seven people are randomly selected from representative groups (e.g., general education teacher, special education teacher)	Oregon Safety Survey

self-assessment methods when it came to schoolwide policies. Where you have flexibility in data collection, you might consider testing different sampling approaches with your fidelity measures. Trying different sampling approaches might be even more relevant if you are implementing more than one systemic model in the same setting (e.g., PBIS, SEL) and each assessment requires commitments of time from the school community.

Fidelity of Specific Schoolwide Practices

As mentioned above, teams may need to measure fidelity of specific practices in addition to systems fidelity checks. Sometimes the original studies or published guides related to specific practices (e.g., Collaborative Strategic Reading) include checklists or tables of critical features that can be used for observations or walkthroughs. Other practices may require the development of observation protocols or checklists, such as the academic vocabulary example above.

Some practices lend themselves to simple tallies (e.g., multiple opportunities to respond, specific positive feedback) or checkboxes (expectations posted on wall) that lend themselves to walk-throughs. Walk-throughs are just a quick snapshot of a given moment, so teams should choose this type of fidelity check for practices they expect to see happening frequently, and in some cases, hundreds are needed over time to give a genuine picture of schoolwide implementation. However, each one is typically under five minutes, and teams can divide and conquer. If multiple people will use a walk-through protocol, it is crucial that they practice rating the same classrooms, and compare results, until they are rating reliably. Though hard copy formats work, online data collection systems make the data analysis easier and quicker. There are online platforms that will help you gather, calculate, and graph data such as PBISApps.org, SurveyMonkey, Google Forms, or Poll Everywhere.

In order to guarantee accuracy of fidelity data it is ideal to have another person observe and collect the data, though sometimes self-report makes more sense in terms of efficiency. Surveying students and staff about the frequency or features of a practice is one option (e.g., how often have you used this graphic organizer this week?), or asking staff members to self-monitor or verify, is another (e.g., did you teach the behavioral expectation lesson of the week?).

Collecting fidelity data also includes things like surveying the buy-in of the staff. The goal is to get a response rate of about 30–40% of your total sample size. Staff buy-in can help give insight into aspects of fidelity such as the efficiency and sustainability of the intervention, and if about 80% of staff are implementing, you have achieved a critical mass that is likely to elicit positive change.

Application – Ways to Collect Fidelity Data

Select an intervention and use the table below (Table 10.2) to consider why you might think about collecting data across the various categories of fidelity data, the ways you can acquire the information, and the tools you could use to collect the information. You may need to consider using existing data or the selection or creation of new data gathering formats/protocols.

Table 10.2 Purpose and Methods for Collecting Fidelity Data

	Why might you need the data?	Ways to acquire the data (select): Expert rating, school community self-assessment, leadership team self-assessment stratified random sample walk-through.	Tool
Participant Responsiveness and Engagement			
Efficiency and Sustainability of the Intervention			
Quality of Delivery Adherence			
Frequency and Duration			

Connection – How to Action Plan with Fidelity Data

Readers may not be surprised to know that as a busy working parent of three (Kelly), caring for my own health can be a struggle! Over the years, when I find myself unhappy with my "current situation," I have found Weight Watchers to be a helpful resource. I tend to be more successful if I attend the weekly workshops, because they include reviewing the data we logged and making a plan for the upcoming week to *address the challenges that led to any lack of fidelity to the program*. For example, when I eat fewer servings of fruits and vegetables, I tend to snack more on junk food that night. When I see that pattern happening, I commit to washing and chopping fruits and veggies on Sunday to get me through the workweek. I know that when I attend the meeting the next week, I will be able to celebrate sticking to my plan. Or, if things did not go so well, I can ask for suggestions to help me stick to it better the following week. For me, and for most MTSS teams, this is a recipe for better outcomes!

Point/Principle – How to Action Plan with Fidelity Data

In general, action planning with fidelity data should start with assessing the systems (e.g., using a fidelity tool such as the TFI), because if your systems are not running according to your chosen model, it will be difficult to support specific practices well. Once systems are functioning effectively, specific practices may also be assessed. If a system or practice is not being implemented with the consistency or critical elements desired, the team must form a hypothesis as to why.

BOX 10.3 PONDERING ON PURPOSE

Use these questions to help you form a hypothesis about why fidelity of implementation is struggling:

- Was enough time allocated to meet?
- Did staff receive enough training?
- Is the intervention too cumbersome to implement?
- Do stakeholders see the connection between implementation and potential outcomes? Is there enough acknowledgement or other "intermediary payoff" for implementing a practice well until it starts to have an impact?

Each possible issue listed in Box 10.3 lends itself to different action steps to address the situation. Utilizing pilot groups and sharing the data with the rest of the staff, and carefully pointing out the connection between fidelity and outcomes, may help increase fidelity.

Many organizations offer protocols for action planning, and some fidelity tools include an action planning protocol as part of the process (e.g., PBIS TFI). One example is Teach to Lead (see https://teachtolead.org), an organization that envisions teachers as leaders in education policy who steer systemic improvements to benefit student learning. They have created a logic model to facilitate the action planning process. On their site under the resource section, they offer leadership and systems planning tools. Their logic model asks the team to determine a problem statement and a goal that addresses the issue. After reflecting and documenting their rationale, the team lists inputs and activities that align with the goal. From this, outputs are determined for the one, three, and six-month mark, along with desired outcomes for the short term (one year), medium term (two years) and long term (two years and beyond).

Just like Kelly in her Weight Watchers example, using an action plan helps to keep you focused on the long-term "wins" even when there are setbacks or "cheat days" along the way. By revisiting an action plan you can hold your team accountable to the "fidelity" of the process you set out to implement, as well as the goals you hope to achieve.

Application – How to Action Plan with Fidelity Data

Review the logic model from the Teach to Lead website as a team. Do you have something like this in place to document the actions you are taking? Consider using your calendar to alert you to the deadlines you set and dedicate time in your team's agenda to using one of the fidelity data collection approaches we described in this chapter to assess your progress in an objective way. This will help you adhere to your process, as well as make the necessary adjustments to ensure your success and ultimate achievement of the outcomes you established in your action planning process.

Conclusion

The fidelity data you collect will drive the action planning of your teams. As always, select a realistic starting point for this work. Teams should choose carefully which specific practices to monitor, when, and how, so as not to become overwhelmed. Starting with an overall systems fidelity check (tools mentioned above) is a great step, and often the results correlate with student outcomes. Planning additional fidelity checks for specific practices may make the most sense for teams in the later stages of implementation (see Chapter 3). Teams should also be cautious not to implement fidelity checks in a way that is overly intrusive, or that makes teachers feel that they are being policed or evaluated. Choose one systems tool, or even one intervention checklist to use with a small pilot group, in order to practice the process of using fidelity measures to action plan. Over time, data collection will become more routine.

Bibliography

Bohanon, H., & Wu, M. (2011). Can prevention programs work together? An example of school-based mental health with prevention initiatives. *School-Based Mental Health Practice*, 4(4), 35–46. Retrieved from http://ecommons.luc.edu/education_facpubs/1/

Bohanon, H., & Wu, M. (2012a). Integration of social, behavioral, and academic initiatives: Part I. *Communique'*, 41(2), 4–5.

Bohanon, H., & Wu, M. (2012b). Integration of social, behavioral, and academic initiatives: Part II. *Communique'*, 41(3), 12–13.

Bohanon, H., & Wu, M. (2019). A comparison of sampling approaches for monitoring schoolwide inclusion program fidelity. *International Journal of Developmental Disabilities*, 65(2), 33–43.

Christ, T. J., Riley-Tillman, T. C., Chafouleas, S., & Jaffery, R. (2011). Direct behavior rating: An evaluation of alternate definitions to assess classroom behaviors. *School Psychology Review*, 40(2), 181–199.

Diamond, A., & Ling, D. S. (2016). Conclusions about interventions, programs, and approaches for improving executive functions that appear justified and those that, despite much hype, do not. *Developmental Cognitive Neuroscience, 18,* 34–48.

Eber, L., Phillips, D., Upreti, G., Hyde, K., Lewandowski, H., & Rose, J. (2009). *Illinois positive behavioral interventions & supports (PBIS) network 2008-09 progress report* (p. 245). La Grange Park, IL: Illinois Positive Behavior Support Network.

Gawande, A. (2010). *The checklist manifesto.* New York, NY: Penguin Books India.

George, H. P., & Childs, K. E. (2012). Evaluating implementation of schoolwide behavior support: Are we doing it well? *Preventing School Failure: Alternative Education for Children and Youth, 56,* 197–206.

Glover, T. A., & Vaughn, S. (2010). *The promise of response to intervention: Evaluating current science and practice.* New York, NY: Guilford Press.

Hall, N., Bohanon, H., & Goodman, S. (2016). Behavioral support: Research-based program reduces discipline problems. *American School Board Journal.* Retrieved from www.nsba.org/newsroom/american-school-board journal/behavioral-support and http://ecommons.luc.edu/education_facpubs/71/

Illinois Positive Behavior Intervention and Support Network. (2011). *FY11 end of the year summary report.* La Grange, IL: Illinois Positive Behavior Intervention Network.

IRIS Center. (n.d.). *How can school personnel determine that they have effectively implemented evidence-based practices or programs?* Retrieved from https://iris.peabody.vanderbilt.edu/module/fid/cresource/q3/p10/

Laxton, T. C., & Sprague, J. (2005). Refining the construct of school safety: An exploration of correlates and construct validity of school safety measures. Retrieved from https://pdfs.semanticscholar.org/9978/500a5a04c21e15bf0f7a7c08960e1059a4e8.pdf?_ga=2.24198782.537865133.1576191704-1403203286.1574713844

Lendrum, A., Humphrey, N., & Greenberg, M. T. (2016). Implementing for success in school-based mental health promotion: The role of quality in resolving the tension between fidelity and adaptation. In R. Shute & P. Slee (Eds.), *Mental health and wellbeing through schools: The way forward* (pp. 53–63). London: Taylor and Francis.

McHugo, G. J. (2007). Fidelity outcomes in the national implementing evidence-based practices project. *Psychiatric Services, 58,* 1279–1284.

Molloy, L. E., Moore, J. E., Trail, J., Van Epps, J. J., & Hopfer, S. (2013). Understanding real-world implementation quality and "active ingredients" of PBIS. *Prevention Science, 14,* 593–605.

National Center on Response to Intervention. (n.d.). *Using fidelity to enhance program implementation* within an RTI framework. Retrieved from https://rti4success.org/sites/default/files/Using%20Fidelity%20to%20Enhance%20Program%20Implementation_PPTSlides.pdf

Pawlowski, A. (2018). *Feeling stressed? It could affect your memory, study finds.* Retrieved from Today website: www.today.com/health/how-lower-stress-high-cortisol-levels-affect-memory-brain-t140593

Reason, J. (2002). Combating omission errors through task analysis and good reminders. *Qual Saf Health Care, 11,* 40–44.

Safran, S. P. (2006). Using the effective behavior supports survey to guide development of schoolwide positive behavior support. *Journal of Positive Behavior Interventions, 8,* 3–9.

Scott, E. (2019, June). *How stress works with and against your memory.* Retrieved from www.verywellmind.com/stress-and-your-memory-4158323

Sprague, J., Colvin, G., & Irvin, L. (1996). *The Oregon school safety survey*. Eugene, OR: University of Oregon.

Vincent, C., Spaulding, S., & Tobin, T. J. (2010). A reexamination of the psychometric properties of the school-wide evaluation tool (SET). *Journal of Positive Behavior Interventions, 12*(3), 161–179. doi:10.1177/1098300709332345

Zimmerman, J. E., Kramer, A. A., McNair, D. S., Malila, F. M., & Shaffer, V. L. (2006). Intensive care unit length of stay: Benchmarking based on acute physiology and chronic health evaluation (APACHE) IV. *Critical Care Medicine, 34*(10), 2517–2529.

11

USING DATA TO MONITOR SYSTEMS AND TARGET INTERVENTIONS

In a Nutshell

- Start with the data you already have.
- Some general outcome measures serve as early warning systems that alert us to issues that will significantly impact students' long-term outcomes.
- Existing data can be used to identify areas requiring further analysis and intervention.
- Data systems allow us to monitor student outcomes.
- Data helps us to make adjustments to our interventions.

Introduction

I (Hank) once met a high school group that was using data, but in the wrong way. The leadership team organized data on student performance to identify students who were struggling the most. So far, this sounds like a noble activity. Ultimately though, the team used the list to identify students who were "too far behind their peers" to warrant support. The school team was trying to find ways to conserve their time by giving up on students who were considered beyond hope. It is important to hold teams accountable to the intent behind the use of data, which is to identify ways to improve experiences and support for *all* students.

Most teams do not have diabolical intent when using data. When used the right way, data can help your team plan and evaluate interventions at every tier of support. Many professions use data effectively to determine the best supports for their end users. For example, there was a time when, according to Charles Duhigg in *The Power of Habit*, the YMCA fitness clubs where not attracting many customers. The leadership of the YMCA looked at perception data from their customers about what they valued. Their customers cared more about connecting with friends, and people at the facility knowing their name, than they did about the age of the equipment. The YMCA focused their energy on helping find ways for people to connect with other patrons and employees, and their membership levels began to increase. Had they invested their time and money into new equipment, it would not have met the needs of their customers, nor had the same positive outcome.

Effective secondary schools use data to plan, monitor, and adjust schoolwide improvement efforts and evaluate outcomes. Sometimes schools can start with the data they already have in hand to begin their schoolwide efforts. In this chapter, we will discuss the different kinds of data you can use to effectively implement your schoolwide interventions. We will then describe ways secondary schools can use data to monitor the progress of students and adjust interventions as needed. The logic behind this chapter can be applied at every level of support (e.g., tier one, tier two) within a tiered schoolwide model.

Connection – Start with What You Have

There is a Chinese proverb that says *the best time to plant a tree was 20 years ago. The next best time is right now.* The same goes with starting an exercise program, it's best to begin as soon as you can based on what you have. You can wait until you have all the equipment you need, however, that will delay your effort. You can begin by walking or running in fresh air for a few minutes a day. Though purchasing that $30 moisture wicking t-shirt might help to make you more comfortable, there is no reason you cannot begin with whatever reliable equipment you have at your disposal. When starting to organize and utilize data for schoolwide systems, start with what you have rather than waiting to purchase all the "bells and whistles."

Point/Principle – Start with What You Have

Starting with the data you have at your disposal is helpful for a few reasons. First, if you are already collecting data, such as grades, attendance, and discipline referrals, you ought to use it for something. Organizing your existing data in a way that aligns with your schoolwide goals will help you to begin to get a sense of the needs and strengths for your setting. Second, once you start reviewing the data you have at hand, you will begin to ask new questions, which can provide more insights into your needs. Third, you will see what additional data you still need to more effectively plan your interventions.

Often teams can get overwhelmed and "drown" in their data or envision overly complex and detailed plans for it. Either way, they get stuck in the planning and organizing stage, and never get to the decision making and action stage. When in doubt, the following mantras may help ease team into data-based decision making: start with simple, and don't let perfect get in the way of better. Any systematic review and use of data are a step in the right direction!

Application – Start with What You Have

We would like for you to consider identifying a specific set of outcomes that are related to the goals of your schoolwide system. Think about decision rules or markers that would identify that students are struggling with the schoolwide curriculum. For example, JoAnne Malloy at the University of New Hampshire identified the following data and markers that were related to a school she was supporting in a research study. Students who were not responding to tier one efforts had one or more of these factors:

- Three or more major office discipline referrals within a four-week period
- Five or more unexcused absences in a quarter
- Two or more class failures in a quarter
- Five to ten nurse visits in a two-week period, and/or
- Six tardies to a class in a quarter

Use Table 11.1 to identify possible data sources for your schoolwide efforts. It follows the CAIRO process that we described in Chapter 7 on communication. This list does not have to be perfect. Use it to help you find ways to begin your schoolwide process with the data you have at hand.

Table 11.1 Planning for Access to Data Sources for Schoolwide Interventions

Data Source	Who needs to be contacted for access?	Who needs to approve the use of the data?	Who needs to be informed about using these data?	Who is responsible for accessing the data?	Who can be out of the loop for now?

Connection – General Outcome Measures
Related to Secondary Schools

General outcome measures can be organized in useful ways to monitor schoolwide systems. I (Kelly) once helped a district with three large high schools that wanted to use the data from a schoolwide reading assessment given three times per year to identify trends. We started organizing the data in a way that we could see average fall to spring gains by particular courses. We also used the data to show how much students gained compared to their starting point in the fall (to ensure that kids who were in need of making the most growth were indeed doing so). One of the schools noted that the students enrolled in course levels implementing more cross-content academic literacy strategies (for example, freshmen enrolled in English 1, Freshman P.E., and Biology) showed larger average gains that other grade levels where less cross-content-area literacy routines were in place. This led to the development and expansion of the role of their Academic Literacy Specialist in order to increase the implementation of common strategies across content areas and grade levels.

Point/Principle – General Outcome Measures
Related to Secondary Schools

As we mentioned in the previous chapter, general outcome measures are data that are aligned to important long-term consequences for students, such as grades, normed assessment scores, attendance rates, and behavioral incidents. Sometimes these outcomes measures can be organized into what is referred to as early warning systems. These data systems do not include every possible data point that a school might collect on student performance. They do focus on data that are related to the import outcomes for students. Below are several examples of studies that found correlations between particular data sets and student outcomes.

- Joseph Allen and his colleagues found that measures of student-teacher interactions are related to student achievement on standardized assessments.
- Arthur Burke, a researcher at the Regional Educational Laboratory Northwest, found in his study that students with attendance rates of 80% or less and a grade point average below 2.0 in 8th or 9th grade were less likely to graduate from high school.
- Researchers Sharon Koon and Yaacov Petscher at Florida State University found that reading scores on the state's standardized assessment could be used to identity students who would score below the college readiness benchmark on the SAT/National Merit Scholarship Qualifying Test and ACT.

- According to two separate research studies by Christenson and colleagues and Jimerson and colleagues, students who had one or more failures in 9th grade English and/or 9th grade algebra were less likely to graduate and more likely to drop out.

Analyzing data patterns can help your district make system-level decisions. Bradley Carl and colleagues looked for ways to identify secondary students who were at risk of failure in the Milwaukee Public Schools. They created what they refer to as the Total Quality Credit (TQC). Rather than predict if a student was on or off track for graduation, their approach provided information on the degree to which students were at risk of failure. The TQC is calculated by assigning a four-point scale to grades (A–F) in English, math, science, and social studies. Higher levels of the TQC were related to higher likelihoods that students would enter some form of higher education following graduation.

According to their work, most students would have TQC scores ranging between 1–16. The latter score being the equivalent of earning four As in four subject areas. They found that the probability of graduating was about 70% for TQC scores of ten (approximately a C+ average) and that a TQC score of eight (core GPA of 2.0 or a C average) was a critical point where there was a considerable drop in the probability of on-time graduation. Analyzing these data allowed their district to create systems to identify and intervene for students considered "at risk."

BOX 11.1 PONDERING ON PURPOSE

- Do you know what data points predict the likelihood that your students will graduate with their peers from high school?
- If the TQC were implemented at your school, what types of interventions would you plan for students who had low TQC scores?

In addition to the types of data described thus far, organizations such as the American School Counselor Association (ASCA), the National Center for School Mental Health, and the National Association of School Psychologists recommend universal screening and preventative programming and instruction related to social-emotional learning and mental health. Schools can ask students to self-reflect on surveys (or have teachers rate them) on social-emotional learning skills, and weave that information into their screening and/or early warning indicators.

There are a variety of validated tools (mostly surveys) school teams can use to screen for mental health concerns, to identify students who may be at risk. Students who are at risk may or may not be demonstrating externalizing behavioral concerns or problems with grades or attendance that would otherwise bring them to the attention of school teams. Universal screening of all students allows schools to either provide mental health services or refer students for support from outside agencies when they suffer from internalizing issues like anxiety or depression, or challenges with things like anger management. Many of the students you will identify have yet to cross a threshold in their behaviors that trigger disciplinary referrals.

An article published by Donohue, Goodman-Scott, and Betters-Bubon outlines the way this type of screening fits within a tiered support framework and includes a useful table of common screening tools. I (Kelly) have worked with schools that use annual screeners, like the Pediatric Symptoms Checklist and the Signs of Suicide prevention program and screening tool, in order to identify students who are potentially at risk for mental health concerns. Counselors, social workers, and school psychologists then respond with a systematic approach to administering individualized follow-up interviews and assigning of responses and interventions based on student needs.

As you can see, there are multiple ways to identify students who need support using data. Much of these data may already be at your fingertips. Certainly, the list provided does not exhaust every option you might have in terms of using data to identify student needs. If you need ideas to help select data sources, visit the companion website for this book. Select data that will help you analyze the aggregate patterns of success for students in your school, as well as screen and monitor for potential intervention. Don't waste time gathering data that you won't be able to use systematically to make decisions.

Application – General Outcomes Related to Secondary Schools

Take a moment to use Table 11.2 to reflect on possible data sets you can use to help identify students in need of support. We encourage you to consider students holistically. There may be students who are achieving significantly beyond other students in local or national norms who are struggling due to social and emotional needs. Students who are significantly performing above their peers also might need additional differentiation and support to help them develop.

Connection – Monitoring Student Needs

No matter what type of doctor you see, there are usually a few similar things they always check. Even before the doctor enters the room, someone will assess your blood pressure, weight, height, and temperature. These are

Table 11.2 Possible Data Sets for Identifying Students Who Need Support

Data Set	Usefulness of the data in relation to your schoolwide approach (1 = not very useful, 5 = very useful)	Location or data system where the data are located

markers related to your health. If your blood pressure or temperature is too high, or your weight has gone up or down drastically since your last visit, the doctor will know that there is something that needs to be covered during your visit. These indicators are red flags that tell the doctor that there may be something wrong in one of your body's systems. Once they have identified there is a need, the doctor may suggest additional tests to determine the nature of the problem. Like screening for these basic health markers, schools can use data to see how the larger system is working. This screening data also helps teams determine if additional data is needed for specific students for more effective problem solving.

Point/Principle – Monitoring Student Needs

Just having the data on your computer or in a desk drawer is not enough. Once you have identified the data you need, as we discussed in previous sections, you need to find ways to organize them. The organization of your data needs to be in a format that can help teams determine if an issue is schoolwide, is concentrated in groups of students, or both. We recommend using graphs and tables to help your team be able to make effective decisions around their data. Graphs and charts tend to work best for monitoring your system as a whole. For example, you may wish to see what percentage of your students are hitting target outcomes in academics and behaviors. If it is below 80%, you may need to strengthen tier one strategies.

Tables tend to work better when identifying specific students and their needs. Table 11.3 provides an example from one combined middle school and high school in Vermont. They reviewed their schoolwide data three times per year. The key markers they selected included MAP reading and math assessments, office discipline referral counts, and the Student Risk Screening Scale (SRSS).

The data were organized into table format that used a color-coding system to tag students in each of these data areas into one of four categories.

Table 11.3 Example of One Secondary School's Monitoring System

Blue Font – Has IEP	Green – Continue Universal Instruction
Orange Font – Has Tier Two/Three Plan	Yellow – Possible Area of Support
Marron Font – Has 504 Plan	Red – Area of Support
Green Font – Has Tier One Plan	More than Two Grade Levels Beyond Proficiency

Student Name	ODR Count	Winter MAP Math Score	Quarter 2 Math Grade	Winder Reading Score	Quarter 2 Reading Grade	Winter MAP Language Usage Score	SRSS Total (0–21)
A.J.	0	229	78	213	84	215	2
B.P.	0	232	91	229	98	223	0
T.T. (Blue Font)	2	201	76	191	89	194	7
B.Q. (Green Font)	0	211	61	207	88	208	2
S.F. (Yellow Font)	2	175	78	191	77	186	11
D.D.	0	235	96	224	95	232	0
A.K.	0	223	92	222	93	218	0

Note. Adapted from Bohanon, Gilman, Parker, Amell, & Sortino (2016). ODR Stands for Office Discipline Referral. MAP stands for Measures of Academic Progress. This table was converted to black and white for the purposes of the book. However, the actual table was developing using color.

For the purposes of this book the colors were transformed into shades for these areas:

1. Continue with the universal instruction, in that area (e.g., math, reading), without additional support
2. Potential area for concern
3. Significant area of concern and needed a plan in place
4. More than two grade levels above the proficient score

Ideally, because secondary schools tend to have large numbers of students and various groups of stakeholders who all need to be included in data analysis. To help organize your data, a data visualization or dashboarding system can be set up that directly links to your student information system, assessment systems, and/or any other place data are stored. Then dashboards, tables, charts, or reports can be automated according to the decision rules your team has established. However, if you do not have an online system that can integrate all of these data sources, you still have an option. As long as each student data collection system uses the same student identification number (e.g., 1535315), then the data can be merged into a common spreadsheet and color-coded, (as shown in Table 11.3) using the VLookup function in Microsoft Excel. An internet search will yield examples of how to use this merging feature in spreadsheets.

Another key recommendation is to build in some data points to monitor your various demographic groups, such as English Language Learners, students of color, various gender identities, or those who have disabilities. If you notice that certain groups of students make up the majority of your intervention groups, but are not the majority of your school, and this is a pattern rather than a one-time event, your tier one team should consider taking some system-wide steps to study and promote equity in your school. The closer your data get to percentages that mirror the percentages of each demographic group in your school population, the healthier your overall tiered system is functioning.

Remember the most important idea to keep in mind when organizing data to monitor students: your purpose. This way students can be quickly assigned to the right type of support or challenge they need. Collecting and organizing data that will help you determine what students need and how to respond. Once you have your data, ask yourself, "Who/how many students need X, Y, and Z intervention?" If your team never progresses to the point of providing a response to the needs the data reveal, you are not yet implementing a schoolwide support model.

Table 11.4 Preparing to Use Data with Your Team (Adapted from Dowdy, Ritchey, and Kamphaus, 2010)

Step	Degree Step is "In Place" 1 = Not in Place 5 = In Place	Possible Next Steps
A team has been charged to oversee your data processes		
The team has identified the goals and purposes of the data you intend to use/ collect		
The team has examined the usefulness of possible data tools based on your goals		
Data tools have been selected that link to your goals		
Interventions have been matched to data you have selected		
A specific action plan and timeline has been developed for data collection		
The team is studying the data, sharing with stakeholders (including district personnel)		

Application – Monitoring Student Needs

Organizing data to screen and respond to student needs can be a big job, especially in larger schools where many data points are collected. It is important for teams to assess their own preparedness to get started. Use Table 11.4 to rate your readiness to organize and use data to respond to students' needs, and plan next steps.

Connection – Adjusting Interventions Based on Data

If you have planted a garden, you know that you cannot just plant seeds, water, and expect success. Successful gardening depends upon monitoring your crops and plants and adjusting as needed. While helping students to grow is not exactly like growing plants, we are tending to the growth and development of our students, and still need to monitor their success and adjust the environment as needed.

Point/Principle – Adjusting Intervention Based on Data

Like gardeners, we need to pay attention to indicators to help us determine what adjustments need to be made for our students. A question that comes up frequently is "How do I know if the intervention is working?" This question demonstrates the importance of developing clear decisions rules, or outcome goals for interventions. In some cases, outcome goals can be created using existing norms. Data related to expected performance and growth in standardized test scores, reading and math fluency, or attendance rates exists. Schools can use these data and create goals that are achievable based on their context.

In many cases, it is important to develop local norms to establish context and inform plans. For example, imagine how the approach might be different in these two cases if the national norm for reading words per minute is 151. In both schools, a student reads at a rate of 100 words per minute. But, in one school, the local norms show the average student reads at a rate of 105 words per minute. In the other school, the average student reads at a rate of 150 words per minute. After considering these local norms, the action for the first school would be to review their entire tier one system, whereas in the second school they will most likely only provide intervention to the one student.

Note that the answer is not to adjust what we consider to be the target outcome for students. Instead, adjust the system to help students achieve that target most efficiently. In the school where the local norms are 105 words per minute, we would not then say the student's reading rate is no longer a concern, we would say that we need a tier one system to address the concern, since it is widespread. The systems schools create to analyze and reflect on their data is just as important as how they gather the data.

BOX 11.2 PONDERING ON PURPOSE

Examine your school and student performance trends.

- Do you serve in an environment where you may need to provide what are typically considered tier two level supports at tier one instead?
- Or perhaps your school has a majority of students who exceed national norms. Do typical tier two interventions get delivered in more of a tier three format (e.g., individualized) given your numbers of students in need?

Application – Adjusting Intervention Based on Data

This will be a longer application section, as we are asking you to utilize your knowledge from chapters 10 and 11 together here. Figure 11.1 provides examples from a high school that was implementing a schoolwide system of intervention for behavior. Their fidelity for schoolwide behavior support was being monitored using the Schoolwide Evaluation Tool. Rob Horner and his colleagues at the University of Oregon found this tool was very useful for monitoring the implementation of schoolwide behavior support. Their research suggested that if teams could get their overall score on all components up to 80% implementation, and teaching expectations component up to 80% implementation, then you were likely to see reductions in behavior problems overall for your school.

The SET included seven components: expectations defined (e.g., identifying three to five expectations for the setting), expectations taught (e.g., staff were teaching expectations to students), acknowledgement system (e.g., students were being acknowledged for appropriate behavior), system for responding to problem behavior (e.g., clear delineation of what behaviors should be managed by administration and those managed in the classroom), monitoring and decision making (e.g., using data for decision making), management (e.g., a team was in place), and district-level support (e.g., access to external coaching).

Outcome data reviewed by the team included reviewing the top three areas for minor-level office discipline referrals (ODRs) by grade level, the top three areas for major ODRs by grade level, and time of day the referral occurred. Data were adjusted for the number of days, average daily enrollment, per 100 students to account for any variability in the data.

Before reading on, take a moment to think about what you would do if these were your data. Table 11.5 provides an area where you can practice your response. We are asking you to consider the strengths and needs for the interventions and outcomes. What kinds of recommendations would you make if you were coaching this school, based on the data?

The leadership team for the schoolwide effort initially took the following steps to address the patterns they saw in both the fidelity and outcome data. How did their recommendations line up with yours?

- Provide training on teaching expectations, acknowledging student behavior, and redirection strategies for redirecting problem behavior for all instructors of first year students.
- Provide an orientation for the incoming 9th grades on the expectations for the school, focusing on expectations related to respect and dress code.
- Provide training to all staff on the overall schoolwide process at the beginning of the year.
- Open a school store in the cafeteria where students could exchange tickets they earned for demonstrating expected behaviors.

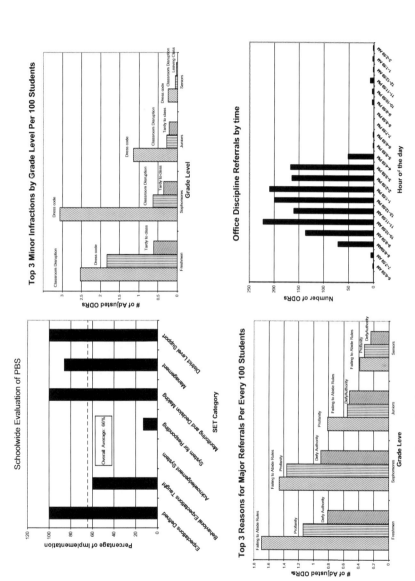

Figure 11.1 Sample Graphs from a Secondary School

Note. **SET** stands for the School-wide Evaluation Tool. ORD stands for Office Discipline Referral. ODR data were converted to per day, per month, per 100 students, per average daily enrollment for consistency across grade-level comparisons.

Table 11.5 Reviewing Fidelity and Outcome Data for Action Planning

Type of Data	Strengths	Concerns	Next steps
Fidelity data			
Outcome data			

Conclusion

The kinds of data you will use for your own planning will depend on the goals of your schoolwide intervention. Look to adjust your intervention based both on reviews of fidelity data, and outcome measures for students. In this chapter we have focused on finding ways to support your schoolwide implementation efforts using data. There are certainly more components to planning with data, but we hope this chapter helped you think through some considerations around using data in secondary schools.

For more information on using data as a part of your schoolwide approaches, look at the book *Advancing Evidence-Based Practice Through Program Evaluation: A Practical Guide for School-Based Professionals* by Julie Morrison and Anna Harms. Another good resource is Kent McIntosh and Steve Goodman's book *Integrated Multi-tiered Systems of Support: Blending RTI and PBIS*. Further, Matt Burns and Kelly Gibbon's book *Implementing Response-to-Intervention in Elementary and Secondary Schools Procedures to Assure Scientific-Based Practices* would be a useful resource as well. Additionally, Rick DuFour and colleagues have a very helpful book called *Whatever it Takes: How Professional Learning Communities Respond When Kids Don't Learn*. For more information on screening related to internalized and externalized behaviors, we recommend Kathleen Lane and colleagues' book *Systematic Screenings of Behavior to Support Instruction: From Preschool to High School*.

Bibliography

Allen, J., Gregory, A., Mikami, A., Lun, J., Hamre, B., & Pianta, R. (2013). Observations of effective teacher–student interactions in secondary school classrooms: Predicting student achievement with the classroom assessment scoring system—secondary. *School Psychology Review, 42*(1), 76–98.

Burke, A. (2015). *Early identification of high school graduation outcomes in Oregon leadership network schools*. Regional Educational Laboratory Northwest. Retrieved from https://ies.ed.gov/ncee/edlabs/regions/northwest/pdf/REL_2015079.pdf

Burns, M. K., & Gibbons, K. (2013). *Implementing response-to-intervention in elementary and secondary schools: Procedures to assure scientific-based practices*. London, England: Routledge.

Carl, B., Richardson, J. T., Cheng, E., Kim, H., & Meyer, R. H. (2013). Theory and application of early warning systems for high school and beyond. *Journal of Education for Students Placed at Risk, 18*(1), 29–49. doi:10.1080/10824669.2013.745374

Christenson, S. L., Reschly, A. L., Appleton, J. J., Berman, S., Spanjers, D., & Varro, P. (2008). Best practices in fostering student engagement. In A. Thomas & J. Grimes (Eds.), *Best practices in school psychology V* (pp. 1099–1120). Washington, DC: National Association of School Psychologists.

Datnow, A., & Park, V. (2014). *Data driven leadership.* San Francisco, CA: Jossey Bass.

Donohue, P., Goodman-Scott, E., & Betters-Bubon, J. (2018). Using universal screening for early identification of students at risk: A case example from the field. *Professional School Counseling, 19*(1), 133–143.

Dowdy, E., Ritchey, K., & Kamphaus, R. W. (2010). School-based screening: A population-based approach to inform and monitor children's mental health needs. *School Mental Health, 2*(4), 166–176. doi:10.1007/s12310-010-9036-3

DuFour, R., DuFour, R., Eaker, R., & Karhanek, G. (2004). *Whatever it takes: How professional learning communities respond when kids don't learn.* Bloomington, IN: Solution Tree.

Duhigg, C. (2012). *The power of habit: Why we do what we do in life and business.* New York, NY: Random House LLC.

Harms, A., Nantais, M., Tuomikoski, K., & Weaver, S. (2019). Designing educational data systems to support continuous improvement. *Association for Positive Behavior Support Newsletter, 17*(1), 2–3.

Horner, R. H., Todd, A. W., Lewis-Palmer, T., Irvin, L. K., Sugai, G., & Boland, J. B. (2004). The school-wide evaluation tool (SET): A research instrument for assessing school-wide positive behavior support. *Journal of Positive Behavior Interventions, 6*(1), 3–12.

Jellinek, M. S., Murphy, J. M., Little, M., Pagano, M. E., Comer, D. M., & Kelleher, K. J. (1999). Use of the pediatric symptom checklist to screen for psychosocial problems in pediatric primary care: A national feasibility study. *Architecture Pediatric and Adolescent Medicine, 153*(3), 254–260.

Jimerson, S. R., Reschly, A. L., & Hess, R. S. (2008). Best practices in increasing the likelihood of high school completion. *Best Practices in School Psychology, 5*, 1085–1097. Washington, DC: National Association of School Psychologists.

Koon, S., & Petscher, Y. (2016). Can scores on an interim high school reading assessment accurately predict low performance on college readiness exams? Retrieved from http://ies.ed.gov/ncee/edlabs.

Lane, K. L., Menzies, H. M., Oakes, W. P., & Kalberg, J. R. (2011). *Systematic screenings of behavior to support instruction: From preschool to high school.* Guilford Press. New York: NY.

Malloy, J. M., Bohanon, H., & Francoeur, K. (2018). Positive behavioral interventions and supports in high schools: A case study from New Hampshire. *Journal of Educational and Psychological Consultation, 28*(2), 219–247. doi:10.1080/10474412.2017.1385398

McIntosh, K., & Goodman, S. (2016). *Integrated multi-tiered systems of support: Blending RTI and PBIS.* New York, NY: Guilford Publications.

Molloy, L. E., Moore, J. E., Trail, J., Van Epps, J. J., & Hopfer, S. (2013). Understanding real-world implementation quality and "active ingredients" of PBIS. *Prevention Science, 14*(6), 593–605. doi:10.1007/s11121-012-0343-9

Morrison, J. Q., & Harms, A. L. (2018). *Advancing evidence-based practice through program evaluation: A practical guide for school-based professionals.* New York, NY: Oxford University Press.

National Alliance on Mental Health. (n.d.). Retrieved from www.nami.org/learn-more/public-policy/mental-health-screening

National Association of School Psychologists. (2014). *Position statement on prevention and wellness promotion*. Retrieved from www.nasponline.org/research-and-policy/policy-priorities/position-statements

Suicide Prevention Resource Center. (2016). *SOS signs of suicide middle school and high school prevention programs*. Retrieved from www.sprc.org/resources-programs/sos-signs-suicide

PART 3

Providing Effective Instruction

12

STRUCTURES THAT FACILITATE ACCESS TO LEARNING

In a Nutshell

- Non-classroom settings contribute to the climate and culture of the school and can support or hinder student outcomes.
- Attendance is important and should be addressed in a systematic way.
- Use research-based approaches to get your students to class on time.
- A well-developed syllabus documents the instructor's explicit expectations for the class.
- Planning and using flexible means of engagement maximizes student participation and learning.
- Using instructional routines broadens the access of your content to all learners.

Introduction

Teachers in one high school were concerned with the unsafe traffic flow in their hallways. To teach the expected behavior for walking in the hallway, they placed blue painter's tape down the middle of the hall and dressed up in construction vests with orange flags. The staff stood in the middle of the hall on the first days of school flagging students to the right (the side traffic follows in the United States). They used some humor to help emphasize how they expected the students to walk through the hallway. The novelty was part of the strategy to engage the students in a way that was far more memorable than simply announcing to walk on the right or having a sign on the wall alone.

We all need some sense of predictability to be successful and to reduce anxiety. Purposeful structures can help students and other members of your community be more successful. Structure can be added to physical settings (e.g., hallways, common areas) or to instruction (e.g., predictable routines for presenting information). Structure also includes being explicit about what you expect from students and staff in your setting.

Connection – Success in Non-Classroom Settings

In one high school, older students had very openly and publicly hazed underclassmen off campus. In response to the problems at the school, the principal developed an advisory team made up of students from a variety of representative groups. One of the issues highlighted in their feedback was that some hazing of students was occurring within the school, in the general commons area. The upperclassmen had taken to sitting on risers and would intimidate underclassmen as they walked past beneath them. The simple solution was for the school to remove the risers from the commons area. While moving the furniture out of the setting did not stop all incidences of bullying, it did reduce a structural opportunity for older students to bully younger ones. Structure in non-classroom settings can have a major impact on the climate of the building.

Point/Principle – Non-Classroom Settings

When we talk about non-classroom settings, we mean any space that is outside of the classroom. These settings can include hallways, common areas, auditoriums, cafeterias, restrooms, and the grounds around the school's campus. One of our favorite tools that can help schools think through creating structure on non-classroom settings is the Positive Behavior Interventions and Supports (PBIS) Self-Assessment Survey, developed by Rob Horner, George Sugai, and Ann Todd at the University of Oregon, particularly the non-classroom section. This instrument includes several key practices that schools can put into place to improve their non-classroom settings. Table 12.1 provides an example of what one high school did in response to reflecting upon this instrument. As a result of the interventions, the school saw a 40–50% reductions in students walking in the hallway after the bell rang, depending on the location. They also saw a 67% reduction in hallway-related office discipline referrals.

Table 12.1 Reflecting on Non-classroom Practices in One Urban High
School Setting

PBIS Self-Assessment Non-Classroom Section	High School's Response
Ensuring that schoolwide expected student behaviors apply to non-classroom settings.	Develop and post specific examples of expectations in hallways (e.g., passing on the right side of the hall, using appropriate language). Create schoolwide on time to class policy.
Teaching schoolwide expected student behaviors in non-classroom settings.	Develop common hallway behavior lesson plans for teachers. Teach expectations during school assemblies. Prompt students in hall to walk to right (dressing in flagman uniforms).
Individuals in charge of supervision actively supervise (move, scan, and interact) students in non-classroom settings.	Staff were asked to visually scan around their classroom areas during passing periods, encourage students to move to class, and greet students at the door. Principal would walk the halls and thank staff for participation.
A process for rewarding expected student behaviors in non-classroom settings is in place.	Students could earn tickets (e.g., Buzzy Bucks) for appropriate hallway behavior. Items could be redeemed in school store. All classes were asked to have a bell ringer activity.
Physical/architectural features are modified to limit (a) unsupervised settings, (b) unclear traffic patterns, and (c) inappropriate access to and exit from school grounds.	The staff taped a blue line down the middle of the hallway to help students know which side of the hall they should walk on.
Ensuring appropriate numbers of students in non-classroom spaces through effective scheduling.	Schedule was changed so that all students started and ended the school day at the same time.

(Continued)

Table 12.1 (continued)

PBIS Self-Assessment Non-Classroom Section	High School's Response
Regularly developing and improving staff's active supervision skills.	Staff were provided training on effective redirection strategies. All staff were provided with a one-page document on effective redirection strategies. Additional training was provided for teachers of 9th and 10th grade students.
Evaluating the status of student behavior and management practices quarterly using data.	The staff reviewed office discipline referral data for "on time to class" and hallway behaviors. Staff also counted the number of students walking in the hallway right after the bell rang.
Involving all staff directly or indirectly in management of non-classroom settings.	All staff were involved in the development of the on time to class policy ("On time to class means students are 100% through the threshold of the classroom when the bell rings").

Note: Adapted from the PBIS Self-Assessment Survey (2009) and Bohanon (2015).

Application – Success in Non-Classroom Settings

As you think you about your own non-classroom settings, what are some areas that you think your school could address? Are there structural or policy changes that could make your non-classroom settings more efficient for everyone in your school? Take a moment to reflect on Table 12.2 to consider how much you think each component is in place, and how much of a priority it might be to you. Should you decide non-classroom settings are an area of focus, we encourage you to complete the entire self-assessment with your staff (you can find it online at PBISApps.org). Completing the instrument and developing an action plan will help your team make sure you have the systems and data procedures in place you might need to be successful.

Connection – Attendance

Think about a time that your friends or family had plans but you couldn't make it. What happened the next time you were together? Perhaps someone tried to catch you up to speed on what you missed. You may have felt left out. No matter how detailed the story, talking over what you missed could never replace being part of the experience yourself. Apply this same principle to your students. When they miss class, it impacts their feeling of belonging and

Table 12.2 Reflecting on Non-Classroom Settings in Your School

Adapted from the PBIS Self-Assessment Non-Classroom Prompt	Level In Place 3 = in place 2 = partially 1= not in place	Level of Priority 3 = high 2 = medium 1 = low
Ensure that schoolwide expected student behaviors apply to non-classroom settings.		
Teach schoolwide expected student behaviors in non-classroom settings to students.		
Individuals in charge of supervision actively supervise (move, scan, and interact) students in non-classroom settings.		
A process for rewarding expected student behaviors in non-classroom settings is in place.		
Physical/architectural features are modified to limit (a) unsupervised settings, (b) unclear traffic patterns, and (c) inappropriate access to and exit from school grounds.		
Ensure appropriate numbers of students in non-classroom spaces through effective scheduling.		
Regularly develop and improve staff's active supervision skills.		
Evaluate the status of student behavior and management practices quarterly using data.		
Involve all staff directly or indirectly in management of non-classroom settings.		

Note: Adapted from the PBIS Self-Assessment Survey (2009)

their comprehension of the material. Just like plans with family and friends, there are countless reasons students miss school. They may have been sick, on a trip, depressed, or caring for another person. They may feel alienated by people at school struggle with transportation, or feel embarrassed by their lack of confidence with their class material. As with all other systemic interventions discussed in this book, when it comes to attendance, there is no one solution to address the needs of every student. You must put some proactive measures in place at tier one. For students who continue to miss class, follow a process to get to the root cause and address the issue at hand to get your students in school.

Point/Principle – Attendance

The issue of attendance is complex, but important to address. Missing just two days per month has a negative impact on student achievement. Students who have poor attendance have an increased risk of dropping out. Unfortunately, many times attendance habits are formed earlier in life. This is not an excuse for secondary schools to ignore the issue as unresolvable. Consider partnering with elementary schools to proactively support students coming in who have a history of chronic absences.

Attendanceworks.org breaks down attendance intervention into three tiers. At tier one, students are missing no more than 10% of school days, or about one day per month. These students are responding well to universal strategies of having a positive learning environment with engaging classes that meet their learning and socio-emotional needs. The second tier, "early intervention," encompasses students who could be categorized as moderately chronically absent (missing 10-20% of school days or two to three days per month). These students need additional engagement, support, and/or action plans tied directly to the reasons for their absences. The third tier, "specialized support," includes students who are missing 20% or more of their time in school. These students need extensive and integrated support, frequently involving several stakeholders to support them, and possibly from outside organizations.

Finding the right solution to chronic attendance can be tricky. Just like with academic interventions, the results will not likely be immediate. It may take weeks, months, or even years of attempting different interventions to make a sustainable difference. Attendanceworks.org outlines five evidence-based components to addressing attendance: engage students and parents, recognize good and improved attendance, provide personalized early outreach, and monitor attendance data. This is a great resource to help your team select schoolwide proactive strategies, and interventions for groups and individual students, as well as a tool to share with parents when engaging them as a partner.

Notice that the recommendations emerging from research do not include detentions or suspensions, or other traditional "punitive" measures. In middle and high schools. These punitive strategies can pose a major challenge for school teams, as often staff, parents, and community members have a difficult time shifting their understanding of how to improve a behavior like attending school. Many adults working in and with schools feel that the threat of a punishment was a driving factor in why they attended classes, even if they did not like the class or feel welcomed there. In reality, many students who do not attend school or who skip classes do so for a multitude of factors. For many students, the punishment or negative impact on their grades is less motivating than the barriers they are avoiding, which reinforces their avoidance behavior, by skipping class.

If a student is faced with a class where they feel bullied by their peers, overwhelmed by the material, and "hated" by the teacher, versus a nice hour in the lunchroom socializing with friends, it is not difficult to imagine him making the "wrong choice." Their choice to avoid a class may become even more appealing for the student" if he has never been explicitly coached by a caring adult on how to successfully navigate his challenges in the classroom. A student who is told by his parents he must take care of his young siblings and get them to school safely may not realistically have the option to attend his first period class, no matter how motivated he might be to get there. A traditional detention or suspension would not address the underlying issues associated with either example, yet this is typically how secondary schools respond to attendance problems.

The types of strategies that gradually make a difference in attendance rates (explicitly teaching social-emotional and behavioral skills, communicating with families, making meaningful connections between students and adults, culturally responsive classrooms, etc.) take more time and effort than traditional punishments, as well as more staff members to be involved. Proactive strategies are sometimes outside the comfort zone of content-focused secondary school teachers. The schoolwide team will need to find ways to provide learning and coaching to the adults in the building that shift mindsets and practices away from a "traditional" model of discipline.

BOX 12.1 PONDERING ON PURPOSE

- How does your school/district monitor attendance data?
- Whose responsibility is it to identify the students who are at risk?
- Do all stakeholders know the process to monitor attendance and their role in keeping students in school?

Application – Attendance

A "quick win" could be to implement the "nudge" intervention. Nudge theory is the idea that it is best to use the most unobtrusive intervention possible. An intervention attempted by the School District of Philadelphia was to send a postcard to parents encouraging them to improve their child's attendance. This "nudge" led to a 2.4% reduction in absenteeism. The intervention worked consistently across elementary and high school settings.

Pull up the attendance data for your district, school, or classroom. Use the Table 12.3 or 12.4, or the one on attendanceworks.org to categorize your student attendance data. Using the intervention resources discussed in this chapter and the planning document below, work as a team to identify possible interventions, the students who will receive them, and the staff member responsible for next steps.

Table 12.3 Attendance Action Planning

Tier (based on # of absences)	# of Students	% of Total Student Body	Names of Students
Tier One (less than one day/month) Satisfactory Attendance			Not applicable for this cell
Tier One (one day/month) At Risk			
Tier Two (two to three days/month) Early Intervention			
Tier Three (more than three days a month) Specialized Support			

Table 12.4 Attendance Action Planning Option Two

Student Name	Tier	Staff Assigned	Possible Need	Action/Intervention

Illustration – Getting Students to Class on Time

Earlier we provided an example about a getting to class on time policy. The staff in this large high school decided that they needed to be aligned on what it meant to be on time to class. Prior to the statement, for some teachers on time meant students had to be in their seats when the bell rang. For other teachers, could still be walking into the room within a minute or so of the bell. This inconsistency was frustrating to students who would be punished in some settings for being a few minutes late, but not in others. The staff knew they needed a new plan, however, it took about three years of discussion for the entire staff to agree on what they meant by being on time! Once they were all in agreement, every classroom door had the policy posted. The policy was the first step in several that decreased problems with tardiness and getting students to class on time.

Point/Principle – Getting Students to Class on Time

The first step to addressing tardiness is measuring the problem with data. There are at least three ways we have seen teams look at tardiness data. The first is to review your current data around the number of students who are tardy. You might look at the time of day, grade levels, and locations. If you do not have a consistent on time to class policy in place, your data may not be very accurate. However, this will at least give you somewhere to start. Second, you could also look at your office discipline referrals for issues in the hallways. Third, you can take "probe" data by occasionally standing in the hall and counting the number of students that pass by a specific location after class has begun. At least three data points are recommended before you start making decisions.

Once you have collected data, you can ask yourself what kind of problem you are having. If more than 15% of the students have one or more tardies/non-classroom office discipline referrals, then you have a tier one problem that will require all hands on deck to improve. If the percentage of students with tardy or non-classroom issues is between 5% and 15% then you have a tier two problem. This will require an intervention that focuses on groups of students and staff. If you have 5% or less students with these issues, then you have a tier three problem. Your response will focus on specific students and staff to help address the issues. You might at some level need to address all three. However, our recommendation is that you put most of your initial effort at tier one, to decrease the overall "noise" these problems are causing in your setting.

Kristina Johnson-Gros and her colleagues found at least three components that, in their study, may have encouraged students to be in class on time. These included:

- Staff being posted at their doors when students entered the room.
- Staff having brief interactions with students during passing periods (e.g., good morning, how are you, good to see you).
- Staff in the hallway encouraging students to move to class.

There were more components to actively supervising students in the hallway. However, these three strategies seemed to be related to the most improvements in students' being on time to class. While more research is needed, this study provides insights into how changes in adult interactions with students can have a positive impact on student outcomes.

Ashli Tyre, Laura Feuerborn, and Jennifer Pierce studied another approach. They had a three-part intervention to addressing being on time. These steps included:

- Explicitly teaching all students what being on time to class meant.
- Providing active supervision in non-classroom settings during transitions (particularly in areas where there were problems for students during passing periods).
- Delivering consistent consequences for being tardy to class.

The consequences included escorting students who were late to class to a specific room. Once in the room, the students signed a postcard that was sent home to their guardian. Then, the students could return to class. Following their intervention, tardiness to class decreased and remained low following implementation. For more information on this type of intervention, we suggest you review the intervention *Safe Transitions and Reduced Tardies (START) on Time* developed by Randy Sprick, available from Safe and Civil Schools (see http://www.safeandcivilschools.com). A word of caution: focusing on consistent consequences alone for tardiness (without the proactive measures) may not produce ideal results. Often these types of punitive approaches can lead to students missing more classes. Depending on how the procedure is structured, some students may skip class altogether or leave school to avoid punishment for being tardy.

BOX 12.2 PONDERING ON PURPOSE

- How does your school/district respond to student tardiness?
- What would it feel like to staff members if the administrators responded to staff tardiness the same way staff respond to students who are late to class?
- What types of approaches to student tardiness approximate what we find acceptable as adults when we are running late?

Application – Getting Students to Class on Time

Take a moment to identify which of the three approaches to collecting data (i.e., reviewing tardy data, office discipline referrals, counting the number of students in the hall) might be useful to your team. Use the CAIRO approach from Chapter 7 to help plan your next steps (if any).

Connection – Preparing Your Syllabus

Meaghan Guiney is a school psychologist by training who has learned some very valuable lessons from Walt Disney and Company. According to Meaghan, Walt Disney is reported to have said, "unarticulated expectations are premeditated disappointments." Disney leaders do not expect that their team members know what is expected of them based on common sense alone. They clearly articulate the goals, expectations, and strategies that employees need to exhibit to be successful. Your school may not be as "magically consistent" as Disney World, but your educators are trying to create a consistent experience for your students that leads to their success.

Point/Principle – Preparing Your Syllabus

One of the key ways you can provide consistent structure for your students is through your course syllabus. We are fans of Randy Sprick's book, *Discipline in the Secondary Classroom*. In his book, he provides a common checklist staff can use to ensure that the school consistently provides information around course expectations. He recommends several key areas of the course that should be explicitly addressed. Table 12.5 provides a list of these factors. We would encourage our readers to look at Randy's book for more information. These components are highly related to other schoolwide efforts.

Table 12.5 Factors that should be Explicitly Addressed within the Course Syllabus

• Course Goals	• Entering the Class	• Communication
• Contact Information	• Tardy/Absence	• Ending Class
• Student Success Traits	• Course Materials	• Consequences
• Rules/Expectations	• Assignments	• Model Projects
• Course Activities	• Due Dates	• Checklists
• Grades/Status	• Late/Missing Work	
• Classroom Procedures	• Materials	

Note: Adapted from Sprick (2013)

Application – Preparing Your Syllabus

Based on the list provided in Table 12.5, how much agreement does your school have on what should go into a syllabus? Take a few minutes to talk about areas where you already have some agreement. Any initial level of agreement is certainly an area to celebrate. Are there other areas that could perhaps increase or improve the structure established for your students and prevent frustration included within your syllabus?

Illustration – Flexible Means of Engagement

My school (Lisa) once had a protocol where teachers observed each other instruct and tallied student engagement. This included raising their hand, being called on, and interactions with the teacher and peers. At the surface level, we all know that we should "engage" all learners in the class, and many teachers use techniques to attempt to increase student participation. But how are we reflecting on the impact of trends across classrooms and grade levels? Following a similar protocol to the one we just described can be really eye-opening when you look at the data trends across the school. We were able to reflect on our engagement of our under-represented students, particularly students of color and students with disabilities, allowing us to create actionable goals for our classrooms. Next, we look at creating structures and interventions to increase student engagement.

Point/Principle – Flexible Means of Engagement

In Chapter 14 we discuss strategies to increase student engagement in more detail, but here we will address some structural factors in lesson design that can promote engagement. Universal design for learning (UDL) is an approach to designing lessons with flexible, barrier-reducing options in mind that all learners can access if needed. UDL becomes part of the structure of the setting that promotes engagement. One of the three guidelines for UDL is "providing multiple means of engagement" with the intent of creating "purposeful and motivated learners." The three subcategories the Center for Applied Special Technology (CAST), a national leader for UDL, suggests focusing on are "recruiting interest, sustaining effort and persistence, and self-regulation." The CAST UDL website breaks down these three categories into specific ways to reduce barriers in these categories. Structuring lessons to include explicit teaching and modeling of engagement, and flexible options for students to choose from, for example, are helpful ways to improve engagement universally. The CAST website contains great resources to explore this style of lesson planning (see http://www.cast.org/).

It is important to structure your routines to include opportunities for students to give feedback, make choices, and explore topics that interest

Table 12.6 Ways to Include Student Voice

Reason for Survey	Possible Survey Tools
Interest Inventories	Inventories based on subject/topic areas such as career interests (See Career) Wonders through the South Dakota Department of Labor
Learning Style Inventories	Connell Multiple Intelligence Survey Riso-Hudson Enneagram Type Indicator (RHETI)
Gauging Prior Knowledge	Anticipation Guides TKWLs: (Think I know, Want to know, Learned) Pre-assessments
Creating Choice in Learning	Identifying subtopics of interest within required topics (i.e., types of poetry within a poetry unit, events within a particular timeframe) Matching student interest with reading assignments for jigsaw activities Surveys to help identify ideal working partners
Feedback	Focus groups 1:1 conferences Rating scales or open-ended questions related to activities and/or instruction
Self-reflection	1:1 conferences Rating scales or open-ended questions focusing on the actions and/or engagement of the student

them. Table 12.6 contains just a few examples of ways to survey students in these areas. You can also create your own instrument using some of the online survey tools mentioned in Chapter 10.

Eliciting feedback from students shows that their contributions to class are valuable and allows them to disclose concerns or needs in a low-stakes way. This will activate their interests and make them feel more supported in the class, helping them to feel comfortable in taking on challenges. We discuss feedback more in Chapter 15.

Application – Flexible Means of Engagement

Consider a unit taught at your school. How are opportunities for multiple means of engagement provided throughout the unit? Using a web diagram similar to Figure 12.1, list out strategies used for each category and reflect on the frequency at which these areas are addressed.

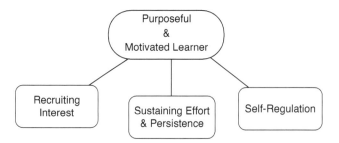

Figure 12.1 Flexible Means of Engagement Areas

Connection – Instructional Routines

Find any kindergarten teacher who seems calm, cool, and collected in the middle of October, and you will likely see evidence of many routines, both behavioral and academic. Ask any child in that classroom, and they are likely able to tell you the process for coming into the room and putting their things away, participating in a math-centered activity, and reviewing the letter of the day in a circle on the rug. They use songs, visual checklists, mnemonic devices, and repetition to help them learn routines early in the year. These teachers can easily plug in new skills (social, academic, behavioral) to the established routines. While these strategies work amazingly well with teens and adults, many secondary teachers have not learned to see the value in establishing routines and sticking to them.

Point/Principle – Instructional Routines

As a new high school teacher, I (Kelly) was guilty of assuming my students had all of the executive function skills and practice needed to learn in any format or structure I chose. I also wanted to try every cool strategy and activity I came across. I found that I was trying new things all the time (in an effort to keep my students from getting bored), but the students and I were always frustrated. I kept having to spend time explaining the directions and walking them through activities step-by-step. Eventually, I changed my approach and instead picked just a few evidence-based strategies and used them as instructional routines on a regular basis. I was delighted to find that my students became more independent. I was also better able to differentiate my instruction.

For the purposes of this book, we define an *instructional routine* as using an evidence-based classroom strategy, as designed (with fidelity), frequently and regularly until students become familiar enough with the strategy that it becomes habitual. An example would be using the Reading for Meaning routine (found in Harvey Silver's book *The Core Six*). This routine includes a graphic organizer where students see a list of statements related to a passage, image, math problem, or other form of text. Students must decide if they agree or disagree with each statement and include evidence from the text in their rationale.

The routine is simple and it lends itself easily to variations and differentiated levels of challenge. For example, students can create some of their own statements related to the text to try to "stump" debate with each other. Students quickly become familiar with the routine, so teachers no longer need to give instructions related to the activity itself. Instead, teachers can focus on moving around the room giving feedback to students.

Instructional routines are not usually complicated, and there are plenty of great books, articles, and online resources available (e.g., the Harvey Silver book mentioned above, Interventioncentral.org, or the What Works Clearinghouse). See the companion website for more examples. However, the key is to choose just enough strategies to routinely address a variety of topics and skills, and then repeatedly use them as they were designed (don't skip steps!). Often secondary teachers are concerned about students getting bored if the structure of the class and types of activities are the same each day or week. However, consistency actually allows students to feel confident and secure (because they know what to expect and how to complete activities) and thus allows the teacher to push, challenge, support, and be creative (within the routine) in ways that are much more efficient. *Instructional routines greatly reduce the cognitive load for students with attentional or executive function challenges.* They can help kids who have been absent to more easily jump back in upon their return. Balance is key. One type of routine is not enough, but if too many are selected, there won't be enough repetition for students to develop new habits.

Instructional routines can be utilized within one classroom but are exponentially more effective if schoolwide efforts are made to replicate them across content areas. Strategies such as common writing process, graphic organizers, academic vocabulary instruction, problem-solving steps, and self-monitoring strategies can be effective schoolwide instructional routines. Imagine the benefits of providing a consistent structure for learning for students who struggle to organize their thoughts and work, those who become bored because they often have to wait for the teachers to explain activities to the whole class, and everyone in between!

Application – Instructional Routines

On your own or with your team, look up a few instructional routines mentioned in this book, or search through Interventioncentral.org, What Works Clearinghouse, or another online database of evidence-based strategies. Pick a strategy you would like to see implemented in multiple subject areas in your school. Complete the following reflective questions.

1. Why did you select this strategy to implement as an instructional routine (what benefit would it provide to learners)?
2. How do you know the strategy is evidence-based?
3. What types of content and/or skills could you pair with this instructional routine?
4. How often would it make sense to use this routine?
5. What would staff members need in order to use this instructional routine, as designed, regularly?

Conclusion

There are various non-classroom and classroom structures that contribute to the overall climate and culture at your school. Having norm-building, explicit conversations about these areas will help prevent misconceptions across stakeholder groups and align everyone around common expectations. Students feel secure and confident when the structures are clear to everyone in the building and they know what to expect throughout the day.

Bibliography

Bohanon, H. (2015). Changes in adult behavior to decrease disruption from students in non-classroom settings. *Intervention in School and Clinic, 15*(1), 12–18. Retrieved from http://ecommons.luc.edu/education_facpubs/39

The Connell Multiple Intelligence Questionnaire for Children. (n.d.). Retrieved from www.ctevh.org/Conf2015/Workshops/412/412a.pdf

Guiney, M. C. (2014). Lessons from the Disney approach to leadership. *Communique', 42*(7), 28–29.

Horner, R., Sugai, G., & Todd, A. (2017). *Positive Behavior Interventions and Support Self-Assessment Survey (v 3.0). Education and Community Supports*, University of Oregon, Eugene, OR. Retrieved from http://www.pbis.org

Israel, M., Ribuffo, C., & Smith, S. (2014). *Universal design for learning: Recommendations for teacher preparation and professional development (Document No. IC-7)*. Retrieved from University of Florida, Collaboration for Effective Educator, Development, Accountability, and Reform Center website: http://ceedar.education.ufl.edu/tools/innovation-configurations/

Johnson-Gros, K. N., Lyons, E. A., & Griffin, J. R. (2008). Active supervision: An intervention to reduce high school tardiness. *Education & Treatment of Children, 31*(1), 39–53.

Rogers, T., Duncan, T., Wolford, T., Ternovski, J., Subramanyam, S., & Reitano, A. (2017). A randomized experiment using absenteeism information to "nudge" attendance. Retrieved from https://ies.ed.gov/ncee/edlabs/regions/midatlantic/pdf/REL_2017252.pdf

Silver, H. F., Dewing, R. T., & Perini, M. J. (2012). *The core six: Essential strategies for achieving excellence with the common core*. Alexandria, VA: ASCD.

Sprick, R. (2013). *Discipline in the secondary classroom* (3rd ed.). San Francisco, CA: Jossey-Bass.

Sugai, G., Horner, R., & Todd, A. (2009). *PBIS Self-Assessment Survey version 3.0*. Eugene, OR: Educational and Community Supports, University of Oregon. Retrieved from https://www.pbis.org/

Thompson, J. G. (1998). *Discipline survival kit for the secondary teacher*. San Francisco, CA: CA; Jossey-Bass.

Tyre, A., Feuerborn, L., & Pierce, J. (2011). Schoolwide intervention to reduce chronic tardiness at the middle and high school levels. *Preventing School Failure, 55*(3), 132–139. doi:10.1080/10459880903472918

What is My Learning Style? (n.d.). Retrieved from www.whatismylearningstyle.com/ https://www.attendanceworks.org http://udlguidelines.cast.org/engagement.

13

DEFINING NORMS TO BUILD COMMUNITY

In a Nutshell

- Take time to identify expectations for your setting.
- Expectations should be developed by involving all stakeholders.
- Select three to five expectations demonstrating the overarching values of the school.
- Consider using non-compliance focused competencies like self-awareness, self-management, social awareness, relationship skills, and responsible decision making.
- How you market your expectations is important. Find creative ways to draw attention to them.
- Explicitly teach and practice the expectations.
- Plan the "rhythm" you will use to teach the expectations (frequency, time of year, etc).

Introduction

We have talked about Zappos, a successful shoe company in the United States, in another chapter. One of the guiding features of the Zappos climate is their 10 core values, which include values such as "create fun and a little weirdness," and "build a positive team and family experience." These values guide their company at every level of their operation. Not only do they try to create a culture around these expectations, they try to hire people who emulate their 10 core values. While no company or organization is perfect, Zappos deliberately focuses on the culture of their work environment. Their

CEO Tony Hsieh believes that if they can get their culture right, then everything else will fall into place for the organization.

We can learn from organizations like Zappos that being clear on expectations can be helpful for everyone. One of the common concerns we hear from secondary teachers is that once students move into the "real world" no one is going to hold their hand. We agree. However, we have noticed that many successful companies (in the real world) are very intentional about the expectations for their culture. Typically, this is seen as setting "norms," or principles that drive the actions of the members of a team or group. Whether it be the acceptable length of time given to respond to an email, or the way ideas are shared, successful organizations, in general, focus on helping their constituents be clear on the expectations that are needed for success.

Connection – How Do We Identify and Learn Expectations?

One winter break I (Hank) went into my university to catch up on some work, and had parked my car in the parking garage. There were maybe two other vehicles in the whole lot. When I returned, I found a parking ticket on my front windshield. Apparently, my tire was touching the yellow line between the parking spots. I was not aware that having a wheel touching the yellow line was a major parking violation. I had been working on my own time, and my reward was a $40 parking ticket. As you can imagine, this was upsetting. I submitted pictures of the event to our parking office with the explanation that I was not aware of the yellow line rule. My ticket was waived, but I did receive a warning that the fine for my next violation would not be remitted. About two weeks later, there was a poster on every wall of the parking garage stating the new yellow line parking rule.

When you have been in a setting for a long time, you may not realize that many expectations are implicit and are not clearly defined. For example, at my (Lisa) old school, teachers were only allowed behind the office partition if invited by the office staff or administration. At my new school, I stood behind the partition awkwardly until someone took notice and asked what I was doing. The office staff laughed when I asked if I could come through to get the form I needed and told me I could help myself.

For both Hank and I (Lisa), a disconnect between our learned expectations and the expectations of others put us in a position where we received a punishment. Members of your community may have had similar experiences. Clarity of expectations, or lack thereof, sets us up for either positive or negative experiences with each other. The proactive, frequent, and clear communication of expectations help us to create positive school communities.

Point/Principle – How Do We Identify and Learn Expectations?

Expectations usually involve the behavioral, social, and emotional skills you expect of all members of your community. Having a core set of expectations that are directly taught to students can lead to improved outcomes. For example, Lauren Molloy and her colleagues found in their research that teaching expectations to students was related to fewer defiance and drug-related discipline problems, as measured by office discipline referrals. There are multiple ways you can communicate and teach expectations to your community. You can use any of the following to help people share the expectations for your setting:

- Staff orientation meetings
- Handbooks
- Lesson plans
- Syllabi
- Assemblies
- Posters
- Providing booster sessions for staff and students
- Pre-correcting/reminding students of expectations prior to major events
- Videos

There are certainly other ways to communicate and teach your expectations. We will discuss multiple ways you can do this with your community in the next sections.

Application – How Do We Identify and Learn Expectations?

Before we begin to develop new expectations, take time to identify any of your current expectations within your school. Many schools have discipline-related codes of conduct or other school improvement goals related to climate. How are you already communicating these expectations with your community? You can use Table 13.1 to help you identify what you are already doing around expectations. For now, focus on those expectations that apply to every student across the school.

Table 13.1 Audit of Your Current Practices Related to Expectations

Expectations for all students	Current methods for communicating and teaching expectations

Connection – Developing Expectations

When you were a young child, you probably were required to follow rules set forth by your parent or guardian. As you became a teenager you might have begun to question some of the rules that you were expected to follow. As you matured, your parent or guardian may have allowed you to have more input in the development of the "rules of the house" as a way to enlist your buy-in and encourage your compliance. If your parent or guardian did not include you in the rule making process, you may have felt some level of resentment. The same holds true when working with adults and adolescents in schools. It is helpful to include all stakeholders in the development of your expectations for your setting.

Point/Principle – Developing Expectation

The Positive Behavior Interventions and Support (PBIS) Blueprint available on the website for the National Center on PBIS provides a very useful framework for developing expectations. Based on their resources and our own research, expectations should have the following qualities:

- Limited to three to five
- Positively stated
- Sometimes uses an acronym to help with memorization
- Could be aligned with competencies or standards such as CASEL Competencies for SEL, Common Core, College and Career Readiness
- Connected to your school spirit/mascot if possible
- Connected to the mission, vision, and/or goals of your school

For example, one secondary school we worked with had the expectations PARR – be productive, appropriate, respectful, and responsible. Another school asks everyone to follow R Code: Be respectful, responsible, and ready. At this point, do not worry about the specifics of what this will look like in action. It is important that you include as many stakeholders as possible in the development of your core expectations. The Comprehensive, Integrated, Three-Tiered Model (CI3T) provides a survey you can use with your community to identify your basic expectations. The instrument is called the Schoolwide Expectations Survey for Specific Settings (see www.ci3t.org/). Another way we have seen schools develop their expectations is by having groups, including students who are on a schoolwide leadership team, place ideas for expectations on sticky notes. Then the teams create histograms of the expectations and develop categories based on major themes.

Lori Lynass and her colleagues looked at expectations at schools that were implementing schoolwide behavior supports across the country and found similarities in expectations. She found that about 60% of these schools had specific expectations for respect, responsibility, and safety. The repeated selection of these concepts demonstrates that they may be highly valued across cultural and regional lines. However, we should not make assumptions of how these expectations present in practice. An action considered "respectful" in one school may very well be considered "disrespectful" in another.

At my old school (Lisa), my students called me "Teacher." When I first entered the school, I assumed it was because they kept forgetting my name. I kept correcting them to the point where I became frustrated. Then it was pointed out to me that it was part of their culture, a way to demonstrate respect for our profession. After learning that, instead of frustration, I felt pride. This is an example of why expectations should be developed with representation from all of your stakeholder groups.

We also encourage schools to be intentional about selecting expectations beyond those typically associated with compliance. For example, Camille Farrington has conducted research that suggests focusing on non-academic skills for adolescents can be helpful for both development and course grades. These skills include developing students' academic mindsets, metacognition, and self-regulatory skills. The four areas Farrington has identified are skills related to: belonging to the community, effort, success being possible, and finding value in work. Making these types of skills a priority can allow teachers and students to operationally define what they "look like" in their community.

Another option is the five competencies identified by the Collaborative for Academic, Social, and Emotional Learning (CASEL) which include self-awareness, self-management, social awareness, relationship skills, and responsible decision making. You can use these skills as the foundation for building the language that your school wants to adopt.

Self-determination skills are another set of skills you can use. To be self-determined, according to Michael Wehmeyer, is the ability to be self-regulated (e.g., self-evaluate), autonomous (e.g., set goals), self-realized (e.g., problem solve), and psychologically empowered (e.g., express wants and needs). As you can see from this list, these skills are very similar to both mindsets and SEL competencies. They are also aligned to many of the speaking and listening standards found in the Common Core State Standards under literacy.

Application – Developing Expectations

Think through what expectations you would like to address in your setting. You can use Table 13.2 to help you organize. Follow these general principles to create expectations:

1. Set a goal for identifying three to five expectations
2. Identify the typical types of issues your school needs to address with students (you can use your office discipline referral data to help identify the issues)
3. Decide on who will be involved in developing your expectations

Table 13.2 *Identifying Your Expectations: Who can Provide Input? How will You Include All Stakeholders?*

Who can provide input?	How will you include all stakeholders?	What kinds of skills do you wish (or your data indicate) your community should hold for each other?	What are some of the non-academic or non-compliance skills you could include on your list?

4. Identify a process for getting input from your community
5. Organize the general expectations into three to five major themes

Connection – Posting What You Expect

Once I (Hank) was driving and noticed a sign that said, "Speed limit 11 miles per hour." I thought, wow, that is odd. Then I realized this particular number was chosen for a reason. Since it did not follow typical speed norms, I took notice and paused to see how fast I was driving. It was a novel way to prompt drivers to remember to follow the speed limit expectations. Having signs that prompt people to your school's expectations is another way to encourage people to live by the norms of the setting.

Point/Principle – Posting What You Expect

Using effective ways to post your expectations helps everyone adopt and practice the expected skills of your setting. Some of these posters or signs will be a part of the evidence-based practice that you adopt and are teaching. For example, some SEL programs may come with posters you can use across all settings in your building. In other cases, you can take the specific expectations from a matrix that you develop and create posters for your setting. Regardless of the source of your prompts, we have found a few general principles that schools have used with some success:

- Keep the font large. One security officer in a school told us that most students will rush past signs that are too small to read from a distance.
- Focus on the specific behavior or skill that you are trying to remind community members to implement in that exact location. Think of restrooms that include signs stating "Employees must wash hands before returning to work."
- Keep the verbiage to a minimum to quickly give the point as people pass by.

- Consider height. If placed too high on a wall, images will not be noticed.
- Posters and signs are designed to prompt behavior community members have already been taught. If you have a poster about a specific skill, it should have already been explicitly taught to members of your community.

To help students generalize the expectations to their everyday life, you can also involve the community. For example, a local grocery store used a school's expectations to create posters about how to behave in the store. This type of community and school collaboration helps to provide consistent reinforcement of desirable behaviors across your setting.

If you are using images, try to make sure they also reflect the cultural and ethnic representation of your setting. Also, be creative! One school had the key expectations posted on the backs of sports jerseys. Another school posted the expectations on the front of stairs for students to see as they climbed them.

The Schoolwide Evaluation Tool (SET) mentioned in previous chapters gives ideas about how to look for evidence that you have effectively taught your expectations. This tool recommends stopping ten teachers at random and asking if they can tell you 67% of the expectations. Your hope is that 90% of the teachers you stop can identify the expectations. You can also stop 15 students at random with the hope that 67% of them can identity 70% of the expectation. There is more to this tool, however, taking a quick formative assessment might give you a way to more frequently monitor the saturation of teaching your expectations.

Application – Posting What You Expect

Use the principles we identified as you consider what and how your expectations need to be posted around your setting. In classrooms, involve your students in the process of identifying the specific skills that should be exhibited by both teachers and students. If you have art, graphic design, or marketing programs in your school, consider involving them in the development of the visual prompts you want to create for your setting. The next section on identifying specific skills to address will also be useful for developing your visual communication strategies.

BOX 13.1 PONDERING ON PURPOSE

- What are some schoolwide expectations that seem to constantly require prompting?
- How could a visual prompt help mitigate this need?
- What are some creative ways to approach visual prompting in your setting?
- What would be the benefits for using videos or other creative approaches in addition to posters?

Connection – Deciding Which Skills to Teach

When I (Lisa) started action research on the self-determination skills of my middle school students, I found that my time as their teacher was taken up by almost everything but the content: getting them in the door faster, helping them bring their materials (or sending them back to their locker to get them), searching through piles upon piles of old papers to find their completed work to turn in, and constant prompts throughout the class period about their voice levels. None of these actions led to discipline referrals, but I was getting an overwhelming amount of "feedback" indicating it was a problem. I needed to explicitly teach my students the skills they needed to access instruction before we could dive into the content itself.

After determining the outcomes I was looking for, I approached this instruction one access skills the same way I approach teaching math or literacy. I used the standards to help me frame the expectations at their developmental level. Our state (Illinois) is one of a few that have stand-alone social-emotional standards. In addition, the Common Core, and some state standards, have speaking and listening standards that are applicable across all settings and domains. For example, 9th graders in English in the state of Oklahoma are expected to "actively listen and speak clearly using appropriate discussion rules with control of verbal and nonverbal cues." I related the self-determination skills I decided to explicitly teach directly back to my school's core expectations. I showed my students how they were not respecting themselves or others if they were not demonstrating those self-determination skills in and out of the classrooms.

Point/Principle – Deciding Which Skills to Teach

After developing your three to five expectations, the next step is to teach what those statements look like more concretely within various school environments. Thinking about what the expectations "look like" throughout the school is an important way to determine what to teach. Using discipline data is important, but sometimes issues that should be addressed are not recorded in discipline data. Schoolwide surveys, suggestion/comment boxes, or stakeholder communication (email/phone calls/in-person meetings) can also hold information about areas that need to be addressed.

As another option, if you are interested in identifying a prepared curriculum, you can use CASEL's *Effective Social and Emotional Learning Programs – Middle and High School Edition* guide (see https://casel.org/). This resource includes an overview of current evidenced-based curricula for social and emotional learning. The program you select should be guided by the kinds of expected skills you hope your students can exhibit.

Keep in mind, if using three to five overarching expectations, you will need to plan ways to integrate them with the program you select in order to use consistent language.

If you are developing your own specific expectations and curriculum, then the next step is for you to develop an expectations matrix. The expectations matrix has two components. In the example in Table 13.3, we have placed the expectations for the school in the headings for the top row. The locations where the skills need to be demonstrated are in the far-left hand column. Each cell should describe what the skills specifically look like. A non-example for describing an expected skill would be to say that being respectful in the classroom means being nice. Everyone is going to have a different interpretation of what nice means.

BOX 13.2 PONDERING ON PURPOSE

- What are some examples of expectations in your setting that are interpreted in different ways by different people?
- What roadblocks or challenges do you feel impact community members' ability to learn/understand the expectations as intended?

To help define the skills to teach, try to determine the positive behavior you would like to see that cannot happen at the same time as the problem behavior. One way to build these matrices is to upload them into an online collaborative platform, such as Google Docs. You can assign team members to complete drafts of each cell for the team to review. You can also share a version of the document with the larger school community to get feedback on the specific skills you want to teach. Make sure that your expectations are culturally relevant. Having as diverse of a group as possible reviewing the matrix would be one step to ensuring the expectations support a diverse array of cultural and ethnic perspectives.

For more information on developing site-specific matrices, we invite you to go to PBIS.org and see their tools for developing schoolwide matrices (www.pbis.org/resource/school-wide-expectations-teaching-matrix). Table 13.3 provides an example of a matrix from one high school. In the table, P stands for the typical problem behaviors you have seen for a specific setting and expectation. The letter T stands for what you want to teach instead of the problem(s) that are occurring. *The problems (P) can be removed once you have developed the matrix.* The school, in this example, aligned their expectations with their state's SEL standards. They also connected specific expected behaviors with self-determination (SD) skills.

Table 13.3 Sample Matrix from One High School

Grid for Schoolwide Expectations (PARR)				
(List locations, settings and activities in this column)	Be Productive (SEL: Goal 1 – self-management, Goal 3 – decision making skills)	Be Respectful (SEL: Goal 2 – social awareness, Goal 3 – decision making skills)	Be Responsible (SEL: Goal 1 – self-management, Goal 3 – decision making skills, responsible behaviors)	Be Appropriate (SEL: Goal 2 – social awareness)
Classroom	P = T = Staying with your task (S.D.: goal setting – breaking down tasks and reviewing steps of task for completion, self-monitoring – checking steps of assignment are completed before submitting)	P = Talking back to adults, graffiti, taking others' property T = Avoid others' property, clean up after yourself (S.D.: self-monitor one's behaviors to maintain interactions that are appropriate and appropriately treating property)	P = Not having ID, uniform, learning materials, tardy, not staying in assigned seating, not following instructions, talking back T = Be on time, follow directions, appropriate remarks, ask for help, think then speak (S.D.: set goals for behavior area needing to be addressed with checklists to complete expectation or task, i.e. remembering ID or uniform)	P = Loud remarks, talking too much in class during quieter activities T = Positive remarks, raise hands, inside voice (S.D.: self-monitor one's behaviors to maintain interactions that are appropriate and appropriately treating property)

(Continued)

Table 13.3 (continued)

Grid for Schoolwide Expectations (PARR)

Hallways	P = Standing to watch a fight. Taking others' items T= (S.D.: self-monitoring and methods to complete task (steps) of utilizing adult support for unsafe situations)	P = Inappropriate language, fighting T = (S.D.: self-monitoring use of appropriate language and behaviors)	P = Garbage in the halls, timeliness, students bunching in areas T = Timeliness to class, keep hallways open, report problems to staff (S.D.: goal setting – breaking down tasks and reviewing steps of task for completion, self-monitoring – checking steps of getting to class on time)	P = Loud voices, lack of uniform, body contact T = (S.D.: self-monitor one's behaviors to maintain interactions that are appropriate and appropriately treating property and others' space)
Lunchroom	P = Not cleaning up T = Place tray in garbage when directed	P = Standing in line fighting, talking back to secretary T = Stay calm, stay in seat, wait your turn	P = Not in correct lunch period, wandering, not following staff directions T = Follow your schedule, stay in lunchroom, listen to staff, throw away trash	P = No ID and uniform, throwing food T = Keep food on tray
Extra Curricular Activities	P = Wandering halls T = Stay in activity	P = Yelling, language T =	P = Excessive trips to lockers, ignoring teachers' directives, cell phone usage T = Be in dress code and have ID	P = Hanging around lockers, running in the hall T = Go directly home or specific locations

Community	P= T=	P = Fighting, intimidating others, throwing trash on the ground T = Non-violent resolutions, throw trash in cans, ask for help. Be respectful on public transportation	P = Blocking sidewalks, jaywalking T = Give pedestrians room, cross at corners and crosswalks	P = Inappropriate language, horse play, sitting on doorways or porches that are not your own T = Use positive language. Recreate in designated areas off private property
Assemblies	P= T=	P = T = Transitioning on time. Stay in the theater. Listen to the program	P = T = Keep the auditorium clean and functional. Respect the equipment of the performers and presenters. Enter quickly and quietly, and a take seat. Leave when excused at end of program. Enter at correct time (wait for breaks in program)	P = T = Applaud at the end of each presentation without whistling, shouting, or yelling
Bathrooms	P = T =	P = T =	P = T =	P = Smoking, litter, graffiti T = Hazards of smoking, keep bathrooms clean (e.g., flush toilets) and smoke free

P= Typical problem   T= What you want the students to do, what you want to teach.

Table 13.4 Blank Teaching Matrix

	Classrooms	Hallways	Lunchroom	Extra Curriculars	Cyberspace
Expectation 1					
Expectation 2					
Expectation 3					
Expectation 4					
Expectation 5					

Application – Deciding Which Skills to Teach

Use the blank teaching matrix (Table 13.4) or your own matrix to identify specific skills you want to teach. Remember to use your data and relevant standards, and non-academic skills (e.g., mindsets). The locations may need to be changed based on your setting. We recommend that you add a cell related to cyberspace and/or social media space.

The items you bullet in the matrix are examples of what the expectation could look like in practice. You will not be able to include every scenario, nor should you. Your matrix is not an exhaustive list; rather, it includes the primary examples of how your school community would like to "live out" your selected expectations. In the next section, you learn ways to explicitly teach the skills you have deemed necessary for your community.

Connection – Teaching What You Expect

A high school teacher was really worried that her students were going to have trouble going to an assembly. She asked her students to line up and wait for her by the door to her room. Next, she ran out of the door and began yelling in the hall while waving her hands. She returned to the room and asked in a calm voice, what would be the problem if we all did that? Then she asked her students how she should have walked in the hall. Rather than yell at her students after they demonstrated a problem behavior, she pre-taught them what was expected. Following the lesson, the teacher reported that her students walked in the hall without disturbing other students.

Point/Principle – Teaching What You Expect

Directly teaching skills and expectations can lead to improvements in your overall school climate. Lauren Molloy found that teaching expected behaviors was connected to decreases in problem behaviors related to defiance of authority. She also found that teaching expectations was connected to decreases in discipline problems related to drug use and possession of controlled substances. This is probably because when time is spent teaching and discussing expectations, discipline becomes less about an "authority" demanding compliance, but rather mutually determined beliefs on how members of a community should act. This approach reduces the power struggles that could occur in more compliance-focused models.

Some components to consider when teaching non-academic expectations or skill sets to students include:

* Having a clear objective related to your schoolwide expectations
* Developing a clear rationale
* *Sometimes* providing non-examples of the skill (what not to do)
* Always providing examples of expectations (what does the desired behavior look like?)
* Some form of demonstration and/or practice of the behavior (teacher models, students all practice together, student volunteers models)
* Providing the students with feedback on their performance of the skill

Secondary teachers may need preparation, such as role playing or coaching, to help them get used to teaching non-academic skills. They are used to being content and academic skills experts. Using staff meetings or preparation periods to review the plans, then checking in and giving feedback and troubleshooting after a pilot attempt, is a good way to ease teachers into addressing behaviors in a proactive way.

BOX 13.3 PONDERING ON PURPOSE

* What are some examples of when you may want to review non-examples of skills with students?
* When might you NOT want to use non-examples?

The following provides an example lesson plan:

Objective: Students will be able to identify and demonstrate respectful behaviors in common areas when presented with a role play situation.

- Expectation: Be respectful
- Location: When talking with adults in hallways, classrooms, and assemblies
- Activity: Role play either with students or staff

Rationale (why this is important): Ask "Why is being respectful to adults important?" (Sample responses include: people treat you the way you treat them, it's nice, everyone is happier.)

- Negative Example:
    - Ask "What does it look like to be disrespectful to adults?"
    - (Sample responses include: yelling back, screaming, cursing, continuing to talk)
- Positive Example:
    - Ask "What does it look like to be respectful to adults?"
    - (Sample responses include: listening while others talk, using inside voice)

Practice: Students practice negative example first then positive. Tell the students (at this point you can discuss the negative example, have a small group demonstrate, or have all students demonstrate).

- Say "We are going to practice the wrong and the right way to _____. First, you are going to show us what being disrespectful looks like in _____. Then, we are going to practice it the right way."
- Say "Remember not to do anything that will get you sent to the office or sent home. Also, remember when I raise my hand you are to stop what you are doing! When I raise my hand, what are you to do?"
- "We will be looking for these sorts of behaviors in the fall. If you follow these expectations, you will have a much better experience at <insert name> High School."

Feedback/Assessment: How will you know they have learned the skill?

- Practice or discuss other situations e.g., "What should you do if asked for your ID in the hall?"
- Give feedback on the skill during unrelated activities (to help generalization of skill)

Table 13.5 Blank Lesson Plan for Teaching Expectations

Objective:

- Expectation:
- Location:
- Activity:

Rationale (why this is important):

- Non-Example (if needed):
- Example:

Practice:

Feedback/Assessment:

- How will you know they have learned the skill?
- Next Steps:

Application – Teaching What You Expect

If you have created your matrix, choose one area of concern for you (or colleagues). Use the lesson plan format provided in Table 13.5 to try to teach one expectation. You can also have students help you in targeting or developing the lesson. You can focus on academic, behavior, or social and emotional skills for your classroom, or on a variety of locations and events (e.g., homecoming, assemblies, major assessment days, Halloween).

Connection – The Rhythm of Teaching

Have you ever been in a class where the teacher only covered a topic once and then tested you on that skill? Can you remember the frustration you might have felt as you realized that, while the concept seemed familiar, you were not able to reproduce the skill? I (Hank) was once in a martial arts class with my son. We were being taught how to use a combination of blocks and punches. The instructor only demonstrated the skill once. Needless to say, my own demonstration was not up to par. Going over the skill once, even with good modeling, was not enough for us to be able to keep up with our classmates. Likewise, your students are going to need ongoing instruction over many of the expectations and skills you hope they will acquire. The rhythm of teaching refers to the frequency and timing of your explicit instruction.

Point/Principle – The Rhythm of Teaching

Think about teaching skills as part of a rhythm that you are trying to follow. For more formalized or packaged programs, such as an evidence-based social and emotional learning (SEL) program, you may have a very set routine to follow. This teaching routine may involve the exact skills and timing you need for developing your students' SEL skills.

Other approaches, such as schoolwide positive behavior support (SWPBS), will encourage you to think about key times of the year and specific skills to teach. Many of these decisions will be based on your schoolwide data. For example, one high school found they needed to re-teach skills related to respect in the classroom following times when students had significant time off, such as January (following a long winter holiday) and April (following a weeklong spring break). While other factors certainly could have contributed to this finding, the school saw statistically significant reductions in office discipline referrals following these two re-teaching events.

You can also focus on transition points between middle school and high school to teaching and re-teaching expectations. For example, Mimi McGrath Kato and her colleagues described a process for focusing specifically on freshmen. She highlights the need for teaching skills such as work completion (e.g., using planner, study plans, prioritizing), moving towards graduation (on-track, reading transcripts), and connecting to the school (e.g., productive coping, getting involved, teacher allies).

As mentioned in Chapter 6 on team development, it can be helpful to have subcommittees to support your schoolwide work. Having a subcommittee on teaching non-academic skills can be useful. This group can be comprised of staff and students who can help develop lessons, as needed, for your school setting. Their role would be to use your local data to identify the specific skills students need to learn to be successful. Developing a common location for storing and sharing lessons can be helpful for this team's work. Resources such as Google Drive can be a very helpful place for your teaching team to keep and distribute their work.

Videos, which can be developed in partnership with students, can also be a useful way to teach non-academic skills with consistency. There is a channel on Vimeo called *Homegrown SW-PBIS Videos* (see https://vimeo.com/groups/pbisvideos) that provides excellent examples of using videos to teach both adults and students skills. There are a few things, in our experience, to consider when developing videos.

- Staff should still directly teach and pre-correct (e.g., remind students of needed behaviors before an activity) students in addition to the videos
- Involve your school's media program if you have one
- Follow a lesson plan format such as the one outlined in this chapter

If you are teaching expectations to students within a SWPBS model, there are two websites you can go to see sample lesson plans. Go to PBIS.org to see secondary school examples of teaching norms in their settings. You can also see example of lesson plans across a variety of settings and occasions (e.g., preparing for exams, hallways, holidays) at Hank's website (www.hankbohanon.net).

Application – The Rhythm of Teaching

You can decide on the rhythm for your teaching of norms and skills based on the kinds of data you are reviewing and the focus of your schoolwide efforts. You can use Table 13.6 to help you identify the kinds of patterns you might be seeing when you develop your teaching plans. Again, if you are using an

Table 13.6 Using Data to Identify Patterns for Teaching Skills

Data Sources	Patterns
Office discipline data • Times of year when most problems occur? • Times of day? • Locations? • Types of behaviors? • What percentage of students are having discipline issues? • Is the proportion of students who are receiving ORDs discrepant from what you would expect based on your school's demographics (e.g., ethnicity, gender)?	
Academic data • What patterns are you seeing in your locally developed core assessments (e.g., rubrics)? • What patterns are you seeing in your disaggregated standardized test scores?	

Social and emotional skills
 	
• What kinds of skills do your screening data suggest that a majority of students need to develop?
  • Internalizing behaviors
  • Externalizing behaviors	

School climate • Based on any climate data (e.g., student connection surveys, safety surveys), what kinds of skills need to be taught or addressed to improve the overall school climate (e.g., bullying, peer-to-peer relations)?	

evidenced-based program that includes a schedule for lessons, you should follow the procedures that have been outlined for you. However, it is also a good idea to use data to make informed decisions about any changes you need to make to your plan. For example, if you are seeing a disproportionate number of students based on ethnicy or gender who are failing or are experiencing high rates of corrective discipline (e.g., suspensions), then your school might need to look at improving culturally relevant instruction.

Conclusion

Do not overlook the importance of dedicating time and resources to setting clear expectations in your setting. By including all stakeholders, you can establish culturally relevant expectations that focus on competencies like self-awareness, self-management, social awareness, relationship skills, and responsible decision making. To ensure all stakeholders know and understand the expectations, use creative marketing techniques including posting reminders strategically. Discuss, teach, and practice the expectations frequently, including providing verbal feedback and praise to reinforce desired outcomes. By planning out the "rhythm" you will use to teach the expectations (frequency, time of year, etc.), you can address trends proactively.

Bibliography

Bohanon, H., Castillo, J., & Afton, M. (2015). Embedding self-determination and futures planning within a schoolwide framework. *Intervention in School and Clinic, 50*(4), 203–209. Retrieved from http://ecommons.luc.edu/education_facpubs/16/

Bohanon, H., Fenning, P., Hicks, K., Weber, S., Thier, K., Aikins, B., … Hoeper, L. (2012). A case example of the implementation of schoolwide positive behavior support in a high school setting using change point test analysis. *Preventing School Failure: Alternative Education for Children and Youth, 56*(2), 91–103.

Center on Positive Behavioral Interventions and Supports. (2015). *Positive Behavioral Interventions and Supports (PBIS) Implementation Blueprint.* Eugene, OR: University of Oregon. Retrieved from www.pbis.org

Collaborative for Academic, Social, and Emotional Learning. (2020, March 27). *Core SEL competencies.* Chicago, IL: Collaborative for Academic, Social, and Emotional Learning. Retrieved from https://casel.org/core-competencies/

Farrington, C. A., Roderick, M., Allensworth, E., Nagaoka, J., Keyes, T. S., Johnson, D. W., & Beechum, N. O. (2012). *Teaching adolescents to become learners: The role of noncognitive factors in shaping school performance–a critical literature review.* Chicago, IL: Consortium on Chicago School Research.

Hicks, S. C., Rivera, C. J., & Patterson, D. R. (2016). Simple steps for teaching prepositions to students with autism and other developmental disabilities. *Intervention in School and Clinic, 51*(3), 163–169.

Horner, R. H., Todd, A. W., Lewis-Palmer, T., Irvin, L. K., Sugai, G., & Boland, J. B. (2004). The school-wide evaluation tool (SET): A research instrument for assessing schoolwide positive behavior support. *Journal of Positive Behavior Interventions, 6*(1), 3–12.

Hubbard, T. L. (2015). Forms of momentum across time: Behavioral and psychological. *The Journal of Mind and Behavior, 36*(1–2), 47–82.

Illinois State Social Emotional Learning Standards. (2019, December). Retrieved from www.isbe.net/Pages/Social-Emotional-Learning-Standards.aspx

Kato, M. M., Flannery, K. B., Triplett, D., & Sueteurn, S. Center for Positive Behavioral Interventions and Supports (funded by the Office of Special Education Programs, U.S. Department of Education). (2018). Investing in freshmen: Providing preventive support to 9th graders. Lessons learned on implementation of PBIS in high schools. In K. B. Flannery, P. Hershfeldt, & J. Freeman, (Eds.), *Lessons Learned on Implementation of PBIS in High Schools: Current Trends and Future Directions* (pp. 54–69). Eugene: University of Oregon Press.

Lynass, L., Tsai, S.-F., Richman, T. D., & Cheney, D. (2012). Social expectations and behavioral indicators in school-wide positive behavior supports. *Journal of Positive Behavior Interventions, 14*(3), 153–161. doi:10.1177/1098300711412076

Molloy, L. E., Moore, J. E., Trail, J., Van Epps, J. J., & Hopfer, S. (2013). Understanding real-world implementation quality and "active ingredients" of PBIS. *Prevention Science, 14*(6), 593–605.

Morrissey, K. L., Bohanon, H., & Fenning, P. (2010). Positive behavior support: Teaching and acknowledging expected behaviors in an urban high school. *Teaching Exceptional Children, 42*(5), 26–35.

National Governors Association Center for Best Practices & Council of Chief State School Officers. (2010). *Common Core State Standards.* Washington, DC: Authors.

Oklahoma State Department of Education. (2019, July). Oklahoma State Standards: English Standards. https://sde.ok.gov/sites/ok.gov.sde/files/documents/files/OAS-ELA-Final%20Version_0.pdf

Wehmeyer, M. (1997). Self-determination and positive adult outcomes: A follow-up study of youth with mental retardation or learning disabilities. *Exceptional Children, 63*(2), 245–255.

Zappo Insights. (2019, September). Zappos 10 core values. Retrieved from www.zapposinsights.com/about/core-values?gclid=CjwKCAjwmZbpBRAGEiwADrmVXiI5xMfwUxkN6OIqKYSav6R0jlV-pGAAA6lG3J9lB5ZAw9GTyYLfhhoCLXEQAvD_BwE

14

INCREASING STUDENT ENGAGEMENT

In a Nutshell

- Teachers have control over the environment which can lead to increased engagement for students.
- Engagement is a learned skill. Students' ability to be engaged varies just as much as other academic skills.
- Explicit instruction in academic mindset and self-determination skills increases others' perception of student motivation and engagement.
- Systematically addressing equity, racial bias, and culturally relevant practices can help to increase student engagement.
- There are instructional protocols and strategies that help encourage student engagement.

Introduction

Being engaged is an issue that crosses many areas of life. According to a Gallop poll, only 34% of American workers feel engaged at their job. As a teacher myself (Hank), there were times I was concerned that I did not have the undivided attention of every student in my class. However, have you ever looked around a faculty meeting to see how many people are actually on task? It is easy to see when other staff members are on Facebook or engaging in online shopping during a meeting. Just because you are physically in the meeting, does not mean you are present mentally.

We worry about engagement for a reason. According to Catherine Bradshaw, student engagement is an important factor of school climate. Christina Cipriano and her colleagues also found that schoolwide approaches can have a positive impact on student engagement, which was connected to improvements in student behavior. Additionally, Nancy Gonzales and colleagues found that school engagement mediated the effects of a schoolwide intervention. John Hattie also reported that improvement in the quality of student–teacher interactions is connected to improving the school experience. Student engagement matters.

Connection – Modeling and Teaching Academic Mindsets

High school graduation has become a calculated process, an algorithm of sorts. Follow these steps and you can get good grades and a diploma. Kids learn how to "do school" rather than how to learn. As a teacher, I (Lisa) stare out at the sea of faces and wonder how many of them are truly engaged. How many of my students are to develop their skills and gain knowledge, not to earn an "A," or go to a "good school." I worry about the disengaged but "successful" students, who follow the right steps, and pass, but to what end?

Point/Principle – Teaching Academic Mindsets

According to many employers and post-secondary settings, students leave school unprepared to independently tackle real-world challenges or navigate roadblocks that may come their way. Teaching academic mindsets provides students with tools to focus on learning as a apply. Students can apply academic mindsets to seek knowledge and drive action rather than a checkpoint on the path to graduation.

Practically speaking, many view engagement and motivation as interchangeable. As teachers, we may determine if a student is authentically motivated or not based on their willingness to complete the task at hand. This is not necessarily the case. Think about a time a student completed an assignment reluctantly. That is not true engagement, nor is it intrinsically motivated. Motivation related to earning good grades, attending a good school, or entering a specific career are considered extrinsic. All of these, though honorable, are separable outcomes, outside motivators for learning. They all come from learned external values and pressures that vary student to student based on culture, family background, community, socio-economic background, and life experiences. Developing a learning mindset is a key to student engagement.

Based on research by Carol Dweck of Stanford University, the academic or learning mindset teaches students to focus on growth of skills and knowledge, rather than "being smart." If a student believes that you must be "smart" to access knowledge, they look at their ability to gain and access information as something restrained by factors outside of their control. This "fixed" mindset makes it appear that no matter their efforts, students are limited by the intelligence they are born with. Having an academic mindset, also called growth mindset, helps set students on a path to engagement.

Teaching students how to have a growth mindset takes time but makes a significant impact in their learning. Some straightforward ways to embark on this process is to have students take a survey to identify their current level of growth mindset. In addition, I (Lisa) always start the school year by teaching my students that their brain is like a muscle. We talk about all the ways they practice and prepare for sports, and how the brain needs "workouts" to become strong. We also review pictures of neurons in the brain and discuss how when you learn something new the nerves grow and connect, making your brain stronger. If you are looking for useful instructional material for teaching mindsets, we recommend the website Mindsets Works (see https://www.mindsetworks.com/), as well as the book *Mindsets in the Classroom* by Mary Cay Ricci. Mary Cay's book includes lessons, assessments, and reproduceable documents that can help teachers provide students with direct instruction around mindsets.

Application – Modeling and Teaching Academic Mindsets

Use Table 14.1 to self-assess the level at which you currently focus on growth mindset in your classroom.

Table 14.1 Classroom Mindset Self-Reflection

	Always	Sometimes	Never
I use surveys and assessments to determine the mindsets of my students.			
I teach my students about metacognition (thinking about their thinking).			
I remind my students to engage in metacognition.			
I teach my students about neural networks in the brain.			
My positively reinforcing statements focus on effort, perseverance, process, and resilience, not intelligence or scores.			
I teach about the struggles people endured before achieving success.			

	Always	Sometimes	Never
When my students say a statement in a "fixed mindset," I help them reword it into a growth mindset.			
I use attribution checklists to help students properly attribute their actions to the results they see.			
I model independent thinking.			
I provide opportunities for my students to engage in procedural, organizational, and cognitive autonomy.			

Using the resources provided, consider incorporating mindset lessons into your instruction. As discussed in Chapter 13, find the "rhythm" that makes most sense for teaching mindset based on the students in front of you.

Connection – Equity for Engagement

We have mentioned the importance of considering issues around equity several times thus far. Equity does not happen simply by setting up a Black History Month display in main office, hosting a Gay–Straight Alliance club, or translating parent communications into students' home languages. Those are all nice, when done well; but they are not enough. Classrooms should include representation of all students' races and cultures in all things: the selected and highlighted texts, authors, scientists, and mathematicians; the types of holidays discussed or celebrated; etc. Representation in curricula seems like an "easy win," however middle and high school classrooms tend to be "steeped in tradition," which sometimes means you will have to "pry *Romeo and Juliet* out of that English teacher's cold dead hands." Facing implicit biases and getting to know our students as individuals separate from the demographics associated with them helps us to make more informed and individualized decisions. The alternative – making presumptions of others – is a dangerous path to wander down as educators if we want to be equitable in engaging our students.

Point/Principle – Equity for Engagement

I (Kelly) wish "being culturally responsive" could be summed up in one section of a book, in a way that was easily understood and acted upon, but it is a deep and complex topic. In general, students learn better when conditions in their schools and classrooms are such that the students feel *respected and valued because of* their race, ethnicity, culture, sexual orientation, and other identities, rather than *tolerated in spite of* those factors (or worse – targeted unfairly or ignored completely). Teachers and other staff members should "assume good intent" rather than judge students based on a set of norms and understandings that may be biased. Very few educators acknowledge holding prejudiced beliefs against certain groups of students, and few believe that their own implicit bias affects their instruction or their students. However, race and other demographic factors often do affect the way staff interact with students.

Schoolwide teams need to explicitly plan for ongoing professional development in the areas of equity, diversity, and cultural competency for the team, school and district leaders, and the staff at large, as well as key stakeholder groups from the community. Supporting those who identify as transgender or gender-fluid is essential. Though some might find it difficult, it is important to discuss issues such as racism, White supremacy, ableism, and homophobia. After speaking with students, be cautious not to disclose their identity with others (including parents). Making moves such as overhauling curricula to be racially and ethnically inclusive, eliminating course levels in order to decrease segregation, or setting policies to allow all students to use their bathroom of choice, can cause all kinds of reactions in people with all different types of backgrounds and views. Changing systems and practices to disrupt racism and discrimination, however, are crucial if we genuinely wish to include and engage all learners.

There are many helpful articles, books, and organizations available to help guide the way. For example, The Ontario Ministry of Education funded the Safe@School Project which has several toolkits and professional learning modules to help teachers address these issues. Harvard's Project Implicit provides an online quiz that will help you confront your attitudes and beliefs around a list of topics related to various stereotypes. Use these tools to develop your own personal awareness and that of your staff.

Application – Equity for Engagement

Choose one of the following options to reflect on your own (or your team's) cultural competence and comfort levels:

1. Choose a syllabus or text from one of your courses. What percent of the authors, scientists, historical figures, artists, musicians, etc. (depending on your content area) are:
    i. From a racial and ethnic group represented by your student population?
    ii. From a racial and ethnic group NOT represented by your student population?

    iii. From a country outside of North America or Europe?

    iv. Part of the LGBTQ+ community?

2. Examine your school data. How closely do the races of your staff mirror the races of your students, in terms of percentages? Why do you think the numbers are proportional or disproportional?

3. Interview a handful of Students of Color and students who identify as LGBTQ+ (with parent permission if you feel that is necessary), and do the same with a few staff members and community members. Ask if they feel the school culture welcomes, values, and supports them, and if they have any suggestions for improvements. Be sure to ask how well and often they see people from their own cultures reflected in the curriculum. A word of caution – NEVER assume someone speaks for an entire population holding a shared identity. One woman does not ever speak for all women across the world.

Connection – Student-to-Teacher Interactions

Think about a job or activity you were involved in where you really felt connected. What was it about the leader, coach, or teacher that made you feel good about your interactions with that person (at least most of the time). For me (Hank), there was a college professor who knew I had flunked out of the music program (turns out you have to practice your instrument). The professor would engage me in conversations about music. He would act very impressed if I knew the name of a piece of music (I did earn a C+ in music history). It was the first time that any teacher highlighted a strength that I had, rather than my weaknesses.

Point/Principle – Student-to-Teacher Interactions

The interactions between students and teachers also may influence how connected students feel to their school, and how well they perform academically. Scott Gest and his colleagues showed that students who are not at first intrinsically motived towards course content could be helped if they related to the teacher. Alternatively, low levels of teacher support and connection with the instructor may undermine student engagement. From the perspective of student-to-teacher interactions, we may have been asking the wrong questions about students and motivation. Rather than ask how to motivate students, perhaps we should ask how to increase the connection between adults and students.

    For example, Joseph Allen and colleagues at the University of Virginia looked at the interactions between teachers and students using a tool called the Classroom Scoring Assessment System (CLASS; see https://curry.

virginia.edu/classroom-assessment-scoring-system). The CLASS is used to student-to-teacher interactions across three areas: emotional support, classroom organization, and instructional support. Joseph found a connection between teacher and student interactions and student achievement. In classrooms with higher scores on the CLASS, failure rates moved from 17% to 11% on standardized test scores. Many of the skills that improve student-to-teacher interactions, as measured by the class, are not particularly complex. For example, teachers could increase engagement by:

- Teachers laughing with students (not at students)
- Giving students a choice on how to respond on assignment
- Providing an out of desk greeting
- Asking about life events like sports (not about their girlfriend/boyfriend)
- Asking students why they answered a question a certain way

There also are other ways to improve student-to-teacher interactions. Clay Cook and his colleagues at the University of Minnesota found that teachers who had five positive interactions for every one negative interaction with students had fewer problem behaviors and increased academic engagement in their classrooms. Some of the positive interactions included:

- Delivering specific praise (e.g., thanks or being on time)
- Providing approval statements
- Using positive non-verbal gestures (e.g., thumbs up) to specific students exhibiting expected behaviors or the entire class as a whole

---

BOX 14.1 PONDERING ON PURPOSE

Why do you think improved student-to-teacher interactions might improve student academic outcomes?

Application – Student-to-Teacher Interactions

As we have mentioned, many of the steps that improve student-to-teacher interactions are not difficult to implement. Consider using a system such as the CLASS to provide feedback and training related to improving student-to-teacher interactions for your staff. You can also apply Table 14.2 as a checklist to rank the steps you could systematically encourage your staff to try (even just one) that might improve student engagement.

Table 14.2 Strategies for Increasing Teacher-to-Student Engagement

Strategies for Increasing Teacher-to-Student Engagement
Rank order the strategies by preference
__ Laughing with students (not at students)
__ Giving students a choice on how to respond on assignment
__ Providing an out of desk greeting
__ Asking about life events like sports (not about their girlfriend/boyfriend)
__ Asking students why they answered a certain way
__ Delivering specific praise (e.g., thanks for being on time)
__ Providing approval statements
__ Using positive non-verbal gestures (e.g., thumbs up) to specific students exhibiting expected behaviors or the entire class as a whole
__ Other_____

Note: Strategies adapted from Allen et al. (2013), and Cook et al. (2017).

Connection – Instructional Approaches

Have you ever heard administrators joke about "formal observation phenomenon"? Also known as, "the one time a year a teacher attempts to use cooperative learning"? The lesson plan looks beautiful, but when the teacher asks the students to get in groups, the students look really confused. They may innocently (or not-so-innocently) ask things like, "Why are we doing this? We never move the desks!" This backfires because the students haven't had practice with the roles, SEL skills, and activities involved in learning together. The activity may look good on paper, but it is evident the students do not know how to engage in the process. Effective instructional approaches such as cooperative learning are wonderful at helping students engage in the classroom. As your read through the following examples, please recall the section on instructional routines from Chapter 12, for a reminder that "rinse and repeat" is important to effective implementation!

Point/Principle – Instructional Approaches

Instruction and student engagement are connected. Adam Lekwa and colleagues discovered a relationship between observer ratings of teacher practices and student engagement. In their study, higher quality instruction and behavior management were associated with higher student engagement. Their analysis of the results for their research revealed that instructional practice scores (as measured by the Classroom Strategies Assessment

System) predicted student academic engagement (i.e., attention and participation during instruction). In the case of their study, behavior management practice scores alone did not. In another study, Justin Cooper and Terry Scott found that what they referred to as high probability practices increased student engagement. These strategies for effective instruction included:

- Asking students questions
- Asking students to comment
- Giving students tasks
- Role plays that engaged students with the class content

In another example, Ann Danielsen found that what she called pedagogical caring and autonomy support was substantially related to students' academic initiative at the class level.

Pedagogical caring included:

- Allowing students to make choices
- Modeling strategies for students

Autonomy support included:

- Helping students to make independent choices

Providing students with frequent opportunities to respond is a great way to keep them engaged. Anita Archer and Charles Hughes provide recommendations for evidence-based explicit instruction techniques that require students to frequently speak, write, or respond in various ways. Both in their book, *Explicit Instruction* and on Anita Archers' website (explicitinstruction. org), you will find video examples of strategies for engaging students during instruction.

The Midwest Positive Behavior Intervention and Support Network (www. midwestpbis.org) also includes some excellent resources on opportunities to respond within the "Classroom Practices" section of their website. The techniques involve teaching students explicit signals and for how to interact with each other and the teacher. Next, the instructor prompts the students on a variety of ways to respond, using a "perky paced" lesson style that keeps all learners consistently interacting with the content. In this approach, the teacher should not talk for more than 40–50% of the lesson. The options for response include choral responding, mini dry erase boards, pair-and-shares, non-verbal signaling, and other techniques. Wait time for thinking is strategically built in to the lesson, as well as techniques to ensure that everyone participates in partner or group activities. Once the students and paired together and are sharing ideas, the teacher moves around the room to monitor responses and highlight the most pertinent or best ideas. Teachers can also revisit misconceptions with the whole group if needed.

I (Kelly) used Anita Archer's REWARDS reading program with high school students, and found that with practice, my students and I really enjoyed the methods. Applying the REWARDS program with my students made the class go by quickly. Students engaged the reading strategies so frequently that they retained them and made progress quickly. Attempting to weave in a few of these strategies consistently and reduce the percentage of time the teacher spends doing the talking would be a good starting point, but teachers should be sure to study the guidelines presented and use the strategies as designed. Approaches for increasing student engagement can be effective tier one "all in" strategies, as evidence exists that they improve both academic learning and behavior in the classroom.

Sometimes, a handful of students in the room repeatedly volunteer to contribute to class discussions. In the book *Total Participation Techniques*, Himmele and Himmele share 26 strategies teachers can implement to ensure every student in the classroom responds.

Technology has also allowed for similar engagement techniques that also track data for the teacher. Plickers is a free online tool. Students can see a graph of the responses and teachers can track students' scores. A few other technology tools that teachers can use to gather student responses include SurveyMonkey, Google Forms, and Poll Everywhere (Polleverywhere.com).

Other resources for engagement include Kylene Beers and Robert E. Probst's book on strategies for both fiction and non-fiction called *Notice and Note*. The routines described in their book help students to be engaged while they are reading and understand what parts of a text are important. The book *Making Thinking Visible* by Ron Ritchhart, Karen Morrison, and Mark Church also includes a variety of routines for increasing student engagement.

Inquiry Circles are also a great way to build student choice into your instruction. In their book *Comprehension & Collaboration: Inquiry Circles in Action*, Stephanie Harvey and Harvey Daniels share a variety of comprehension and collaboration strategies that make excellent instructional routines.

There are also many teaching strategies that involve movement to help students stay active and remember important information. For example, you can find many videos online that show how Total Physical Response and/or Whole Brain Teaching can be used in secondary settings. Other books that teachers have found useful in helping to build engagement in their classrooms are *Teaching Content Outrageously* and *Teach Like a Pirate*.

Application – Instructional Approaches

With so many tools available, it could be easy to try to do all in one lesson or select a new approach every day. Rather than try every strategy at once, pilot one at a time and practice it until it becomes intuitive to both you and your students.

BOX 14.2 PONDERING ON PURPOSE

What is one evidence-based approach you have found useful in your work increase engagement for secondary level students?

Conclusion

There are many factors that affect a student's ability and motivation to engage in the classroom. It can be overwhelming to read through a chapter like this one. Imagining the amount of learning, planning, professional development, and coaching it would take to implement these strategies schoolwide consistently could be offputting. The good news is, there are common threads among the approaches. The keys to engagement include developing strong relationships with and between students and setting up the learning situation in a way that all learners can actively participate in the lesson. Choosing one factor or strategy to start with, and developing it systematically, is a good antidote to feeling overwhelmed!

Bibliography

Allen, J., Gregory, A., Mikami, A., Lun, J., Hamre, B., & Pianta, R. (2013). Observations of effective teacher–student interactions in secondary school classrooms: Predicting student achievement with the classroom assessment scoring system—secondary. *School Psychology Review*, *42*(1), 76–98.

Ames, C. A. (1990). Motivation: What teachers need to know. *Teachers College Record*, *91*(3), 409–421.

Anderman, L. H., & Midgley, C. (1998). Motivation and middle school students. Retrieved from http://eric.ed.gov/?id=ED421281

Archer, A. L., & Hughes, C. A. (2011). *Explicit instruction: Effective and efficient teaching.* New York, NY: Guilford Press.

Barbetta, P. M., Heron, T. E., & Heward, W. L. (1993). Effects of active student response during error correction on the acquisition, maintenance, and generalization of sight words by students with developmental disabilities. *Journal of Applied Behavior Analysis*, *26*, 111–120.

Beers, K., & Probst, R. E. (2013). *Notice & note: Strategies for close reading.* Portsmouth, NH: Heinemann.

Bradshaw, C. P., Waasdorp, T. E., Debnam, K. J., & Johnson, S. L. (2014). Measuring school climate in high schools: A focus on safety, engagement, and the environment. *Journal of School Health, 84*(9), 593–604. doi:10.1111/josh.12186

Bremer, C. D., Kachgal, M., & Schoeller, K. (2003). Self-determination: Supporting successful transition. *Research to Practice Brief: Supporting Secondary Education and Transition Services through Research, 2*(1), 1–4. Retrieved from http://www.ncset.org/publications/researchtopractice/NCSETResearchBrief_2.1.pdf

Burgess, D. (2012). *Teach like a pirate*. San Diego, US: Dave Burgess Consulting.

Carnine, D. W. (1976). Effects of two teacher-presentation rates on off-task behavior, answering correctly, and participation. *Journal of Applied Behavior Analysis, 9*(2), 199–206.

Cabeza, B., Magill, L., Jenkins, A., Carter, E. W., Greiner, S., Bell, L., & Lane, K. L. (2013). *Promoting self-determination among students with disabilities: A guide for Tennessee educators*. Nashville, TN: Vanderbilt University.

Cipriano, C., Barnes, T. N., Rivers, S. E., & Brackett, M. (2019). Exploring changes in student engagement through the RULER approach: An examination of students at risk of academic failure. *Journal of Education for Students Placed at Risk (JESPAR), 24*(1), 1–19. doi:10.1080/10824669.2018.1524767

Collaborative for Academic, Social and Emotional Learning (CASEL). (2015). State scan scorecard project. Retrieved from www.casel.org/state-scan-scorecard-project

Cook, C. R., Grady, E. A., Long, A. C., Renshaw, T., Codding, R. S., Fiat, A., & Larson, M. (2017). Evaluating the impact of increasing general education teachers' ratio of positive-to-negative interactions on students' classroom behavior. *Journal of Positive Behavior Interventions, 19*(2), 67–77. doi:10.1177/1098300716679137

Cooper, J. T., & Scott, T. M. (2017). The keys to managing instruction and behavior: Considering high probability practices. *Teacher Education and Special Education,* 0888406417700825. doi:10.1177/1098300716679137

Cooper, K. (2014). 6 Common mistakes that undermine motivation. *Phi Delta Kappan, 95*(8), 11–17.

Council for Exceptional Children. (1987). The winds of opportunity: Chicago CEC convention 1987. *Teaching Exceptional Children, 20*(1), 68–71. doi:org/10.1177/004005998702000121

Danielsen, A. G. (2010). Perceived support provided by teachers and classmates and students' self-reported academic initiative. *Journal of school psychology, 48*(3), 247–267. doi:10.1016/j.jsp.2010.02.002

Mindset Works. (n.d.). Decades of scientific research that started a growth mindset revolution. Retrieved from www.mindsetworks.com/webnav/whatismindset.aspx

National Gateway to Self-Determination. (n.d.) What is self-determination? Retrieved from www.ngsd.org/everyone/what-self-determination

Dweck, C. (2015). Carol Dweck revisits the growth mindset. *Education Week, 35*(5), 20–24.

Gest, S. D., Welsh, J. A., & Domitrovich, C. E. (2005). Behavioral predictors of changes in social relatedness and liking school in elementary school. *Journal of school psychology, 43*(4), 281–301.

Gonzales, N., Wong, J., Toomey, R., Millsap, R., Dumka, L., & Mauricio, A. (2014). School engagement mediates long-term prevention effects for Mexican American adolescents. *Prevention Science, 15*(6), 929–939.

Harter, J. (2018). Employee engagement on the rise in the U.S. Gallup. Retrieved from https://news.gallup.com/poll/241649/employee-engagement-rise.aspx

Harvard Extension School. (2019, December). 10 emerging skills for professionals. Retrieved from www.extension.harvard.edu/professional-development/blog/10-emerging-skills-professionals

Harvey, S., & Daniels, H. (2009). *Comprehension & collaboration: Inquiry circles in action.* Portsmouth, NH: Heinemann.

Harvey, S., & Daniels, H. S. (2009). *Comprehension and collaboration: Inquiry circles for curiosity, engagement, and understanding.* Portsmouth, NH: No. Heinemann.

Hattie, J. (2008). *Visible learning: A synthesis of over 800 meta-analyses relating to achievement.* London, England: Routledge.

Himmele, P., & Himmele, W. (2017). *Total participation techniques: Making every student an active learner.* Alexandria, VA: ASCD.

Johnson, D. W., & Johnson, R. T. (2011). Cooperative learning. In D. J. Christie (Ed.), *The Encyclopedia of Peace Psychology.* John Wiley & Sons. Retrieved from http://ecoasturias.com/images/PDF/ponencia_zaragoza_David_Johnson.pdf

Jones, S. M., & Bouffard, S. M. (2012). Social emotional learning in schools from programs to strategies. *Social Policy Report, 26*(4), 1–22. Retrieved from www.acknowledgealliance.org/wp-content/uploads/srcd-policy-brief-sel-in-schools.pdf

Kagan, S., & Kagan, M. (2009). *Kagan Cooperative Learning.* San Clemente, CA: Kagan Publishing.

Lekwa, A. J., Reddy, L. A., & Shernoff, E. S. (2019). Measuring teacher practices and student academic engagement: A convergent validity study. *School Psychology Quarterly, 34*(1), 109–118.

National Gateway to Self-Determination. (n.d.). What is self-determination? Retrieved from www.ngsd.org/everyone/what-self-determination

Pogrow, S. (2010). *Teaching content outrageously: How to captivate all students and accelerate learning, grades 4–12.* Bridgewater, NJ: John Wiley & Sons.

Project Implicit. (n.d.) Retrieved from https://implicit.harvard.edu/implicit/takeatest.html

Reinke, W. M., Herman, K. C., & Stormont, M. (2013). Classroom-level positive behavior supports in schools implementing SW-PBIS: Identifying areas for enhancement. *Journal of Positive Behavior Incentives, 15*(10), 39–50.

Ricci, M. C. (2013). *Mindsets in the Classroom.* Waco, TX: Prufrock Press.

Ritchhart, R., Church, M., & Morrison, K. (2011). *Making thinking visible: How to promote engagement, understanding, and independence for all learners.* Hoboken, NJ: John Wiley & Sons.

Ryan, R. M., & Deci, E. L. (2000). Intrinsic and extrinsic motivations: Classic definitions and new directions. *Contemporary Educational Psychology, 25,* 54–67.

Safe@School. (n.d.) Lesson plans and toolkits. Retrieved from www.safeatschool.ca/resources/resources-on-equity-and-inclusion/racism/tool-kits-and-activities

Salend, S. J. (2011). *Creating inclusive classrooms: Effective and reflective practices* (7th ed.). Upper Saddle River, NJ: Merrill Prentice Hall.

Schloss, P. J., & Smith, M. A. (1998). *Applied behavior analysis in the classroom.* Boston, MA: Allyn & Bacon.

Schreiner, M. B. (2007). Effective self-advocacy: What students and special educators need to know. *Intervention in School and Clinic, 47*(5), 300–304.

Stang, K. K., Carter, E. W., Lane, K. L., & Pierson, M. R. (2009). Perspectives of general and special educators on fostering self-determination in elementary and middle schools. *The Journal of Special Education, 43*(2), 94–106.

Stefanou, C. R., Perencevich, K. C., DiCintio, M., & Turner, J. C. (2004). Supporting autonomy in the classroom: Ways teachers encourage student decision making and ownership. *Educational Psychologist, 39*(2), 97–110.

Sutherland, K. S., Alder, N., & Gunter, P. L. (2003). The effect of varying rates of opportunities to respond to academic requests on the classroom behavior of students with EBD. *Journal of Emotional and Behavioral Disorders, 11*(4), 239–248.

Sutherland, K. S., & Wehby, J. H. (2001). The effect of self-evaluation on teaching behavior in classrooms for students with emotional and behavioral disorders. *The Journal of Special Education, 33*(3), 161–171.

Transforming Education. (n.d.). What is a growth mindset, and why does it matter? Retrieved from www.transformingeducation.org/growth-mindset-toolkit/

van Uden, J. M., Ritzen, H., & Pieters, J. M. (2014). Engaging students: The role of teacher beliefs and interpersonal teacher behavior in fostering student engagement in vocational education. *Teaching and Teacher Education, 37*, 21–32.

Wehmeyer, M. L. (1995). The Arc's self-determination scale: Procedural guidelines. Retrieved from www.thearc.org/document.doc?id=3671

West, R. P., & Sloane, H. N. (1986). Teacher presentation rate and point delivery rate: Effects on classroom disruption, performance accuracy, and response rate. *Behavior Modification, 10*(3), 267–286.

What is a growth mindset, and why does it matter. (n.d.). www.transformingeducation.org/growth-mindset-toolkit/

Wolman, J. M., Campeau, P. J., Mithaug, D. E., & Stolarski, V. S. (1994). *AIR self-determination scale and user guide.* Retrieved from www.ou.edu/content/dam/Education/documents/miscellaneous/air-self-determination-user-guide.pdf

Yang, C., Bear, G. G., & May, H. (2018). Multilevel associations between school-wide social-emotional learning approach and student engagement across elementary, middle, and high schools. *School Psychology Review, 47*(1), 45–61.

Yemen, G., & Clawson, J. G. (2003). *The locus of control.* The University of Virginia Darden School Foundation. Retrieved from https://faculty.darden.virginia.edu/clawsonj/General/SELF_ASSESSMENT_TOOLS/OB-786_Locus_of_Control.pdf

15

IMPROVING ACADEMIC AND BEHAVIORAL PERFORMANCE THROUGH FEEDBACK AND ACKNOWLEDGEMENT

In a Nutshell

- We are always providing feedback, be purposeful about it.
- Consider the culture of students' families and their views on feedback and acknowledgement.
- Use feedback and acknowledgement intentionally to reinforce desired behaviors, or prevent undesired behaviors.
- Feedback must be timely, specific, genuine, age appropriate, and given frequently.
- Acknowledgement comes in a variety of formats. Use the format that is valued by the person you are acknowledging. Aim for a 5:1 ratio of positive interactions to corrective statements.
- Use data to reflect on feedback and acknowledgement to establish cycles of improvement in implementation and effectiveness.
- Don't forget the adults in your setting.

Introduction

According to the book *Lead with LUV*, Southwest Airlines spends a great deal of energy on providing feedback to their employees by acknowledging their behavior. For example, they have parties for employees to acknowledge their hard work and print compliments from customers in their magazine. These celebrations are designed to encourage their team members to continue to carry out behaviors that are helpful to their customers and their company. Sometimes we hear that when students enter the "real world" of work that no one is going to praise them for their efforts. The truth of the matter is providing feedback and acknowledgement of the work of employees is a sign of a successful organization. Southwest's approach follows Albert Bandura's statement that what is rewarded is repeated. Feedback, as Ken Blanchard the author of *Lead with LUV* stated, is *the breakfast of champions*!

Feedback, a potential form of acknowledgment, happens whether we intend it or not. It comes in many forms and does not necessarily need to be tangible or verbal. Experiencing success in an endeavor can encourage us to keep trying even when the task is difficult. Regardless of its form, feedback can help encourage students to develop new behaviors and skills. Schools can use feedback as part of instruction to encourage academic, behavioral, and social and emotional skills. Many feedback strategies can be easily incorporated into instruction and tend to provide quick and easy "wins" when done correctly. Remember this sentence: aspirin does not cure every headache, but it's still useful.

Connection – What We Know about Feedback, Acknowledgement, and Outcomes

I (Lisa) once read a study by Richard Miller, Philip Brickman, and Diana Bolen on attribution theory. Before the study, they took data on the cleanliness of classrooms and noted they were all equal in terms of their "cleanliness." Over the course of a week, the teacher, principal, and janitor made specific praising comments to a class about the cleanliness and tidiness of each classroom. In another classroom, the researchers taught the students about the effects of litter and asked them to keep their room clean. After a few days, the classroom that was provided praise and acknowledgement continued to be significantly cleaner than other classrooms where student praise was not a focus, even weeks later. They repeated the study by providing specific positive feedback to students regarding their ability and motivation to complete a math task and got the same results. Students who received praise outperformed their peers who were simply taught how to complete a math related task.

Howard Wills and colleagues found in their study that increases in specific praise and decreases in reprimands, along with other effective teaching strategies, increased students' on-task behavior. Wendy Reinke, Keith Herman, and Melissa Stormont found in their research that teachers who had higher levels of reprimand and used general praise (rather than specific) felt more exhausted and less effective than their counterparts who had higher positive to negative ratios. These studies provide evidence that specific and positive praise can improve outcomes and maintains them over time.

Point/Principle – What We Know about Feedback, Acknowledgement, and Purposeful Outcomes

Joseph Allen and colleagues suggest that feedback includes what we share with students based on their performance on academic tasks. The goal of quality feedback is to challenge students and expand their understanding of a concept. Along with other instructional factors, quality feedback for students has been associated with higher standardized test scores. Justin Cooper and Terry Scott suggest that providing students with feedback is part of an effective way to manage both instruction and behavior.

While praise alone is nice, using specific praise is what makes the most difference. To understand the difference, try this. If you are sitting with a colleague, tell them, "There is something about you that I appreciate." Awkward! Now, tell your colleague "I really appreciate that you … (e.g., are so helpful to me, etc.)." Though they may feel happy to hear you appreciate them, the second version will probably enhance their delight and increase the chances of them repeating the behavior in the future. Telling students "good job" is vague, and they may either not know, or misunderstand what you are praising.

Feedback also comes in the form of natural consequences and impacts whether we repeat behaviors. For example, Glen Dunlap and his colleagues implemented a study where they modified activities to be meaningful to students. This made the reward less extrinsic because the outcome of the task itself was rewarding.

There are times when external rewards can help you to develop new skills. Charles Duhigg described in his book *The Power of Habit*, that all habits involve a cue or prompt, a routine, and some type of reward. Many teachers worry that tangible rewards will decrease motivation or undermine students' success later in life, but balance is key. When students are not showing signs of intrinsic motivation, rewards paired with specific feedback can help "get the ball rolling" with an academic or behavioral skill. External rewards can help students gradually start to experience the social connectedness and internal feelings of success that are paired with a target skill.

Application – What We Know about Feedback, Acknowledgement, and Outcomes

It is almost impossible to name a behavior that is done for no reason at all. People typically engage in behaviors to access an object, escape or avoid something unpleasant, gain attention (good or bad), or because they are over- or under-stimulated. Learning why a person is engaging in a behavior can help connect you to a solution or meaningful outcome that might address the students' needs. Use Table 15.1 to choose a strategy to try out, perhaps with a student with challenging behaviors, and reflect on the outcomes.

The climate and culture of the classroom and school is important in establishing strong feedback and acknowledgement cycles. Feedback and acknowledgement that encourages us to repeat behaviors we already do is easy to receive. Valuable feedback, however, often includes confronting an error or false assumption. Without a strong growth mindset, feedback

Table 15.1 Matching Intervention Strategies to Students' Function of
Problem Behavior

Function of student's undesired behavior	Strategy	Examples that increase feedback and acknowledgement
Access an object (e.g., cell phone, computer games)	• Use surveys to determine preferred content/methods to incorporate in lesson • Outcomes lead to something purposeful (social, tangible, preferred activity, object)	• Use web-based quiz software • Allow student to engage in debate • In math class, allow students to complete word problems to figure out how to save money for a video game system (Xbox, Playstation, etc.)
Escape or avoid	• Errorless learning • Allow the student to escape task, in the short run • Assignment expectations match student skills and expectations (independent, guided, frustrational level) • Task interspersal (mixing hard and easy tasks, preferred and non-preferred)	• Have your target word on the board and tell students "I'm looking for a word." • Allow a student to ask for a break if they are frustrated • Check the level of assignment and consider your students' ability levels before you have them engage in the assignment. Provide support accordingly. • Build momentum by starting with more accessible problems before taking on challenges • Change between familiar and unfamiliar problems on a math assignment
Attention	• Incorporate social interaction • If/then social reward • Cooperative groups	• Allowing students to socialize as a part of group activities • If you let me start on time, I will give you some time back to socialize at the end of class • Assigning students to roles in their success zone (e.g., reporter if they cannot read or write well, timekeeper, task manager)

(Continued)

Table 15.1 (continued)

Function of student's undesired behavior	Strategy	Examples that increase feedback and acknowledgement
Over or under stimulated	• Breaks (biofeedback) teach students to pay attention to signs of biological needs (yawning, hydration, alertness, heart rate, muscle tension) • Self-check (self-monitoring)	• Everyone stands up and stretches for one minute after 45 minutes of work. Use stretching, yoga, mindfulness breaks, individualized breaks, relaxing music during independent work, sound blocking headphones, dividers, etc. • Teacher sets a random timer. When the timer goes off, student checks "yes" or "no" to being "on tasks."

could trigger defensiveness and even trigger undesirable behaviors. In addition, the culture of the students and their families are important to consider. Some cultures have different expectations and perceptions of feedback and acknowledgement and how it is presented. For peer-to-peer feedback to be positive and effective, students need to be taught how to provide feedback and the climate must support a growth mindset.

Connection – How to Provide Feedback

According to a large-scale meta-analysis from John Hattie, feedback has a major positive impact on learning, but only when done well. It is one of the top influencers of student achievement, yet studies show that a third of feedback given is actually detrimental to performance. Examples of this can vary in severity. For example, many teachers may have experienced giving an overarching comment like "everyone is doing a great job right now" to a quiet classroom and then a minute later all the students are chatting. Without an understanding of why the teacher commented, the students assumed their work was "done" and began socializing. Or, while trying to seek an explanation for a correct response the teacher asks "why did you respond this way?", only to have the student erase their work assuming it was wrong. It's important to give feedback, but not just any feedback. It must be timely, specific, genuine, age appropriate, and given frequently (which varies depending on whether learners are acquiring a new skill or practicing for fluency or maintenance).

Point/Principle – How to Provide Feedback

Feedback can take many forms, but it should be given in a way that guides the learner toward a goal, and the goal must be clear. In order to make feedback valuable and effective, make sure there is an opportunity to keep improving performance. Providing feedback only in summative assessments such as a final exam, when students cannot make improvements, is not worthwhile.

Provide feedback in a way that helps the learner feel coached and supported. Ideally, students know where they are in the progression of skills moving toward a learning goal. If so, they can determine where they are "stuck" or struggling and ask for feedback in those areas. Daniel Wilson created a "Ladder of Feedback" (see http://www.pz.harvard.edu/) that was turned into a protocol by Project Zero Classroom's Making Learning Visible. The ladder walks participants through the steps deemed "best practice" for giving high-quality feedback that will improve outcomes for the person receiving it. You can find more detailed information about this protocol and the steps on their website, but the steps are summarized below.

- **Clarify** – ask questions to understand
- **Value** – what stood out as strong
- **Raise Questions & Concerns** – questions and thoughts – not judgements
- **Suggest** – build upon existing ideas
- **Thank** – share what you learned

These general guidelines sound logical on paper but consider the high school teacher who sees 150 students per day. The traditional model of feedback may include: students turn in the essay, the teacher grades 150 essays and writes many corrections on each one. A week later, the student glances at their score and throws it in the garbage because the class has moved on. By taking these larger assignments/assessments and breaking them into smaller parts, teachers can provide specific goals for each component. The students then use the feedback to improve on the assignment as a whole or create a more developed final product.

BOX 15.1 PONDERING ON PURPOSE

- Think of a larger summative assessment you might give students. Make a list of specific skills you typically provide feedback on within that assessment.
- How can you build in opportunities to give that feedback prior to the final submission of the assessment?
- How might that feedback strengthen student outcomes both for the assignment and in future performance?

I (Kelly) developed a few symbols to highlight areas where students either nailed the assignment (e.g., I underlined their evidence) or needed to make some progress (e.g., I circled problem areas related to skill 1 and put an asterisk next to problem areas related to skill 2). I stopped writing comments or correcting things for the students, and instead planned workshop time in class where they could review the skills and examples, and work in pairs, individually, or with me to redo sections and resubmit.

I also focused on improving my verbal feedback, with a shift from comments like "Good job!" to statements like, "Wow, you chose a great quote to show why that argument is weak!" I found quick ways to formatively assess how students were progressing, using bell ringers, exit slips, and quick dry-erase activities during class. Each of these provided a chance for me to give quick feedback, or have learners self-assess: "Check your response, does it include X,Y, and Z? If so, you are right on track!"

To maximize the effectiveness of feedback, model your instruction like a coach instead of a judge. A coach "runs drills" (isolating skills that need practice) and gives frequent feedback to tweak performance. The summative assessment is then like the actual game. During the game the coach may cheer from the sidelines and provide small amounts of feedback, but now the team/players' performance is judged and they are provided points for their final performance.

In order to be able to give effective feedback, assessments and instruction must be well designed. We suggest beginning by revisiting the plans and goals for the content you are seeking to improve, then plan opportunities for students to practice and receive feedback along the way. Students should know their learning goals and have opportunities to self-assess. In order to track performance within the gradebook, teachers can be creative to include scores related to the application of feedback or include smaller skill-specific assessments. Ideally, students will not take a summative (graded) assessment until formative assessments indicate they are ready to perform well.

Application – How to Provide Feedback

Consider the methods you use to provide feedback utilizing the following lists. How frequent is feedback provided to students? Is it tailored to the needs of the students? Does the feedback involve specific evidence? Is feedback used for the teachers (diagnostic, planning) as well as the students (development of skills)?

- Format for Feedback
  - Verbal (in person, recorded)
  - Non-verbal (handwritten, tech-based, using pictures, words, symbols)
  - Public vs. private

- Source of Feedback
  - Teacher
  - Peer
  - Self
  - Community "experts"

BOX 15.2 PONDERING ON PURPOSE

- With a colleague, each select a piece of student work to practice providing feedback using Harvard's Project Zero Feedback Ladder through role play (see http://www.pz.harvard.edu/).
- This practice works best with an authentic assignment (word problem, writing assignment, etc.).
- Have one colleague be the teacher and the other be the student.

Connection – Providing Acknowledgement

Many people, especially educators in secondary settings, make statements against acknowledgement (rewarding good behavior). Consider the disdain for "everyone gets a trophy" culture. This uproar comes from a tainted perspective of what true acknowledgment could and should be. I (Lisa) love to do triathlons. They take a lot of time, energy, and commitment. Almost every triathlon I have entered provides the finisher with a medal. I doubt anyone would complete in a triathlon just for the medal. But given a choice, I would select to sign up for a race that provided one over a competition that did not. Sometimes the existence of the acknowledgement does not change the behavior, but at the very least it makes engaging in the behavior more enjoyable and satisfying, making it more likely to be repeated.

Point/Principle – Providing Acknowledgement

What's wrong with this scenario? A teacher wants the students to complete 20 worksheets, so he provides a cookie for each completed worksheet. Let us guess. You are thinking:

- I don't believe in/our school does not allow tangible rewards.
- The student will become unhealthy due to the high sugar diet.
- We should not have to reward students for doing their work.
- There might be a cookies shortage, then what will we do?

We could go on, but the larger and more important question is why is the student doing 20 worksheets? Tangible rewards are the ones that most people take issue with, and we do understand why there are concerns. Often, the reward is not tied to the learning target and does not add meaning to the task or the outcome.

In his book *Drive*, Daniel Pink talks about two kinds of rewards. The first kind involves if/then rewards. For example, if a person does something that is desirable, then that individual will earn something. Daniel suggests that this is where we typically need to start when we support a new skill. For example, students might be told they can have five minutes to socialize at the end of class if they begin their work on time and stay on task. Framing can be instrumental here. Consider the difference it makes if you propose the reward by explaining it as a self-regulation strategy. "When we have a hard task to do, we can reward ourselves after we complete it." Offer a personal example such as treating yourself after reaching a workout goal or dinner out after a long and tiring workday.. Now picture it as a bribe. "If you all do this worksheet I'll let you talk later." A simple strategy of pairing the if/then reward with a self-determination strategy turns this method into a life skill for self-motivation and goal setting.

The second type of reward involves "now that …". In this case, students may not have known that a reward is coming, but they receive it based on their performance. For example, one high school teacher told her students that since they did a great job on their civics assignment, they could have a debate instead of quiz. The students did not know the debate was coming, but it was a reward for their performance. These students had already been taught and acknowledged for being responsible in the class. This can be paired with a reminder about how doing your best even when you think no one is looking can pay off. Again, a great life skill lesson.

Here are a few things to consider when thinking about specific praise as a form of acknowledgement and reward:

- Keep your praise to corrective statements to a 5:1 ratio.
- Be specific with your praise (for example, "Thank you for being respectful and showing me your ID when I asked for it.").
- Recognize students immediately after seeing behavior.
- Be genuine: Convey sincerity with tone of voice and body language, message, and choice of behavior to acknowledge (avoid patronizing).
- Tokens or points can be useful as a concrete representation of a job well done. However, we recommend not taking away rewards that students have earned as a form of punishment.
- Use vicarious reinforcement. Acknowledge a student who is meeting your expectation when others are not: "I really appreciate the productivity of group one. You all have your books open and are taking notes." As the other groups get on task, praise them.

- When given a choice between acknowledging students for completing a tedious task, or making the assignment more engaging, focus on making the work more appealing.

As already mentioned, with acknowledgement, framing is important. Token economies (e.g., tickets, points that can be turned in for rewards) frequently generates the most pushback from educators, especially in secondary settings. However, if used intentionally, they can be effective. For example, I (Lisa) had a student once who struggled with social interactions with peers. The student would frequently not be able to accurately identify whether or not they had a "good" day. The student was not making the connection to the impact his behaviors had on those around him. We created a point system tied to five specific "high impact" desirable behaviors we wanted to increase. The student reported that he really liked the point system because it helped them in a concrete way to determine if he had a good day. As a reward, the student selected a few activities that involved peers, as well as a few smaller "quick win" items. When he earned a quick win item, he also received one to share with a peer, which reinforced positive relationships. One of the larger "prizes" was earning the opportunity to have a root beer float while watching a Netflix show of their choice with a peer during lunch. It took about six weeks to earn this acknowledgement, but it was motivating to the student, reinforced positive interactions, and gave the student a concrete way to monitor a more abstract concept (positive peer interactions).

Acknowledgement does not need to be verbal or concrete, but the desire for acknowledgement is at the core of most relationship issues regardless if they are personal or professional. Gary Chapman wrote the book *The 5 Languages of Appreciation in the Workplace: Empowering Organizations by Encouraging People.* He also has other versions of this book that apply the same concept to relationships with teenagers and with children. According to Gary, people have five ways in which they show appreciation. The way most people show appreciation may not necessarily match the way they want to receive appreciation. The five languages are words of affirmation, acts of service, receiving gifts, quality time, and physical touch. Some students or co-workers might respond better when you verbally acknowledge their actions, others might be encouraged by a fist bump or high five. Many high school teachers dismiss the idea of rewarding a student. But, think about a time someone acknowledged you, using one of the language we just shared, that was most meaningful to you. Think about the impact it had on your emotional connection to that person and/or that task/action at hand.

Application – Providing Acknowledgement

Clay Cook and his colleagues found that in classrooms in their study where teachers gave five positive praises for every one negative correction, there were fewer disruptions and increased academic engagement. Do you follow this 5:1 ratio of acknowledgement? When you provide consistent, proactive acknowledgement, it might make corrections easier to accept.

You can use data to reflect on how you provide acknowledgement. For example, I (Hank) once had one of my students watch me teach for 20 minutes and count how many positive to negative statements I made. The feedback from these data helped me to reflect on my own teaching. Other strategies might include moving a paper clip from one pocket to another every time you make a specific praise statement to a student and moving it back once you make a corrective statement. You could also use a golf counter application on a smartphone or watch to keep track. You can select whatever strategy works best for your setting.

Another option is to take a quiz on "The Languages of Appreciation in the Workplace." This tool can help you discover which appreciation manifestation you value most. Knowing what your students (and colleagues) value can help you provide them with acknowledgement they will most appreciate and recognize.

BOX 15.3 PONDERING ON PURPOSE

- How do you like to receive acknowledgement from others?
- Is this the same way you give others acknowledgement?
- Does the amount of acknowledgement you receive (plenty, not enough) impact the quantity and quality of effort/work you do for that person/company?
- Consider how acknowledgement impacts your spending habits. What marketing strategies have worked on you? Why?

Select an acknowledgement strategy to implement and use Table 15.2 to help you reflect on your practice.

Table 15.2 Reflecting on Your Acknowledgement Strategy

Prompt	Your reflection
What acknowledgement strategy did you try this week?	
What was the impact on the student's or students' behavior (if any)?	
How did you feel about using the strategy?	
What could you improve next time you try the strategy?	

Connection – Schoolwide Feedback, Acknowledgement, and Purposeful Outcomes

My wife and I (Hank) sometimes respond differently to requests from our children. If one of our sons asks my wife for a piece of candy and she says no, they will come to me, leaving out that they have already asked their mom. At first, I would allow them to have the candy. Eventually I caught on. The inconsistency between the adults in the house was discouraging unified expectations of behaviors. Our boys needed to know we would give a consistent response. This goes for our students as well.

Point/Principal – Schoolwide Feedback, Acknowledgement, and Purposeful Outcomes

When providing feedback schoolwide, the key is having routines, a culture of growth mindset, and clear expectations for tasks whether academic or behavior-related. You can use Table 15.3 to reflect on your school's overall approach to providing feedback to students.

When planning schoolwide acknowledgement, there are typically three levels to think about: immediate, frequent acknowledgement, unpredictable intermediate boosters, and schoolwide. How you address these levels can vary based on the climate, culture, and goals of your setting. Table 15.4 is an example of the levels of acknowledgment you can use in your school.

Table 15.3 Feedback Schoolwide

Consideration	Notes	How will implementation and/or effectiveness be monitored? How often?
Which feedback routines/systems/ protocols will we use as a school? For example: peer feedback protocols, feedback ladder, formative assessment routines (exit slips, stop lights, "3, 2, 1").		
What formats do we use to provide feedback? (verbal, written, non-verbal cues, peer, teacher, self, etc.)		
How do we share/document/ communicate schoolwide feedback routines/procedures and/or protocols for consistency?		

The first level involves immediate, high-frequency acknowledgements. For example, schools have used wristbands, tickets, or imitation coins or dollars that students can earn when an adult sees them doing an expected behavior. These can be submitted for drawings for prizes at the class, department, or school level. Other schools have created school stores where students can purchase school supplies or school-spirit-related items (e.g., pens, t-shirts, backpacks). The key here is that students do not have to wait until the end of the month to be recognized, they are being provided with immediate and frequent feedback and acknowledgement for their behaviors. Often students are more interested in collecting the tokens than turning them in. The concrete token also serves as a good reminder for adults to look for appropriate behavior from their students.

The next level of acknowledgment is unpredictable intermediate boosters. These are less frequent than the tokens but can work with them. For example, some schools have used their tokens to have drawings for larger awards such as preferred parking spots for vehicles or the sky box award. The staff boxed off an area in the school's gym and the student could invite friends to the "sky box" where they would be served drinks and snacks during a sporting event. In another example, a student won the opportunity to sit on a couch at the midfield line during the school's (American) football games with two friends and share food and drinks. Another school had postcards set up in the office. Teachers would write in the student's name, check off the behavior from the list of three to five expectations and the office would mail the card home. These rewards did not cost much, but they went a long way towards building a positive culture in the schools.

The final type of acknowledgement would be schoolwide. These can be developed based on setting goals for the whole school. For example, one school held a school dance because they had reduced their office discipline referrals by a pre-set amount. Another had a schoolwide BBQ and invited community vendors to set up booths around the school's outdoor field. Schoolwide acknowledgments help schools to focus on building a positive culture that celebrates expected behavior. Table 15.4 provides an example of how one school developed their action plan for acknowledgements at all three levels.

Application – Schoolwide Feedback, Acknowledgement, and Purposeful Outcomes

Review Table 15.4. Consider who your school might create a schoolwide acknowledgment plan for your school. How might you or your team pilot some of these approaches to gain support from other members of your community?

Table 15.4 Reinforcement Matrix for Planning Purposes

Type ESHS Example	What it is	When will it happen?	Where can/will it happen?	Who will be implementing?	Notes
High-frequency "Gotchas"	Students earn tickets from staff and turn them in for tangible items.	Beginning of the year staff get nine tickets with nine tickets. They can use a request form for more. Give in class and hallway.	Class and hallway, store. Turn in once per week.	All staff. Ticket is worth a quarter. Maybe have a Spartan's club parent to support.	Donations system for turning in and new tickets out. Stocking the store.
Unpredictable/ Intermittent "Boosters" *Targeted behaviors, times, and locations were chosen from referral data.*	Tickets from store are drawn weekly, names of teacher and student are called during loud speaker. Student earns a prize. Prizes include: parking spots, five minutes extra for lunch, doughnut time. Pictures also should go on the wall.	One per week during announcements. Six and third periods. Make sure we do this during Sept., Oct. and Feb. and March, and May. Randomly pull teachers, weekly, and then pull at least two during the month in off months.	Office and board in hall. Go to class or buzz down.	Administration will designate person to do this weekly. Discipline deans will support this action.	

(Continued)

Table 15.4 (continued)

Type ESHS Example	What it is	When will it happen?	Where can/will it happen?	Who will be implementing?	Notes
	Administrator randomly checks with third and six period classes to look for specific behaviors around disrespect, insubordination, dress code, or truancy. Or, ask if 80% of the class can state the big expectations.				
Attention-grabbing "Celebrations" Months were chosen from referral data, criteria from AYP.	Focus on two celebrations. We would look for a 10% reduction between the months of October and February. Dances, movies.	October and February	Gym is OK	Supervision schedule	Student council and leadership team will support this effort.

Note. Adapted from the Illinois Positive Behavior Support Network

Conclusion

Using feedback and acknowledgement effectively is a low cost, high impact strategy to make significant changes in your school. We have offered a variety of factors you can consider when focusing on improving feedback, acknowledgement, and purposeful outcomes for your students. Use the best practices (e.g., systems, data) we outline throughout the book to implement these strategies in your setting. Be sure to set goals for implementation and use data to monitor the effectiveness of your work.

As a reminder, all the strategies and theories related to feedback and acknowledgement of students also goes for the adults in your building too. Leaders and colleagues can create strong climates and culture for the adults in the building by applying these methods to each other. If you know your colleague's appreciation language is gift-giving, imagine how far bringing them a cup of coffee to thank them for showing you a new strategy might go. Another colleague might appreciate a personalized thank you email that copies the principal. Leadership can recognize teachers that implement systems with fidelity with a week in a coveted parking spot, or for going above and beyond the call of duty with a free lunch or donated gift certificate. Don't allow yourself and your colleagues to get buried in all the things you "haven't done." Recognize the things you have done.

Bibliography

Allen, J., Gregory, A., Mikami, A., Lun, J., Hamre, B., & Pianta, R. (2013). Observations of effective teacher–student interactions in secondary school classrooms: Predicting student achievement with the classroom assessment scoring system—secondary. *School Psychology Review, 42*(1), 76–98.

Bandura, A., & Walters, R. H. (1977). *Social learning theory* (Vol. 1). Englewood Cliffs, NJ: Prentice-hall.

Blanchard, K., & Barrett, C. (2010). *Lead with LUV: A different way to create real success.* Upper Saddle River, NJ: Pearson Prentice Hall.

Cannella-Malone, H. I., Tullis, C. A., & Kazee, A. R. (2011). Using antecedent exercise to decrease challenging behavior in boys with developmental disabilities and an emotional disorder. *Journal of Positive Behavior Interventions, 13*(4), 230–239.

Chapman, G. D., & White, P. E. (2012). *The 5 languages of appreciation in the workplace: Empowering organizations by encouraging people. Rev. and updated.* Chicago, IL: Northfield Pub.

Cook, C. R., Grady, E. A., Long, A. C., Renshaw, T., Codding, R. S., Fiat, A., & Larson, M. (2017). Evaluating the impact of increasing general education teachers' ratio of positive-to-negative interactions on students' classroom behavior. *Journal of Positive Behavior Interventions, 19*(2), 67–77.

Cooper, J. T., & Scott, T. M. (2017). The keys to managing instruction and behavior: Considering high probability practices. *Teacher Education and Special Education, 40*(2), 102–113.

Duhigg, C. (2012). *The power of habit: why we do what we do in life and business.* New York, NY: Random House LLC.

Dunlap, G., Foster-Johnson, L., Clarke, S., Kern, L., & Childs, K. E. (1995). Modifying activities to produce functional outcomes: Effects on the problem behaviors of students with disabilities. *Journal of the Association for Persons with Severe Handicaps, 20*(4), 248–258.

Hattie, J. (n.d.). Feedback in schools. Retrieved from www.visiblelearningplus.com/sites/default/files/Feedback%20article.pdf

Loehr, J., Loehr, J. E., & Schwartz, T. (2005). *The power of full engagement: Managing energy, not time, is the key to high performance and personal renewal.* New York, NY: Simon and Schuster.

Making Learning Visible. (n.d.). Ladder of feedback. Retrieved from www.making learningvisibleresources.org/uploads/3/4/1/9/3419723/ladder_of_feedbackguide.pdf

McLeskey, J., Barringer, M.-D., Billingsley, B., Brownell, M., Jackson, D., Kennedy, M., … Ziegler, D. (2017). *High-leverage practices in special education.* January. Arlington, VA: Council for Exceptional Children & CEEDAR Center.

Miller, R. L., Brickman, P., & Bolen, D. (1975). Attribution versus persuasion as a means for modifying behavior. *Journal of Personality and Social Psychology, 31*(3), 430–441. doi:10.1037/h0076539

Pink, D. H. (2009). *Drive: The Surprising truth about what motivates us.* New York, NY: Riverhead Books.

Reinke, W. M., Herman, K. C., & Stormont, M. (2013). Classroom level positive behavior supports in schools implementing SW-PBIS: Identifying areas for enhancement. *Journal of Positive Behavior Interventions, 15*(1), 39–50. doi:10.1177/1098300712459079

Saaris, N. (2016). *Effective feedback for deeper learning.* Retrieved from www.actively learn.com/post/effective-feedback-for-deeper-learning

Wills, H. P., Caldarella, P., Mason, B. A., Lappin, A., & Anderson, D. H. (2019). Improving student behavior in middle schools: Results of a classroom management intervention. *Journal of Positive Behavior Interventions, 21*(4), 213–227.

16

RESPONDING TO ACADEMIC AND BEHAVIORAL NEEDS

In a Nutshell

- Response cycles use a problem-solving process to take action at all three tiers of support.
- Expand teachers' capacity by strengthening their "toolbox" of academic, behavior, and social and emotional support skills.

Introduction

When firefighters arrive on the scene of a fire, they make several important decisions. These decisions include determining how many firefighters should be put on the job of preventing the fire from spreading and how many should rescue people from the burning building. No matter how effective the intervention to stop the fire is, there may still be people that need to be rescued. The rescue work tends to be very intense. Even with our best efforts to create effective schoolwide climate for our community, there are still going to be students who need support. Certainly, it is a good use of our energy to prevent as many issues for our students as possible. Unfortunately, our best prevention work will not be enough to prevent every problem our students will come across.

Schools should focus on detecting students who do not respond to our initial efforts and still need support. In order to be successful, staff need support to be able to fulfil your school's mission for helping every student be successful. Schools can prepare their staff to be able to respond to the needs of students academically, behaviorally, emotionally, and socially. In this chapter, we will discuss ways to prepare your team and staff to detect and respond to students' needs.

Connection – Response Cycle Overview

While prevention is the best medicine, sometimes people do become ill. As discussed in Chapter 11, when you see a doctor they measure your symptoms by collecting various types of data. At first, they may measure your temperature and survey you about your pain level on a scale of one to ten, or go through a checklist of symptoms. The doctor then may recommend a treatment plan, such as taking Ibuprofen. If the fever and symptoms clear up within a week, the response is complete. If not, the doctor may try a different medication, or collect additional data, such as blood counts, and then prescribe a new treatment. The cycle continues as needed. A similar cycle of response occurs within a schoolwide tiered system of support.

Point/Principal – Response Cycle Overview

The response process we recommend involves using the problem-solving method. In Chapter 1 of this book we identified the steps for problem solving. These steps include, according to Anna Harms and her colleagues in the state of Michigan:

1. Identify the problems in your setting;
2. Analyze the problems in your setting;
3. Develop a plan for addressing the problem; and
4. Implementing plan and evaluate the plan.

The first question to address is: What is the problem and for whom? For example, we once worked with a high school where 95% of the students had one or fewer office discipline referrals to the office. However, only 60% had an overall grade point average of 2.0 (on a 4.0 scale). In this setting, behavior only needed to be addressed in small groups or with individual students, however, academically the response involved addressing what was not working for a large portion of the students within the core curriculum.

Application – Instructional Response Cycle Overview

Consider what you are already doing to identify students who are not responding to your core curriculum. What, kinds of data are you using to identify and monitor the progress of your student? If you have a team in charge of responding to students' needs, find out who they are and what data they are using for their process. This is a time when having an organizational chart as we describe in Chapter 9 comes in handy. Also, some of the data that we have suggested Chapters 10 and 11 might be of use to your team members as well.

Illustration – Response Cycle – Tier One – In the Classroom

I (Kelly) was co-teaching a large English class where we were using a school-wide writing strategy to teach students how to write a claim and support it with evidence. We gave a formative assessment where students had to read a text and write a paragraph that included a claim, evidence from the text, and reasoning. We looked over the students' responses, and grouped them into two categories: those primarily in need of support in developing a claim, and those primarily in need of support in selecting and incorporating evidence. Students who had been absent worked on the formative assessment in their first day back to school and joined a group the next day based on their performance. We taught targeted mini lessons with each group, and then reassessed when we saw their responses improving in the mini lessons. Our response progress took time to implement, but it paid off for our students in the long run.

Point/Principle – Response Cycle – Tier One – In the Classroom

A common challenge in secondary settings is that teachers feel pressured to "get through the content." As a result of this pressure, they teach, assess, and move on to the next topic regardless of the results. Step back from content for a minute and consider if your content is being delivered using high-leverage instructional methods. The Collaboration for Effective Educator Development, Accountability, and Reform (CEEDAR) Center (https://ceedar. education.ufl.edu/); the Innovative Resources for Instructional Success (IRIS) Center (https://iris.peabody.vanderbilt.edu/); and TeachingWorks (http://www.teachingworks.org/) have in-depth resources related to high-leverage practices. Ideally, teachers work together with students to short- and long-term goals for skill development, use instructional routines including modeling, discussion, metacognition, explicit instruction, and feedback to make progress toward that skill, and use formative assessment continuously to identify areas for whole group and small group targeted lessons. Students should not be referred for tier two supports until you are sure that tier one instruction is effective and implemented with fidelity.

The same response cycle should be implemented for students who are struggling with attendance, behaviors, or social-emotional learning skills. To implement response cycles, we need to support teachers in learning to use efficient, reliable methods to teach, formatively assess, and monitor student performance. We also need to help them implement an evidence-based strategy at tier one before referring a student out for intervention. For example, you might have a class where a few students are often using their cell phones at inappropriate times, others are coming late to class, and others are talking over the person who has the floor during discussions. In response, the teacher could start a simple game where expectations are clearly defined, and students earn points each day for sticking to the guidelines. Low- or no-cost reinforcements can be earned for "winning" the game (reaching a set goal) such as five minutes at the end of class for a funniest storytelling competition or a "My Life in Numbers" share-out. The teacher can monitor the points, and possibly tally the problem behaviors on a sheet of paper, to see if behaviors are improving.

We also need to make sure our teachers are prepared to respond to students when problem behaviors occur in real time. According to the Crisis Prevention and Intervention Model (see www.crisisprevention.com), student responses usually follow phases of escalation. These phases include anxiety, defensive behavior, risk behavior (e.g., acting out), and tension reduction (e.g., student is exhausted from outburst). While providing sufficient training on how to respond to every issue is beyond the scope of this book, we will include some of our more commonly used strategies to redirect students when problems arise. Many of these strategies were adapted from a book by Allen and Brian Mendler called *Power Struggles*. This book is a great short read on strategies for preventing problems from escalating for students.

Here are some of the book's strategies, and a few we have found effective:

- **Use privacy, eye contact** (do not force eye contact), **and proximity** (about three feet) when correcting.
- **Start with something positive** – what is the student doing right? Or what is the student next to him doing that is right? Praise that behavior specifically.
- **Assume the student did not know the expectation** (assume innocence until proven guilty).
- **Use humor** – this is not sarcasm (e.g., you know, sometimes my arms just fly around too, are you OK now? – Is this really being safe in the hall?).
- **Stay out of content** when you ask for something or give a direction. When the students says, "why" or "who are you" simply wait a moment and repeat the direction. You must be willing to wait it out, if not, do not use this strategy!
- **End with a teachable moment**: "Was that an example of being safe?" "What did you need to do instead?"

When attempting to redirect groups, try the following:

- **Acknowledge those who are on task**. When the rest come back, thank them. The same can be done for individual students: look for anything they are doing right, and point that out. When the student stops the problem behavior, thank them for their self-control without having to be told what to do (hint: start with something positive).
- **Stop, wait** for instructional control, **remind and re-teach** expectations.

BOX 16.1 PONDERING ON PURPOSE

- Refer back to Chapter 8, when you "cleaned out your closet" of practices. Are the remaining practices considered "high leverage?"
- Which instructional strategies have you implemented that help to impact both academic and behavior outcomes in the class as a whole?
- What strategies have you tried that seem to help redirect students without escalating problem behaviors?

Application – Response Cycle – Tier One – In the Classroom

What types of coaching and support might teachers need to become more comfortable with the response cycle? Brainstorm a list of ideas that might help teachers develop a wider repertoire of strategies at tier one, prior to referring students for added layers of support beyond the classroom.

Connection – Instructional Response Cycle – Groups of Students

Sometimes it is helpful to identify needs by a group. For example, my (Hank) home community identifies elderly residents who need extra support during winter months. The local government finds ways to match them with teenagers who can check in on them and provide support such as shoveling snow from their sidewalks. In this case, matching groups of people to support needs is efficient for both the older adults in need of care and the youth who are looking for purpose.

Point/Principal – Instructional Response Cycle – Groups of Students

When we think about our responses to students who are still struggling, one area to focus on is students with similar support needs. Typically, we are talking about roughly 10–15% of the population. Sometimes these interventions are considered to be group level supports. By group, we mean programs that meet the specific needs of students, but are not necessarily individualized for each student. Sometimes these interventions are also thought of as tier two interventions. We adapted the following list of features of tier two support from the work of the Missouri Schoolwide Positive Behavior Support Network (see https://pbismissouri.org/tier-2-overview/).

- Students can access the supports throughout the school year
- Initial steps should begin within 72 hours of identifying the student's need

- Interventions should fit within classroom procedures and not require excessive amounts of time for teachers
- The skills staff need to learn to implement the interventions should be easily acquired and related to high-quality instruction
- Interventions should be aligned with tier one practices
- All staff should know about the interventions, and should understand their part in implementation
- Interventions are, for the most part, standardized across students. Minor changes can be made to improve outcomes for students
- Interventions are matched with the issues underlying the student's problem (e.g., seeking attention, decoding multisyllabic words inefficiently, avoiding work that is too difficult, being over- or under-stimulated)
- Interventions should be included within the master school schedule (e.g., a student could take a math intervention course one period and then attend their algebra 1 course)
- Interventions are organized by whether or not the students' issues are related to the ability to perform the needed skill, or will to perform the needed skill (see Chapter 2)

Northfield Middle and High School School in Vermont that we referenced in Chapter 11 (Table 11.3) has a tier two group level intervention program. Their process is called the teacher advisor action planning process (TAAP). Their team includes the teacher, the identified student, a tier two team representative, the referring teacher, other related services (e.g., special education, nurse), and other individuals as needed. A major member of the team is the teacher advisor. Each instructor is given between 10–14 students to be a part of their advising group. The goal of the advising group is to give each student in their building at least one adult with whom they meet on a regular basis. These individuals also serve as advocates for their students. The TAAP meetings are called if (a) the schoolwide data indicate a need, or (b) a teacher has a concern for a student who is not already receiving tier two or three supports, or (c) a teacher thinks a student needs supports beyond tier one. These interventions typically run for nine weeks. The plans are reviewed every three weeks to determine the student's progress and the level of fidelity for implementation of the plan. The interventions are selected from a common intervention protocol. The protocol aligns each intervention with the function or need related to the student's issue. Table 16.1 provides examples of what these interventions entail. The table includes:

- The intervention type
- Function of behavior
- Referral criteria

Table 16.1 Sample of Inventory of Group Level Interventions. Adapted from the work of Northfield Middle School and High School, VT

Current Group Intervention	Function				Referral Criteria	Frequency/ Intensity of Intervention	Resources Needed (staff, space, $, time)	Schedule for Checking Progress	Effectiveness Measured (success criteria/goal)	EXIT Criteria
	Adult att.	Peer att.	Work avoid	other						
Check In and Check Out	X			X	5 ODRs for minors in one Quarter Effective Support Team (EST) referral"	Check sheet for feedback at end of every class Morning/ Afternoon check in/out with CICO Coordinator	Staff Coordinator Three Hours Daily	Safety – Daily for five days Trust – Weekly for four weeks Independent – Weekly for four weeks	Meeting CICO requirements to advance in program	Safety five days at 80% Trust four weeks at 85% Independent four weeks at 90%
Social Skills Group	X	X			EST/504/IEP referral	Odd/Even Weekly	Teacher	Quarterly or three-week intervals for three recurrences, total of nine weeks	Increase in positive social interactions Fewer office discipline referrals	Teacher record EST/504/ IEP Plan requirements
1:1 Tutoring	X	X	X	X	EST/504/IEP referral	EST/504/IEP Plan requirements	Tutors	Three-week intervals for three recurrences, total of nine weeks	Higher Grades HW Comp increase Increased organization	EST/504/ IEP Plan requirements
Skill Center Instead of Electives	X		X		EST/504/IEP referral"	EST/504/IEP Plan requirements	Teacher/ IA to run workshop	Three-week intervals for three recurrences, total of nine weeks	Higher Grades HW compliance increase Increased organization	EST/504/ IEP Plan requirements

- Frequency/intensity of intervention
- Resources needed (staff, space, $, time)
- Schedule for checking progress
- Effectiveness measured (success criteria/goal)
- Exit criteria

The team monitors implementation and outcomes through an online form. Students are referred for more intensive interventions if they do not make progress with these initial interventions. Additional interventions that we typically see at this level include REWARDS reading intervention (www.voyagersopris.com/literacy/rewards/overview), Check In and Check Out (see Leanne Hawken (2014) in the reference section), and/or the Behavior Education Program (see Deanne Crone (2010) in the reference section). For a more detailed list, visit the companion website.

Application – Instructional Response Cycle – Groups of Students

A good place to start for your team might be to inventory what you already have in place for groups of students who are not responding to your universal support. You can use the blank version of the matrix we just discussed (Table 16.2) to help you identify what you already have in place. Take time to think about how each intervention might address the needs of your students.

BOX 16.2 PONDERING ON PURPOSE

- What processes is your school using that match student needs with interventions?
- How has understanding why a student is struggling affected the way you match students to interventions?

Connection – Instructional Response Cycle – Individual Students

Even with the best group level interventions, sometimes we still need to respond to individual students' needs. For instance, I (Hank) was a guest in a high school to provide professional development. As I walked out of the training room, I saw students who were kissing right outside of the door. In order to intervene, I asked them where I could find the bathroom. The students stopped momentarily and pointed down the hall. Then they started kissing again so I said, "I am new here, could you show me where

Table 16.2 Blank Matrix for Planning Group Level Interventions

Current Group Intervention	Function/Problem				Referral Criteria	Frequency/ Intensity of Intervention	Resources Needed (staff, space, $, time)	Schedule for Checking Progress	Effectiveness Measured (success criteria/goal)	Exit Criteria
	Adult attn.	Peer Attn.	Work Avoidance	Other						

the bathroom is?" They were disappointed but stopped kissing and walked me to the restroom. I am sure I totally ruined their moment! However, using a competing behavior (they could not walk me to the bathroom and kiss at the same time!) I was able to stop the kissing and allowed them to save face. I imagine it could have been a different interaction had I confronted them directly about their smooching.

Point/Principal – Instructional Response Cycle – Individual of Students

Sometimes individual responses to students require teams to help develop plans. For example, Northfield Middle School and High School also has an intensive support team that provides both tier two level and tier three level intervention. The team consists of the teacher's advisor we just mentioned and other standing group members. The teams have been trained on problem-solving approaches that were related to student's underlying needs. Student problems are identified using:

• Interviews
• Reviews of behavioral and social and emotional screening data
• Attendance
• Academic performance data

The goal of the team is to provide intensive support for students based on:

• Entrance criteria
• Progress monitoring
• Reviewing fidelity of implementation of the plan

The most intensive interventions are facilitated by individuals with the most specialized skills (e.g., special education teachers, school counselors). The interventions are available to all students whether or not they have an identified disability or diagnosis. The plans also run for a nine-week period. Progress monitoring and implementation fidelity are checked every three weeks. Interventions include approaches such as check in and check out, homework club, skill development, and a community-based hands-on experiential program where students could gain course credit (e.g., gardening, community service).

In terms of the intensive individual interventions, some of the most common ones we see at the secondary student level include:

• Wilson Reading Program (https://www.wilsonlanguage.com/)
• Mentoring
• Credit recovery

- Social skills training
- Homework labs
- Person-centered planning, such as Project RENEW (Rehabilitation for Empowerment, Natural Supports, Education, and Work – see https://iod.unh.edu/projects/rehabilitation-empowerment-natural-supports-education-and-work-renew)
- Functional behavior assessment/behavior intervention plans
- Check in/check out
- Behavior Education Program

For an additional case example of tiered interventions that includes Project RENEW, please see the bibliography for the article by JoAnne Malloy and colleagues. Also, see the website accompanying this book for a master list of resources for individualized supports.

Application – Instructional Response Cycle – Individual of Students

One strategy we have found to be helpful in developing the comfort levels of staff with redirection strategies is to allow them to try one on their own. Ask your staff, or even yourself, to try one of these strategies over the next week. Reflect on how the students responded to the approach. Ask the staff to share how the student's response differed from other times when perhaps they used more confrontative strategies.

Connection – Preparing Your Team to Respond

If you have worked at Starbucks Coffee as a barista, you likely received a considerable amount of training. For example, one of Hank's friends reported that he received over 50 hours of professional development per year. For example, one training that Starbucks provided to their employees was how to respond to unhappy or disgruntled customers. The process was called the LATTE method. When a customer became upset in some way, the employees were coached to listen to the customer, acknowledge the complaint, take action by solving the problem, thank the customer, and then explain why the problem occurred. If Starbucks provides training on how to respond to people who are having problems, it may be a good idea for all of us who work with people to think about developing some new skills.

Point/Principal – Preparing Your Team to Respond

There is certainly a wide literature base for preparing your staff and teams to respond to students' needs. For the purposes of this book, we are going to cover just a few that we have seen to be employed most often.

- **Go over strategies with staff.** Before you ask staff to be able to respond to student needs, make sure you have provided professional development.
- **Provide coaching.** Few of us can play the piano or a sport without feedback from someone who can show us the way (e.g., coaching). One of the most effective instructional coaching systems we have seen is by Jim Knight at the University of Kansas. We recommend seeing more information about their approach at https://kucrl.ku.edu/kansas-coaching-project-kcp
- **Have staff pilot or experiment with strategies.** Evan Dart and colleagues suggests that one way to help teachers to see which interventions might work best for them is to "test drive" them before they fully commit to an approach.
- **Give feedback and allow for self-reflection.** Having staff reflect on their experiments with interventions and responses allows them to assess what works and what does not. Consider asking staff to keep a reflection journal as a part of the professional development process.

Application – Preparing Your Team to Respond

We invite you to review some of the resources that we have mentioned along with those we provided on the book's companion website, to support your students with more intense needs. While we know these lists are not exhaustive, perhaps they give you a sense of some of the tools that are available to support students in secondary schools. Some of these resources are also very useful to consider for use with your core curriculum (e.g., The Strategic Instructional Model, see https://sim.ku.edu/sim-curricula). As you review these lists, determine if there are any resources that might be useful to the needs of your students and staff members.

Conclusion

Even with the best tier one practices in place, you will still have students who struggle. It is essential to have a response process in place to detect students that need help. Responses should include systematic approaches. Responses also include staff reactions to students when problems occur in real-time, allowing for redirection. Taking the time to prepare your staff to understand your systematic and in the moment response practices will be beneficial to your team.

Bibliography

Bohanon, H., Gilman, C., Parker, B., Amell, C., & Sortino, G. (2016). Using school improvement and implementation science to integrate multi-tiered systems of support in secondary schools. *Australasian Journal of Special Education*, 40(2), 99–116. doi:10.1017/jse.2016.8

Crone, D. A., Hawken, L. S., & Horner, R. H. (2010). *Responding to problem behavior in schools: The behavior education program.* New York, NY: Guilford Press.

Dart, E. H., Cook, C. R., Collins, T. A., Gresham, F. M., & Chenier, J. S. (2012). Test driving interventions to increase treatment integrity and student outcomes. *School Psychology Review, 41*(4), 467–481.

Hawken, L. S., Bundock, K., Kladis, K., O'Keeffe, B., & Barrett, C. A. (2014). Systematic review of the check-in, check-out intervention for students at risk for emotional and behavioral disorders. *Education and Treatment of Children, 37*(4), 635–658.

Knoster, T. (2013). *The teacher's pocket guide effective classroom management* (2nd ed.). Baltimore, MD: Paul H Brookes.

Malloy, J. M., Bohanon, H., & Francoeur, K. (2018). Positive behavioral interventions and supports in high schools: A case study from New Hampshire. *Journal of Educational and Psychological Consultation, 28*(2), 219–247.

Mendler, A., & Mendler, B. D. (2011). *Power struggles: Successful tips for teachers.* Bloomington, IN: Solution Tree.

Stein, M., Kinder, D., Silbert, J., Carnine, D. W., & Rolf, K. (2017). *Direct instruction mathematics.* London, England: Pearson.

Uber, P. A. (2019). Doling out mental healthcare with your latte: Do Starbucks employees have more emotional intelligence than your physician? *Psychology Today.* Retrieved from www.psychologytoday.com/us/blog/critical-decisions/201211/doling-out-mental-healthcare-your-latte

INDEX

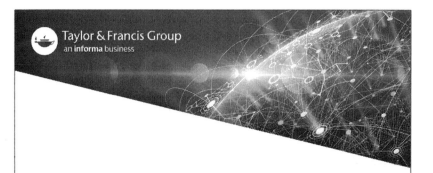